P9-AQQ-535

ADVOCACY
FOR
CHILD MENTAL HEALTH

Advocacy
for
Child
Mental
Health

Edited by **IRVING N. BERLIN, M.D.**

A little knowledge that *acts* is worth infinitely more
than much knowledge that is idle. KAHLIL GIBRAN

BRUNNER/MAZEL, Publishers   NEW YORK

IN APPRECIATION

We are indebted to The Grant Foundation
for the funds which made much of the work
on this book possible.

ANDERBILT UNIVERSITY
CAL CENTER LIBRARY

JUL 1 1987

ASHVILLE, TENNESSEE
37232

Copyright © 1975 by Irving N. Berlin

Published by BRUNNER/MAZEL, INC., 64 University
Place, New York, New York 10003

All rights reserved. No part of this book may be reproduced
by any process whatsoever, without the written permission
of the copyright owner.

Library of Congress Catalog Card No. 74–78716
SBN 87630–096–4

MANUFACTURED IN THE UNITED STATES OF AMERICA

Preface

The editor and writers of this book are all former officers, directors, and committee chairmen of the Joint Commission on Mental Health of Children.

The official publications, overwhelmed by the mass of material available, have not, in our opinion, dealt with a number of specific and important issues, especially those related to operational child advocacy and the knowledge base required for the development of such programs.

We have thus selectively emphasized our major concerns and biases not dealt with in official volumes.

It is our hope that this book will be informative to both our colleagues and legislators, but especially to citizen leaders in the movements for realizing children's needs and human rights.

IRVING N. BERLIN

ACKNOWLEDGMENTS

To my wife, Roxie Berlin, for her encouragement,
judicious editorial help, collaboration, and infinite
patience.
To Jessimai Strange for her gentle editorial assistance.
To Jeanette Ashby, our always good-natured, strong
right arm in this as in other publications.
To Yvonne Weedin, who helped Jeanette.

(i do not know what it is about you
that closes and opens; only something in me understands the voice
of your eyes is deeper than all
roses) nobody, not even the rain,
has such small hands.

e. e. cummings

Foreword

It has been said that the quality of our nation can be judged in large part by how we treat our children.

Sadly, American children do not receive the attention they deserve. Our national statistics bear this out. Part of the blame for our failures must be placed on the frenetic pace of our society.

But even more important, as ADVOCACY FOR CHILD MENTAL HEALTH clarifies, is the fact that our society concerns itself too much with cures and not enough with prevention. If we could find and diagnose problems before they develop, we could assure our nation's children of healthy development at what is the most important and formative stage of their lives.

It was for this reason that I introduced legislation in the 1960's which led to the development of the Joint Commission on the Mental Health of Children as well as provisions to assure early and periodic screening, diagnosis, and treatment of impoverished children under Medicaid.

Those who would hope to understand the problems and progress in the mental health of children should read ADVOCACY FOR CHILD MENTAL HEALTH.

It is an important statement which, bringing light to the problems of mental health, hopefully will move policy makers to formulate solutions.

ABE RIBICOFF
United States Senate

Introduction

A new war has quietly started in the U.S. It is being carried out by a dedicated group of citizens, including mental health professionals, who are determined that the momentum created by the Joint Commission on the Mental Health of Children for meeting the needs of children shall not die. They feel strongly that the Joint Commission's findings and recommendations must not suffer the fate of the reports of the seven White House Conferences on Children and Youth. They are fighting under the banner of child advocacy raised by the Joint Commission. Much of the war is underground, but it is also being fought in the offices and hearing rooms of the Congress, state legislatures, and local political leaders. The fighters need fresh ammunition and this timely book on child advocacy provides it in abundance.

The history of the creation of the Joint Commission is itself a demonstration of the forces that must be fought in this war. The earlier Joint Commission on Mental Health and Illness had neither the time nor the money to be concerned with the problems of children. It was not until the assassination of President John F. Kennedy that a flurry of top-level interest in better children's services arose. Because Kennedy's assassin had been diagnosed in childhood as severely emotionally disturbed but had never had the recommended treatment, Senator Abraham Ribicoff proposed the so-called Oswald bill, to provide services to prevent more Oswalds. A small group met with the Senator and persuaded him that an up-to-date study of the fundamental needs of children in the U.S. should be a first step. The legislation to authorize a multidisciplinary study was substituted and was attached as an amendment to the Social Security bill of 1965. At the end of the final Senate-House conference committee meeting on the bill, H.E.W. Secretary Wilbur Cohen had to call to the conferees walking out the door, "Hey, come back. We have one last amendment to consider." He was at the same time calling attention to a recurrent manifestation of the low priority which children's programs have. And there aren't many Wilbur Cohens around to call the decisionmakers' attention back to the mental health needs of children.

Probably the most important principle underlying the tactics of the child advocacy war is that one cannot separate child mental health from health. Both of these cannot be separated from education. All three cannot be separated from the cultural and social forces influencing the development of children. In addition, the Joint Commission found that the services dealing with these developmental areas are most neglected during the child's first three years of life. It is in this age period that the brain is growing faster than it ever will again and is most readily available to remedial inputs.

We know a great deal about constitutional vulnerabilities and their much greater response to corrective approaches in these early years. We know about critical or optimal periods in early development of key human functions but, as this book highlights, for the most part we are not applying this knowledge. One goal of the advocacy warriors is to emphasize prevention in this crucial age period.

If we look at our child-rearing and service systems in light of those values which Americans hold dear—life, liberty, and the pursuit of happiness—statistics tell us we are not making it possible for close to 20 million of our youngsters to achieve them. By leaving them hampered with physical, emotional, and educational handicaps, we can offer them only a form of half-life; they are locked-in from liberty by limited choices; they are locked-out from many paths in the pursuit of happiness.

The small number of fighters for the children who can't fight for themselves are only the vanguard of what is needed. They must have an army of service providers on the firing line with the children and their families. Possibly we need a new concept of a Department of Defense. In the hopeful future when the battles are won, the names of the editor and his collaborators in this volume—Berlin, Bazelon, Norman Lourie, Pierce, Prugh, and the others—will be known as the new version of advocate generals.

REGINALD S. LOURIE, M.D.
President, Joint Commission on Mental Health of Children
Professor Emeritus, Child Health and Development
Children's Hospital, National Medical Center (Washington, D.C.)

Contents

Contributors

BAZELON, DAVID L.

Chief Judge, U.S. Court of Appeals, Washington, D.C.; Director, Joint Commission on Mental Health of Children; member, Council of National Institute of Mental Health.

BERLIN, IRVING N., M.D.

Professor of Psychiatry and Pediatrics, Head of Division of Child Psychiatry, University of Washington School of Medicine; Director, Joint Commission on Mental Health of Children; President-Elect, American Academy of Child Psychiatry.

BERLIN, ROXIE, M.S.W., PH.D.

Consultant in early childhood education and development of parent participation programs, Seattle School District and Highline School District, Washington.

DE BUNO, THEODORE, M.D.

Deputy Director, Syracuse State School, Syracuse, New York.

JORDAN, KENT, M.D.

Associate Clinical Professor, Department of Psychiatry, University of California San Diego at University Hospital.

LOURIE, NORMAN V., A.C.S.W.

Executive Deputy Secretary, Pennsylvania Department of Public Welfare; Director, Joint Commission on Mental Health of Children.

MORSE, WILLIAM C., PH.D.

Professor of Education and Psychology, University of Michigan, Ann Arbor; Director, Joint Commission on Mental Health of Children.

PIERCE, CHESTER, M.D.

Professor of Education and Psychiatry, Harvard University; chairman and member, Committee on Children of Minority Groups.

PRUGH, DANE G., M.D.

Professor of Psychiatry and Pediatrics, University of Colorado Medical Center; Director, Joint Commission on Mental Health of Children.

RICHMOND, JULIUS B., M.D.

Professor of Child Psychiatry and Human Development and Professor and Chairman, Department of Preventive and Social Medicine, Harvard Medical School; Psychiatrist-in-Chief, Children's Hospital Medical Center; Director, Judge Baker Guidance Center, Boston, Massachusetts; Vice President, Joint Commission on Mental Health of Children; President, American Orthopsychiatric Association.

WALZER, STANLEY, M.D.

Assistant Professor of Psychiatry, Harvard Medical School, Boston, Massachusetts.

We shall not cease from exploration
And the end of all our exploring
Will be to arrive where we started
And know the place for the first time.

T. S. ELIOT

1

We Advocate
This Bill of Rights

IRVING N. BERLIN, M.D.

The Bill of Rights, the first ten amendments to the Constitution, guarantees civil liberties to adult Americans, now beginning at age 18. In recent years, through legal action, children have been afforded some rights of adults.

Children's special needs have not been a major concern of our country. Child labor laws and universal education are related to industrialization and a way to keep unneeded child workers out of the labor market but off the streets. The recent trend toward mass college education for two to four years also appears to be related to reducing youth unemployment in a country so mechanized it no longer can employ many people in industry or agriculture.

Human values, conservation of human life, and elimination of hunger, poverty, disease, racism, and ghettos are yet to become major national priorities.

Absence of developmental rights

"Children are our greatest resource for the future," is often said, but rarely meant. White House conferences on children, held regularly since 1903, have brought *no* major legislative action. The many wise and foresighted recommendations have been an exercise in futility for the well-qualified child care and child development specialists involved. Implementation of recommendations with programs that well could have prevented or reduced crime, delinquency, drug use, and alienation of youth has had low priority. Unlike Russia, the Scandinavian countries, and Mainland China, the United States has not demonstrated commitment through national programs to the healthy development of all of its children. Existing programs for disturbed and malfunctional children ignore developmental knowledge and remediation methods and have become fragmented. Programs for the poor become poor programs. In contrast, what is necessary for the nurturance, even survival, of our democracy are child development programs which use our present knowledge to facilitate the development of effective, responsible adults.

Children's right to buy

Perhaps the preeminent right currently extended U. S. children is to spend money, to influence parent purchases, to buy outright clothes, records, and breakfast and snack foods. Children and youth are the largest purchasing force in the nation. With the right to purchase should come the right to consumer protection and, certainly, protection from buying illicit drugs. Children are good business. It is better business to protect our investment in them and their future by planned child development-oriented programs.

Poverty, racism, child health, and mental health

A quarter of our nation is poor! Children and youth under 25 make up one-half our population. Children today are the victims of our society's overwhelming sociocultural and economic problems.

Poverty and racism are major societal, health, and mental health problems. Poverty and racism are closely tied to physical and mental illness in both adults and children. Our infants and young children in poverty, of all races, are the most vulnerable and suffer the most.

Recent data quoted by the Joint Commission on Child Mental Health [3] reveal that the death rate of infants in ghettos, Appalachia, and the poor South is twice as great as in middle-class neighborhoods. In general, the infant death rate of poor Blacks is twice that of even poor whites and many times that of nonpoor whites. School failure and school dropout rates are at least ten times greater in the poverty population than in the middle-class population.[3] Delinquency and crime are essentially problems of the poor, and of Blacks, Spanish-speaking Americans, and American Indians.

Recent studies by Cravioto, DeLicardie, and Birch [2] have shown that prenatal maternal malnutrition and infant malnutrition are major factors in the physical ill health and mental retardation found in many youngsters in the poverty population. Cravioto's research, validated by research of others, indicates that such malnutrition, primarily protein and vitamin deprivation, leads to fewer brain cells, thus to smaller brains, and in turn, to smaller head size as well as smaller body size of children who are significantly nutritionally deprived. The President's Commission on Mental Retardation has stated it is likely that the etiology of most mental retardation is socioeconomic. That is, nutritional deprivation and sociocultural stimulus deprivation, rather than hereditary causes, account for most of our retarded children. Minority children are the most frequent victims.

We also know that the incidence of premature birth is almost ten times as great among the poverty population as it is among the middle-class population. These infants are at much greater risk of brain defects and of physical and neurological problems and have fewer chances for survival. Many will never be able to work and learn effectively.[4] Our persistent lack of concern with regard to adequate nutrition and prenatal care for mothers, and nutrition for poor and minority babies and children, is a national disgrace.

Economic exploitation of Blacks, Spanish-speaking Americans, and American Indians has historically led to racist attitudes toward these people. Racist attitudes today lead to strife, violence, and continued segregation and impoverishment of ethnic minorities long the victims of white society. Continuation of racism results in serious mental health problems for all races, especially the white, and stands in the way of progress to benefit all people. Discriminatory practices in work, education, housing, health, and welfare mean that most Americans will, in reality, be deprived of those rights denied minorities. Racism is the only infectious *mental* disease, and it must be eliminated!

National priorities——not for children

The priorities of our nation, as revealed through national and state spending, have never at any time in history demonstrated concern for children. Even today, education, welfare, and health budgets are rarely designed to benefit children most at risk. Such budgets never equal those for manned space flight or defense.

Today our nation faces increasing stress from technological problems which can no longer be dealt with by further technology, such as pollution of the earth, overpopulation, and deterioration of inner cities. Increased poverty and hopelessness of a large underfed, unemployed, and futureless population create enormous problems. Their children cannot cope with these burdens; they cannot learn in a society without a place for them. No work, no pride, and no earnings result in a turning to crime and drugs. Today technology has made it difficult for most youngsters in all socioeconomic classes, but especially minorities, either to find jobs or to train for jobs which represent meaningful future careers. The work force continues to shrink and mechanization of all industrial and agricultural processes continues to increase. In our increasingly complex world, with mounting national tensions, our young people have fewer options for a useful and meaningful life.

We pay little attention to the impact of our world upon our citizens and especially upon the next generation. We find ourselves in a nation where our children are increasingly poor, are increasingly dropouts, are increasingly delinquent and drug addicted, are increasingly mentally defective, and are increasingly mentally ill. These facts of life today are not realized or believed by a nation still living with the Horatio Alger dream that "any person can become President." These realities affect not only the poor and minorities, but increasingly are spreading to middle-class white children from families of white and blue collar, business, and professional backgrounds. We must face these facts. This volume will document these facts. *The time is now for a stand on behalf of our children.* We therefore propose this Bill of Rights.*

---

* In part derived from the rights developed by the Joint Commission on Mental Health of Children.

A BILL OF RIGHTS

We hold these truths inalienable for all children:

ONE: The Right to Be Born Wanted.

TWO: The Right to Be Born Healthy.

THREE: The Right to Live in a Healthful Environment.

FOUR: The Right to Live in a Family Whose Basic Economic Needs Are Met.

FIVE: The Right to Continuous and Loving Care both at Home and in School.

SIX: The Right to Acquire Intellectual and Emotional Skills for Effective Citizenship.

    a. The Right to Dignity in School.

    b. The Right to Humane and Concerned Treatment Under the Law and by Courts.

    c. The Right to Child-Centered Divorce and Custody Laws.

SEVEN: The Right to Meaningful Employment.

EIGHT: The Right to Diagnostic, Treatment, and Rehabilitative Care through Facilities which are Appropriate to Children's Special Needs and Which Keep Them as Closely as Possible within Their Normal Social Setting.

NINE: The Right to Racial and Ethnic Identity, Self-Determination, and a Real and Functional Equality of Opportunity to the Above Rights.

TEN: The Right to Political Participation through Education for Informed Citizenship.

The Bill of Rights explained

ONE: THE RIGHT TO BE BORN WANTED. The right must exist for each individual family to determine whether they are psychologically, emotionally, physically, and financially able to have another child. A new child should not be a burden to the family. When planned for, the baby can have the love and attention from a family that wants a child to be born into it. Too many children are born into an environment and into a home setting of such poverty and chronic ill health and—in all socioeconomic classes—

to such depression and apathy that they cannot possibly grow up physically and emotionally healthy. In such environments, they acquire enormous physical and psychological scars which later lead to a variety of handicaps that make living, learning, and working in society difficult, if not impossible.

TWO: THE RIGHT TO BE BORN HEALTHY. This includes the right to a healthy and well-nourished mother and father, particularly a mother who, during pregnancy, has adequate medical care and nutrition so that the child is protected from an interrupted pregnancy or premature birth or infections. Premature birth is a major cause of retardation and, along with infections, produces a variety of birth defects. Maternal malnutrition produces infant malnutrition with physical and mental retardation and varieties of mental illness. In our nation, each child has the right to be born in good health and nutrition.

THREE: THE RIGHT TO LIVE IN A HEALTHFUL ENVIRONMENT. A healthful environment is free of malnutrition for all family members, free of debilitating diseases such as T.B. and emphysema, and free of infections. It is an environment free of rats, garbage, and sewage as carriers of disease, and free of lead poisoning. A healthful environment provides decent housing, fresh breathable air, sanitation, heat in winter, play and recreation space for children. A healthful environment is free of the venom of racism and the resulting discrimination in work, housing, health, and education services. It must be free of the ghetto!

A healthful environment includes national and local environments of reduced anxiety about poverty, racism, ghettos, overpopulation. It is one which is concerned with the healthy growth of children in healthy families. The quality of life must revolve around human values, not financial gain.

FOUR: THE RIGHT TO LIVE IN A FAMILY WHOSE BASIC ECONOMIC NEEDS ARE MET. In the midst of plenty, hunger and poverty mean national lack of concern. Every family must have basic financial support to provide for itself adequate food, clothing, housing, and health care.

The child must be born into a family where he or she is wanted and can be supported physically and psychologically. Family pride and cohesiveness depend on the adults' knowledge that they can provide for their children adequately—that they can feed, house, and clothe them and care for their health.

In particular, the vicious cycle of poverty, depression, and apathy must be broken. It means that wages and prices must be balanced so that food, clothing, shelter, and medical care are guaranteed for all. Prevention of disease and disorder as well as treatment for already acquired illnesses are major basic economic concerns.

FIVE: THE RIGHT TO CONTINUOUS AND LOVING CARE BOTH AT HOME AND IN SCHOOL. Concern and loving care are essential to healthy development of the child. At home, this means parents who understand the needs of the infant and young child and are prepared to nurture the infant, to provide the security and stimulation that can occur only when parents have hope for the future and little anxiety about the economics of day-to-day living. Parental anxieties, the sense of helplessness and powerlessness, massive health and nutritional problems affect abilities to parent all children. Current anxieties about life and our vulnerability to destruction from pollution, internal strife due to racial discrimination, massive poverty, and threat of wars devitalize most parent-child relations. Research shows that much of adolescent troubles reflect their sense of a futureless society in which there is general unconcern about humans. A massive sense of powerlessness and the resulting need to acquire possessions as a bulwark against fears are contrary to the traditional values of human concern and human interchange that make democracy viable.

Children must have optimal opportunities for learning and developing their curiosity and capacities for exploration. This requires family access to early childhood education. Large cities with their crowding and suburbia with its isolation of individuals permit few natural avenues for exploration, learning, and socialization in the first few years of life.

Preschool programs need to be available to all and to be staffed by knowledgeable persons dedicated to facilitating development through the child's play and exploration.

The mutual goal of parents and educators is to provide age-appropriate experiences and stimuli from birth on, experiences and stimuli required to help the child feel safe to explore, to relate to others, and to assert his or her individuality.

SIX: THE RIGHT TO ACQUIRE INTELLECTUAL AND EMOTIONAL SKILLS FOR EFFECTIVE CITIZENSHIP. The right to develop potential interests, skills, intellectual abilities through effective teaching and learning is essential. As the child grows, we need an educational system geared to helping each child to find the kind of learning and work he needs for his personal growth and sense of effectiveness. Especially, each child must experience the kind of learning situation which encourages that youngster to learn to collect information, then to apply it to solving problems as a way of life in a complex and problem-ridden society.

When we talk about the right to acquire the intellectual and emotional skills necessary to achieve individual aspirations and to cope effectively in our society, we are talking about the right to learn in school how to work in useful occupations while still in school. Children have the right to be dealt with by educators who are skilled in understanding children and in helping them directly and through working together with their parents to find each child's own greatest capacities and abilities. All children must experience mastery to feel effective. A sense of effectiveness is rarely experienced by most children today.

SEVEN: THE RIGHT TO MEANINGFUL EMPLOYMENT. A society which is more and more technically organized and mechanized must find ways for its children to learn to work in useful occupations. It follows that youngsters have a right to actually have such work available as they reach adolescence. This means no discriminatory practices based on race or sex. Therefore, the health, education, and welfare enterprises of our society must become major avenues for gainful, valued, and meaningful employment for our children and youth. Fine craftsmanship in all the trades must be given due value and respect in order to engage those youngsters with these unique talents. Race as a bar to employment in every field must be ended!

EIGHT: THE RIGHT TO DIAGNOSTIC TREATMENT AND REHABILITATIVE CARE THROUGH FACILITIES WHICH ARE APPROPRIATE TO CHILDREN'S SPECIAL NEEDS AND WHICH KEEP THEM AS CLOSELY AS POSSIBLE WITHIN THEIR NORMAL SOCIAL SETTING. Care which keeps them within their normal social setting means there must be a health maintenance and care system geared to prevention of illness and maintenance of health. Such a system must follow children from birth on, and be concerned with the prenatal factors leading to disease and disorder. That system must integrate all the services needed for each child and his family. Such a health maintenance system must be available to all, at all times. Nothing short of a total health system will be concerned with prevention of illness as well as its treatment. One aspect of such a system is that it can, and must be able to, bring together on behalf of the child and the family all the resources required to deal with any particular health or mental health problem. It means that the necessary medical and other treatment facilities must be available. Well-trained personnel must also be available. All of these treatment facilities must not only be responsive to the needs of the child but also responsive to the needs of the family, keeping the child within its normal social setting as much as possible to encourage the child's recovery and return to the best possible functioning no matter what the illness is.

NINE: THE RIGHT TO RACIAL AND ETHNIC IDENTITY, SELF-DE-TERMINATION, AND A REAL FUNCTIONAL EQUALITY OF OPPORTUNITY TO THE ABOVE RIGHTS. In all of the above, we must be aware that we are talking about the right of the children of minorities to contribute, from their ethnic background, information which helps give those children and therefore all other children the dignity and respect due to each child and citizen. It means that we begin to look carefully at what racism has done to our society today as a major issue to be understood and resolved. The impact of racism today exists despite civil rights laws. It has critical, harmful effects upon all citizens and all children. Black children of the ghettos, Spanish-speaking American children, American Indian children, Oriental children and those of all other minorities still find it impossible to get employment or an education that will lead to a meaningful life. They have never been and still are not an accepted important part of our pluralistic society. It is only as all of the children in a minority are encouraged that they begin to contribute to the learning of all children, each from his or her own background, and that some mutual respect begins to be prevalent rather than the hatred and alienation that currently exist. We as adults must find the means to begin such interchange and provide the models for such mutual respect, consideration, and human concern. Mutual learning and respect rest on equality of opportunity to work, housing, quality education, and health care.

TEN: THE RIGHT TO POLITICAL PARTICIPATION THROUGH EDUCA-

TION FOR INFORMED CITIZENSHIP. The right of children to be educated early to become participant citizens in their world means first that education must become a problem-solving system and children must be taught how to think about problems and to learn the methods for solving problems. Every aspect of the education system must be geared to teaching children how to gather data and to use that data to understand and work on problems of concern to them. They need to learn to examine problems which confront them and to learn to determine what the solutions might be for them. It means that the educational system and the family support system must be so geared that children see a vital role for themselves as citizens in society and learn to use themselves as citizens. Only then will their voices and votes help determine the kinds of policies under which they and their children can live.

Not all the ten rights are specifically covered in this volume. Our intent is to provide a background which reveals major issues and some possible solutions. Selected methods of approaching problems and clearly revealing issues which affect institutions and individuals are presented.

The intent of the chapters that follow is to make vivid the inequities that exist. These writings emphasize that advocacy of these rights is not only possible and feasible, but is, in fact, urgent and necessary for our own survival.

REFERENCES

1. BIRCH, H., & RICHARDSON, S. A. The relation of handicaps to social and obstetrical factors in all children living in one city. Presented at the American Academy of Cerebral Palsy, December, 1965.
2. CRAVIOTO, J., DELICARDIE, E. R., & BIRCH, H. G. Nutrition, growth and neuro-integrative development: An experimental and ecologic study. *Pediatrics*, 1966, *38*(Suppl.).
3. Joint Commission on Mental Health of Children. Report. *Crisis in Child Mental Health*. New York: Harper and Row, 1970.
4. KNOBLOCH, H., RIDER, R., HARPER, P., & PASAMANICK, B. Neuropsychiatric sequelae of prematurity. *Journal of the American Medical Association*, 1956, *161*, 581.
5. PASAMANICK, B., & LILIENFELD, A. M. Association of maternal and fetal factors with development of mental deficiency. I. Abnormalities in the prenatal and perinatal periods. *Journal of the American Medical Association*, 1955, *159*, 155.

I am neither a wise man nor a visionary
nor one who stands alone—I have merely
studied and put what I have learned into
order.

Talmud, Tractate Pesachim

2

Children in the Seventies: Developmental Findings and Recommendations from the Joint Commission on Mental Health of Children

IRVING N. BERLIN, M.D.

Extent of the problem

In the United States today, no less than 12 to 13 percent of all children between the ages of five and nineteen have mental health problems severe enough to require some kind of professional intervention. This fact is established by information now available from the Office of Biometry of N.I.M.H., the study of Glidewell and Swallow,[8] and the latest school and juvenile court findings. This means that during the '70s, at least six million children per year will require treatment. Some experts in school guidance feel this estimate is low.

Statistics from studies of preschool children indicate that children in poverty populations have a much higher incidence of health problems. These statistics show that at least 50 percent of children in poverty populations have general health problems and 30 percent have mental health problems. In the suburban pre-

11

schools studied, the incidence of mental health problems indicated by disturbed and withdrawn behavior is estimated at 20 to 25 percent. Bateman [2,3] and others found that between 20 and 30 percent of all children studied in the schools have poor motor development and that about 15 percent have perceptual motor problems. Twelve percent of the school-age children studied have psychological problems of sufficient severity to seriously interfere with their learning.

Problems of the infant and small child

NUTRITION IN PREGNANCY, BIRTH, AND INFANCY. Maternal malnutrition during pregnancy is directly related to infant mortality, birth defects, and prematurity. Difficulties during and after birth such as anoxia, malnutrition, and death during the first year are clearly related to poor care given during delivery and the neonatal period in poverty areas and an inadequate diet provided for mothers and infants in the poverty population.

Prematurity has been shown to be a major cause of a youngster's mental deficiency and of failure to grow and mature normally, to learn effectively and thus to become a useful citizen. Prematurity and low birth weight have been causally related to malnutrition of the mother.

Research on infant and child malnutrition indicates very clearly that the frequent anemia due to iron deficiency and massive protein deficiencies markedly affect the activity level of the child, its capacity to investigate the environment, to play, to talk, and to walk. The child's low energy level interferes with the capacity to socialize with playmates. The capacity to learn in preschool and school settings is therefore also seriously impaired.

INFANT RHYTHMS: NEED FOR DEVELOPMENTAL HELP TO MOTHERS. Studies indicate that both genetic and environmental factors may produce infants who are particularly sensitive to normal sensory stimuli such as light and noise in the home, who are fussy, not cuddly, and thus do not live up to the particular requirements and expectations of the parents. These infants are especially likely to become difficult for their mothers. Similarly, infants with minimal brain dysfunction or slowed developmental rate who are very irritable and unpredictable in their sleeping habits are likely to so tire their mothers that they cannot be very warmly attentive to them. These infants are poorly understood in terms of their developing feeding and sleeping rhythms. As a result, as their particular needs for food and sleep become more stabilized and regulated, these changes may not be perceived as development proceeds. Nobody is observing the infant to determine emerging patterns of behavior which could help mother, through a more predictable pattern, feel more rested and able to relate in a more relaxed and nurturant way to the infant. Such difficulties in regulation of behavior patterns in infancy may separate the mother and child in their feelings of closeness and begin, therefore, to set up a circular process of poor mothering on the one hand and poor response and development in the child on the other.

EFFECTS OF MATERNAL DEPRIVATION ON THE INFANT AND YOUNG CHILD. Very close review of investigations under way on deprivation of nurturance to the infant and small child indicates that deprivation at critical stages of development may be so crippling that by the time a child is three the effects of deprivation may not be reversible, although they may be somewhat ameliorated. These investigations are so compelling that several task forces recommend a major emphasis on preventive efforts before age three. Although these problems are more obvious at the poverty level, they are also reported with great frequency in the suburbs in mothers who are depressed as a result of having unwanted children or who have marital or other problems which reduce their sense of adequacy. They find that their worries and depression interfere with their usual awareness of their babies' needs and their usual capacity for playful tenderness. However, such mothers in the suburbs usually feel they must not complain about their babies and their feelings of depression to their physicians. Conversely, physicians are usually not trained to recognize maternal troubles and fail to inquire about mothers' pleasure in their infants unless a crisis occurs.

FAILURE TO THRIVE: A SIGN OF THE TIMES. Investigation of the "failure-to-thrive" syndrome has implications for the problems of infant deprivation of nurturance. While evidence exists that a few scrawny children are genetically unable to digest their food because of enzyme deficiency, the overwhelming evidence from both psychologic and behavioral studies is that failure to thrive results most often from great maternal ambivalence or uncertainty about a particular youngster. An infant who is unwanted may, because of the lack of stimulation and attention necessary to thrive, grow, and regulate its sleeping and waking patterns, begin to fuss, cry, and be sleepless. Thus, it does not gain weight. This indicates to some physicians and to others that somehow the mother is unable to be maternal. As a result, the mother feels labeled as a failure without being helped to change her behavior toward the infant, which could often then alter the baby's behavior. This in turn increases the amount of estrangement between mother and baby and the incapacity of the mother to relate to the child in a nurturant, stimulating way is increased and the likelihood that the process might be reversed is decreased.

In short, failure of a baby to thrive and failure to reach the clearly defined developmental landmarks should be warnings to health personnel of possible troubles in mother-child relationships. They should look into the mother-child interactions to find ways not only of helping the mother relate to the child, but also of helping medically with some of the child's most distressing behavior. Intervention that occurs early enough helps the mother and permits reversal of the process of deprivation.

CHILD ABUSE: THE UNWANTED CHILD—THE IMMATURE PARENT. A series of studies on child abuse indicates that the abused and seriously hurt child is often the one child in a family who is particularly unwanted, although when the victim is removed from the home another child may be abused. He or she may not be the result of the present marriage, may have been a premature child with all its special problems, or may have been born out of wedlock. Investigations show that children who begin to be abused use the abuse and being hurt as a way of being involved with parents who would otherwise ignore them. Thus they tend to arouse more anger and hostility and create a greater threat to their lives.

The studies of Kempe and his co-workers [23] and the Polanskys [21] indicate that it is often possible, if the health care professionals pick up signs of child abuse early and report it to the appropriate agencies, to begin an effective intervention program with the family. These studies show that the parents usually have a history of being severely physically beaten as children and have received little tender nurturant care. They have the previous life experience to guide them in the care of their infant. These parents view the two-year-old's "No," which is normal child behavior, as if it were stubborn, deliberate adult contrariness. Sometimes removing the particular child from the family to a foster home or an institution geared to give such a child remedial care reverses the developmental retardation and the child begins to develop more normally and to thrive with warmer and more encouraging relationships. Especially the child needs to learn how to interact with adults in a way that will bring forth nurturant, playful, and tender behavior rather than punishment.

A critical issue with foster parents and institutions which requires professional help is that at first the abused child will use the tactics learned in relating with the abusing parents to arouse anger and hostility in the caretaker adults. Close monitoring of the course of the child's development in the new situation may be vital for effective intervention.

DAY CARE: A DEVELOPMENTAL RESOURCE. Recent investigations of day care show a number of impressive findings. In one setting, day care for infants of working mothers in the poverty group was provided. The children received individual nurturance from a number of adults and were provided a wide variety of sensory and motor stimuli with other children. These children socialized with peers very early. At ages three and four, they had much higher IQs when compared with a control group. The control group was made up of children of middle-class university graduate-student parents. These children of the same age, but not in the day care program, were repeatedly tested at the same time as the day care children. The experimental day care children were not only brighter, but better able to relate to both children and adults. They were able to investigate creatively and with sustained interest not seen in their uninvolved siblings or even in the normally bright middle-class control group children. One of the issues raised for further investigation was the effect of active, involved personal stimulation of the experimental children versus the passive TV stimulation of many of the control children and siblings of the experimental group.

Stress in the infant and small child

Collation of a variety of research studies has led the Joint Commission task forces on the infant-to-preschool child, the school-age child, and the adolescent to begin to assemble a kind of developmental, diagnostic early warning system for both the physician and other health-related persons in the community. All studies indicated that stress on the infant and child may be first noted in the way the adaptive equilibrium of the child is altered. Differences in response to stress depend in part upon hereditary and constitutional factors. Under similar conditions, the very vigorous and muscular child may not be so greatly affected by stress in his adaptive equilibrium as the listless and less vigorous child or infant. Investigators agree that malnutrition affects growth and vitality and the attainment of developmental landmarks in most children. They also agree that severe physical stress and severe illness can cause both psychological and social repercussions. Thus when a child is hospitalized or separated from mother, signs of stress usually appear. The length of stay in the hospital, how much separation from parents is enforced, the severity of the child's illness, and the capacity of hospital personnel to be nurturant and supporting to the child, spending time with the child, may determine both the severity of the stress and how long it will affect the child after return home. The physician and other health-related professionals need to be alert to signs of stress.

EARLY WARNING SIGNS. Some early warning indicators of stress, while known to most physicians, bear reemphasis. In early infancy, disturbances often are noted by changes in the usual patterns of eating, sleeping, and elimination. Anorexia (starvation) and overeating may point to problems. Eating of nonedible material, such as hair, plaster, or dirt, is usually an indication of severe physiologic or psychologic stress. Early and continuous sleeping problems and colic may be indications of minimal brain damage but more often are related to central nervous system immaturity or to severe psychological stresses usually associated with temporary or occasionally prolonged inability of the parenting person to adequately nurture the infant. Chronic constipation is also indicative of physiological and psychological problems. As previously mentioned, delayed growth and signs of malnutrition are very critical indicators of stress.

Some organ system symptoms, particularly those of the gastro-intestinal tract, skin, and respiratory tract, are particularly important as early warnings. Chronic vomiting, rumination (vomiting and reswallowing of food), poor food absorption, skin rashes which do not heal, chronic wheezing and runny noses with sustained weight loss as well as colds and chronic, poorly-defined illness are predictive of later problems in physical health and mental health. The sudden occurrence or reoccurrence of these symptoms often signals acute onset of stress.

DEVELOPMENTAL DELAY PREDICTS LATER PROBLEMS. Delayed development of landmarks has powerful, predictive significance. Marked retardation of several functions during the first year of life is important. These functions include development of curiosity noted by eager looking and grasping at three to five months; in the area of vocalization, making repetitive sounds at three to six months, and saying a few words around age one; motor coordination and beginning use of hands for investigation, usually occurring at the time of sitting up and crawling at about eight months; finger-thumb opposition and the precise handling of objects which usually occurs about the time of walking at around twelve months; and development of sphincter control of bowel and bladder occurring at about eighteen months to two years of age. Marked delay in these functions may all be warnings of impending difficulties. Health care personnel who are trained to inquire about socialization can closely follow a child's social and intellectual development. Their inquiries lead to responses about the smiling, cooing, vocalizations, verbalizations, and play which indicate undisturbed development. Disturbances in the relationships or unusual stress on family or child may be revealed by recurrent fear of others, anxious desire to be constantly alone, loss of speech or reduction in the amount of vocalization, significant decrease in alertness and interest in the environment or family members as well as by severe head banging. These are early signs of psychological difficulty which require prompt attention.

Many investigators have found that the mother who can not easily play with, or talk and sing to her child is very likely to have a child with emotional problems. Such a child develops speech late, after two years of age, and uses it poorly for communication. As one investigator pointed out, a "talking environment" is a prerequisite for learning language.

OTHER SIGNS OF STRESS. One of the more serious indicators of stress at either the physiological or psychological level is loss of previously acquired skills like walking, talking, bowel control, etc. Prompt investigation frequently reveals a recent illness or injury, or alienation from the mothering person for various reasons such as marital problems, death of a parent or sibling, or divorce. Prompt intervention in a crisis with attention to the mother's needs and help in her interactions with her child bring rapid resolution of stress, while failure to intervene may lead to irreversible changes.

Problems in preschool socialization. It is difficult for the physician or other helping person to become aware of disturbances in a child's capacity to play, to investigate, to explore his environment, and to relate to peers and to family members. However, regular inquiries made of the parent when the child is brought in for examination may reveal important data. To play, to investigate, and to socialize are the child's primary developmental tasks in his preschool years. They are necessary for developing sensorimotor skills and social mastery of the environment. Repetitive, robot-like play, indifference to new toys and objects, fear of learning new skills such as using a scooter or trike, and refusal to interact and play with age mates often indicate troubles.

Overreaction. Persistence of overreaction to minor stresses, great sadness, impulsiveness with marked violence, and incapacity to tolerate any frustrations may be critical indicators of difficulties on the psychological level and from retrospective studies have implications for a child's well-being and effectiveness in later life.

Constant restlessness, inability to be still, a frenzy of movement without reduction in tension may be indications of neurophysiological disturbances. Often these children do not respond to efforts at distraction, comfort, or punishment. They appear driven. These problems require very early diagnosis so that treatment and management plans may be started as early as possible. Effective treatment and management help the child and the worried family. Behavior change may be marked and completely alter the child's capacities for learning and socializing.

The school-age child and stress

For the young school-age child, early warning signs are difficulty in separating from mother to go to school, so-called school phobia, temper tantrums, marked isolation, asocial, hostile, and impulsive behavior, as well as inability to relate to teachers or classmates. Especially critical are problems in learning. Research studies indicate that physicians, nurses, and teachers who follow children closely are able to make diagnostic assessments which have great predictive value. Thus youngsters who are hyperactive, hyperaggressive, and violent frequently elicit an environmental reaction which interacts with their genetic and psychological state to produce delinquent behavior.

Similar evidence exists that early asocial behavior plus withdrawal occurs in children who later become adolescent psychotics, that is, schizophrenics. Such children are noted in the primary grades to be withdrawn, unable to play with classmates, and poor learners. While the school bears a major responsibility for identifying these youngsters, the health care professionals are often in the first line of problem detection.

The school setting also exposes a child's insecurities when he passes from one grade to another and thus to a new teacher. Especially traumatic for some children is the transition from grade school to junior high school. The change from having one teacher who acts as a parental figure all day to having a new teacher every period may be difficult. Such transitions may be special problems for children from disorganized families who need stable attachments to function effectively. The child who cannot make such transitions begins to disintegrate in the junior high school setting, to act up, and to have learning difficulties. Persistent school refusal may also occur. These symptoms must be understood not as isolated phenomena but rather in terms of the child's developmental history and current developmental needs to separate from mother and fears of loss of support. Pressures to learn in school, to socialize with peers and to become independent, sexual fears in adolescence brought on by needing to undress in gym, new demands for intellectual effectiveness and independent strivings in adolescence may all precipitate school phobia.

PSYCHOPHYSIOLOGICAL MANIFESTATIONS. Many psychophysiological problems which manifest themselves in the school-age child have a strong emotional component related to stress from school and home. Sex differences in learning readiness, which have been noted by investigators as early stability of the autonomic nervous system in girls and instability in boys, result in earlier learning readiness in girls. Parenthetically, this nervous system instability from birth on in boys as contrasted to girls has been related to the higher incidence among boys of mental illness and problems in reading, speech, and learning. Many large-muscled, hyperactive boys are not ready to sit still long enough to be able to begin to learn to read and write. Stable perceptual and motor integration may not occur developmentally until age nine or ten. As a result, the school's uniform curriculum may contribute to such a youngster's increased hyperactivity and learning difficulties. The health and mental health professionals who are aware of this problem can help by alerting the school to reduce the kinds of expectations and stresses faced by such a youngster, especially those resulting from encounters with uninformed and poorly attuned female teachers.

SEXUAL MATURATION: EMOTIONAL PROBLEMS. Early sexual maturation also creates problems. Intellectual immaturity, coupled with the minimal education and information provided in schools and homes about their own physiology and anatomy and about sexuality in general, increases the problems and self-doubts of these youngsters. Sudden changes in behavior of pubescent students may be warnings of increased stresses and may be part of normal adolescence. Learning problems, open masturbation, withdrawal from friends and family, fear of undressing in gym, and school phobia may be both warnings and signals for help.

Studies of unmarried mothers, especially of junior-high and young high-school age, show that most of these girls are seeking some kind of closeness and nurturance rather than the usually disappointing sexual experience. Studies of the fathers reveal confusion about sexuality, longing for warmth and closeness, as well as a drive for sexual relief and satisfaction. Both partners need help to mature and find satisfying relationships during adolescence so that as adults they may be nurturant parents.

ABRUPT BEHAVIOR CHANGES: A WARNING. Any abrupt change

in the usual patterning of a child's learning and social behavior should be a warning both to the school and to the physician that the child is experiencing something unusual. Experience clearly shows that sudden withdrawal as well as violence may be premonitions of the onset of acute psychosis, suicide, or homicide.

The role of health and mental health personnel

Persistence of the signs described requires evaluation and action. Health caring professionals need to use their knowledge of the child's development and their understanding of the parents and possible family problems to make a comprehensive assessment. Physicians and nurses can evaluate the need for intervention and the means available to help the family and child. One of the most pervasive dangers is our optimistic tendency to believe that problems will fade away and that parents need not be concerned about particular problems. We depend on an unrealistic belief that the child will outgrow them. Because of this, observations of the young child are often not continuously recorded in order to make assessment possible. There is now powerful evidence that continued, prolonged, or repeated stress from any cause before age three may result in irreversible damage. Such continued stress especially interferes with the child's capacity to learn, to develop sensorimotor skills, a sense of competence and a capacity to relate to others. Thus the individual is greatly handicapped throughout life.

Many health care professionals are able to work effectively with distraught and disturbed mothers. Others have neither the time nor the desire and lack needed information about community resources available for parents who need such help. When physicians, nurses, or agencies refer parents, the need to keep in touch with the parents and the mental health professional or agency to see how things are going continues. Such contact gives parents a sense of continued interest and concern, which reduces the parents' feeling of self-blame or blame by an authority and permits them to use help more effectively.

For example, with a premature infant, if the physician or nurse helps the mother to handle and stimulate the infant in the hospital and works out a stimulation program with the nursing staff, some of the handicaps of prematurity are reduced. The mother is also not afraid of the infant when it comes home. Public health nurses can help the family with the crisis of a premature infant. Under a physician's direction they can anticipate the problems of fussing, poor eating, and sleeping due to the maturational state. They can also find housekeeping help for the sleepless mother so her family is taken care of, thus assuring better mother-infant and mother-family relations.

Infants who are excessively sensitive to stimuli are very difficult to cuddle. Such infants or those who fail to thrive give the mother a sense of incompetence and failure. Often a physician or a nurse can demonstrate how playing with, talking to, and providing frequent interaction with a difficult baby may reverse the process. Many mothers do not know how to play with and talk to their infants. They require demonstration and encouragement to make such efforts. The professionals' complimentary comments about a mother's efforts and a few moments taken to observe new mother-child interactions can reinforce a mother's capacity to nurture. This is effective primary prevention.

In all of these problems, perhaps best exemplified in child abuse, the professionals' knowledge of community agencies, readiness to act on behalf of the abused child, and capacity for supporting the agency by continued interest in a child may help the agency anticipate and follow through on problems, relying on their expert advice about developmental needs and responding to their concern and encouragement by increased efforts with a difficult child.

The physician's diagnostic efforts to assess signs of stress at any age and to collaborate with schools and other agencies in intervention often relieve parents' burdens. Parents usually know continued problems exist, but they need authoritative sanction to begin to get help for the child and themselves so the problems can be resolved. For this reason, continued monitoring by physician or public health nurse as an authoritative figure may be vital to continued treatment and collaborative effort by family and agency.

Some recommendations from the task forces

A WANTED CHILD. All studies show a clear relationship between general health and mental health. As has been pointed out by one of the task forces, perhaps the least expensive mental health intervention is birth control, which permits women of any age not to have children who are unwanted and not to be forced into the position of being a nonnurturant mother, especially if they still need nurturance themselves. Difficult marital or financial situations may reduce the nurturance of a resented infant and therefore affect his mental health.

LEGALIZED ABORTION. The same task force also recommended legalizing abortion as a critical mental health strategy. Establishment of the right to have a wanted child as expressed by many state medical societies and the American Public Health Association is a vital factor in insuring that the child is indeed likely to have the important experiences with its mother which are requisite to optimal development.

HIGH RISK REGISTERS. Other task forces have recommended establishment of high risk registers. These community data banks would make available to health care personnel and concerned agencies necessary information about youngsters who had birth injuries, were premature, or had congenital or genetic problems. Data would also be collected about minimal brain damage, malnourishment at birth, instances of child abuse or neglect, and other physical and psychological problems which might be predictors of developmental difficulty for a child and should be known by health and mental health professionals and relevant agencies. Such knowledge would permit ongoing evaluation and prompt intervention. Registers already in use have demonstrated possibilities for secondary prevention which may be essential for helping a child to grow more normally. Identification through numbers rather than names would help preserve the required confidentiality.

BETTER HOSPITAL PROCEDURES. Some task forces expressed the concern that hospitalized children be taken care of by their own mothers so psychological stress of hospitalization and surgical procedures could be reduced.

GENETIC COUNSELING. Several of the task forces have recommended genetic counseling, especially to those families in which inborn errors of metabolism, youngsters with XYY chromosomes or with XXY Klinefelter's syndrome have occurred.

NEW PROFESSIONAL EDUCATION AND TRAINING. Much discussion

took place in the Joint Commission and the task forces about how to involve medical schools and schools training all the other helping professions in teaching developmental diagnosis and comprehensive child care in a way relevant to each profession so that early detection of developmental problems and intervention might be more prevalent. Physicians especially not only require effective training in developmental diagnosis and family intervention methods but must be kept abreast of research findings that will enhance their diagnostic and therapeutic skills.

The training of indigenous workers as aides to both teachers and health workers has also been stressed as a way of dealing with manpower needs. Training of teachers and pupil personnel workers in developmental diagnosis is emphatically recommended. The key roles of health care professionals in all of these endeavors, that is, to spearhead prevention and intervention efforts on behalf of the child and his family and to lead the way in helping train the needed auxiliary medical manpower, are evident in all of the recommendations.

Clear needs, clear prevention and intervention methods: Now a people's mandate

This brief review of the problems, the needs, and some ways of meeting these needs of all children reveals the need for commitment—a commitment of health and mental health professionals to prevention and early intervention strategies; a commitment to new strategies of health and mental health care delivery to those most in need; a commitment to develop large numbers of well-trained paraprofessionals to perform the many health care tasks they can do well for patients.

Such commitments require a new dedication to health and mental health care by educational institutions, professionals and, above all, the Congress and the Federal Administration.

The mandate must be a financial one—strong, whole-hearted, and adequate. We must "orbit the earth and land on the moon" for children; we must secure their birthright in health, mental health, and basic economic security from hunger, so they can in fact assure our future as a democracy.

REFERENCES

1. BAYLEY, N. Developmental problems of the mentally retarded child. In I. Philips (Ed.), *Prevention and Treatment of Mental Retardation*. New York: Basic Books, 1966. Pp. 85–110.
2. BATEMAN, B. An educator's view of a diagnostic approach to learning disorders. In J. Hellmuth (Ed.), *Learning Disorders*. Vol. 1. Seattle, Washington: Bernie Straub and Jerome Hellmuth, 1965. Special Child Publications of the Seattle Seguin School. Pp. 219–239.
3. BATEMAN, B. An overview of specific language disabilities. *Bulletin of the Orton Society*, 1965, *15*, 1–12.
4. BELOFF, J. S., & KORPER, M. The health team model and medical care utilization. *Journal of the American Medical Association*, 1972, *219*, 359–366.
5. BIBER, B., & FRANKLIN, M. B. The relevance of developmental and psychodynamic concepts to the education of the preschool child. In J. Hellmuth (Ed.), *Disadvantaged Child*. Vol. 1. New York: Brunner/Mazel, 1967. Pp. 305–323.
6. FRIEDENBERG, E. Z. *Coming of Age in America*. New York: Pitman, 1964.
7. GIL, D. *Violence Against Children*. Cambridge, Mass.: Harvard University Press, 1971.
8. GLIDEWELL, J., & SWALLOW, C. *The Prevalence of Maladjustment in Elementary Schools*. (A report prepared for the Joint Commission on Mental Health of Children.) Chicago: University of Chicago, July 26, 1968.
9. HARRELL, R. F., WOODYARD, E. R., & GATES, A. I. Influence of vitamin supplementation of diets of pregnant and lactating women on intelligence of their offspring. *Metabolism*, 1956, *5*, 555–562.
10. HUNT, J. MCV. The psychological basis for using preschool enrichment as an antidote for cultural deprivation. In J. Hellmuth (Ed.), *Disadvantaged Child*. Vol. 1. New York: Brunner/Mazel, 1967. Pp. 255–299.
11. KEITH, H. M., & GAGE, R. P. Neurologic lesions in relation to asphyxia of newborn and factors of pregnancy: Long-term follow-up. *Pediatrics*, 1960, *26*, 616–622.
12. KNOBLOCH, H., & PASAMANICK, B. Distribution of intellectual potential in infant population. In B. Pasamanick (Ed.), *The Epidemiology of Mental Disorder*. Washington, D. C.: American Psychiatric Association, 1959.
13. KNOBLOCH, H., & PASAMANICK, B. Evaluation of consistency and predictive value of 40 week Gesell developmental schedule. In G. Shagass and B. Pasamanick (Eds.), *Child Development and Child Psychiatry*. Washington, D. C.: American Psychiatric Association, 1960. P. 10.

14. KNOBLOCH, H., & PASAMANICK, B. Genetics of mental disease: Symposium: 1960. 2. Some thoughts on inheritance of intelligence. *American Journal of Orthopsychiatry*, 1961, *31*, 454–473.

15. KNOBLOCH, H., & PASAMANICK, B. Mental subnormality. *New England Journal of Medicine*, 1962, *266*, 1045–1161.

16. KNOBLOCH, H., & PASAMANICK, B. Syndrome of minimal cerebral damage in infancy. *Journal of the American Medical Association*, 1959, *170*, 1384–1387.

17. KOCH, R. A. Diagnosis in infancy and early childhood. In I. Philips (Ed.), *Prevention and Treatment of Mental Retardation*. New York: Basic Books, 1966. Pp. 44–58.

18. MARANS, A. E., & LOURIE, R. Hypotheses regarding the effects of child-rearing patterns on the disadvantaged child. In J. Hellmuth (Ed.), *Disadvantaged Child*. Vol. 1. New York: Brunner/Mazel, 1967. Pp. 17–41.

19. NELSON, M. M., & EVANS, H. M. Protein deficiency and pregnancy in rat. *Nutrition Review*, 1955, *13*, 152.

20. PINNEAU, S. R. Infantile disorders of hospitalism and anaclitic depression. *Psychological Bulletin*, 1955, *52*, 429–452.

21. POLANSKY, N., & POLANSKY, N. The current status of child abuse and child neglect in this country. Report to the Joint Commission on Mental Health for Children, February, 1968.

22. President's Task Force on Early Child Development. *A Bill of Rights for Children*. Washington, D.C.: Department of Health, Education and Welfare, 1967.

23. STEELE, B. F., & POLLOCK, C. B. A psychiatric study of parents who abuse infants and small children. In R. E. Helfer and C. H. Kempe (Eds.), *The Battered Child*. Chicago: University of Chicago Press, 1968. Pp. 103–147.

24. STOTT, D. H. Infantile illness and subsequent mental and emotional development. *Journal of Genetic Psychology*, 1959, *94*, 233–251.

25. TAYLOR, R. W. Depression and recovery at nine weeks of age. *Journal of the American Academy of Child Psychiatry*, 1973, *12*, 506–510.

26. THURSTON, D., GRAHAM, F. K., ERNHART, C. B., EICHMAN, P. L., & CRAFT, M. Neurologic status of 3-year-old-children originally studied at birth. *Neurology*, 1960, *10*, 680–690.

27. TOMPKINS, W. T., & WIEHL, D. G. Maternal and newborn nutrition studies at Philadelphia Lying-in Hospital. Maternal Studies. II. Prematurity and maternal nutrition. In Milbank Memorial Fund. *The Promotion of Maternal and Newborn Health: Papers Presented at the 1954 Annual Conference of the Fund*. New York: Milbank, 1955. P. 25.

28. WENDER, P.H. *Minimal Brain Dysfunction in Children*. New York: Wiley-Interscience, 1971.

29. WINDLE, W. F. Effects of asphyxiation of fetus and newborn infant. *Pediatrics*, 1960, *26*, 565–569.

The aim of every science is foresight (prévoyance).
For the laws established by observation of
phenomena are generally employed to foresee their
succession. All men, however little advanced, (and
we may take comfort from this) make true
predictions, which are always based on the same
principle, the knowledge of the future from the
past. For example, all men predict the general
effects of terrestrial gravity (for example, when we
jump off the earth we come back to it, or at least
some of us do!) and a multitude of other
phenomena sufficiently simple and usual for the
least capable and attentive spectator to be aware of
their order of succession. The faculty of foresight
in each person is measured by his science.

A. COMTE in *System of Positive Polity*
(New York: B. Franklin, 1966, vol. 4.)

3

Child Development:
A Basic Science for the
Child Health Professions

JULIUS B. RICHMOND, M.D.
STANLEY WALZER, M.D.

Society continues to look to physicians and other health care
workers for solutions to new health problems. Throughout most
of this century, the primary requirement of the professionals was
to cure disease; to do this, they also had to clarify the causes and
develop a way of classifying diseases. However, in recent years
society has come to expect more of the health care professional.
The concept of health has broadened from simply the absence of
disease.

The constitution of the World Health Organization defines
health as "a state of complete physical, mental, and social well-

being. . ." Such a definition emphasizes that preoccupation with issues of sickness is insufficient for health professionals of this decade. More attention must be directed to defining those factors which help prevent illness and contribute to normal growth and development. The total development of any individual is determined by an interaction of a biologically endowed organism with the environment and the people in it. Consideration must therefore be given to biological, psychological, and sociocultural factors. The health care professionals need to reorient themselves from the exclusive consideration of biological development to a consideration of all aspects of the life of the child.

At the same time that we were called upon for a more unified approach to health care, child health workers were embarked on various fragmented courses. Biological development had been considered apart from issues of child ecology and child-rearing practices as they influence the development of the child. It becomes evident that if we are to be responsive to the demands of modern society for total health care, we must reintegrate the broader aspects of child development into the mainstream of health care. Perhaps we can deal more adequately with the problem if we turn to history in order to understand how we came to be this way.

The history of modern child health care

Prior to 1920 there was a concern with general child development and child welfare, with particular attention to child care practices and the living conditions of the family which affected the child. With the coming of the scientific revolution (which followed the industrial revolution), the interests and priorities of health care were reordered. There were rapid advances in research in microbiology, epidemiology, biochemistry, physiology, and pharmacology, which brought about the establishment of our present research culture. So effective have these efforts been that, as a consequence, one can compare infant-child illness and death statistics between 1900 and today and see the enormous differences. Research advances made possible the isolation of specific causative agents of disease and the development of specific cures, and led to an increased understanding of immunology and the development of immunization procedures for diseases of childhood. The new knowledge of nutrition and metabolism made it possible to prevent many nutritional disorders and to treat metabolic disturbances. The priorities quite properly shifted to applying the new and emerging knowledge from biology to the saving of lives.

In this atmosphere of disease-oriented pediatric training, a number of research institutes in child development were established. Of prime importance was the establishment of the Society for Research in Child Development, which offered a significant scientific forum for communication among workers in the interdisciplinary field of child development. This organization facilitated the publication of a number of notable monographs in child development, as well as the journal, *Child Development*, which has served as a catalyst for all segments of this field. It is significant that the monographs and the journal of this organization have not been utilized sufficiently as resources for teaching child development to physicians in schools of medicine or in training programs for nurses, public health personnel, pediatricians, or child psychiatrists.

Dr. Samuel Levine, in his presidential address before the American Pediatric Society,* summarized the period we have just described as follows:

> From 1920 to 1950, many of us lived through and participated in what might be called the "Golden Age of Curative Pediatrics"—prophylactic immunization, the widespread use of vitamins, nutritional knowledge, water and electrolyte metabolism, discovery and availability of antibiotics, isolation and synthesis of hormones, tranquilizers and diuretics, plus an ever-growing body of scientific knowledge, led to radical changes in both the scope and direction of modern pediatrics.

He also noted:

> While a major revolution has taken place in community and individual child health needs during the past couple of decades, pediatric education would appear to be still plugging along in the pattern of the late 1920s or, at best, the early 1930s.

---

* Pediatric Education at the Crossroads. *American Journal of Diseases of Children*, 1960, *100*, 651–656.

Thus, although there have been broad changes in the health care requirements of our society, these changes have not been reflected in the teaching of our health care personnel. Our commitment to total health care determines that we foster an understanding of factors contributing to normal growth and development as well as an understanding of all those factors contributing to ill health. Our health professionals must be interested in all aspects of a child's welfare; they must emphasize the psychological and social aspects of an individual's development and not direct themselves exclusively to the biological factors.

In recent years, it has become clear that the usual classifications of causes of illness and death are no longer sufficient. Current pediatric diagnosis also needs to be concerned with child ecology or environment and child-rearing practices and their consequences for the development of the child. A number of rapid sociological changes have made the need for understanding total development of children rather urgent.

The Selective Service statistics for World War II indicated a relatively high incidence of psychological and social ineffectiveness in our young adults. This became a national concern. It seemed a reasonable expectation that those of us in the child care professions might be in a position to minimize such unfavorable human development. Also, the increased mobility of our population and disruption of the extended family resulted in parents' increasingly looking toward the child care professions for help with their child-rearing practices.

At the same time, rapid urbanization came upon us, with all of the complications of rearing children in increasingly dense population areas of our cities. Simultaneously, there occurred a movement of health care professionals from the rural and inner city areas toward the suburbs. Thus, a large number of children with increasingly complex social, psychological, and biological problems were left relatively unattended medically, especially in central city and rural areas. The practitioners remaining in these high—in the ghettos—and low—on the farms—population density areas, in order to provide an adequate level of health care, were under increased pressure to understand how the psychosocial and biological variables interact.

Problems in teaching child development

There have been numerous efforts to help pediatricians, family physicians, and other health-caring professionals to better understand the psychology and social development of the children under their care. These efforts have increased as our rapidly changing society has brought about more complex interactions between physical and psychosocial variables. However, many health care professionals have found it difficult to comprehend fully the nature of the psychosocial variables and to define them in a way which would make it possible to consider methods of prevention and intervention.

Furthermore, the academic community has been extremely resistant to incorporating into medical and paramedical curriculums new ways of dealing with problems of children that were not disease oriented. Pediatricians, family-caring physicians, nurses and others, because of their own lack of expertise and the deficiencies in their training, naturally turned to those mental health professionals who were trained in working with the psychological and social problems presented by child patients and families.

Unfortunately, the stage of development of child psychiatry, social work, and clinical psychology has ill equipped these disciplines to provide the child development background required by the medical practitioners. In fact, child development as a basic science is usually not included in the basic training of any of the mental health professions. These professions have grown out of a concern for the disturbed child and adult. As a consequence, these fields have been relatively rich in theory drawn largely from the retrospective reconstructions of personality development elicited from the treatment experience. They are relatively short on direct empirical observations of the development of children, which are necessary to design more effective intervention-prevention models. The theoretical ideas, poorly based in observational or experimental data, offered the family physician or pediatrician by mental health workers are in contrast to the "scientific" research approach of the biological-medical model. Small wonder, therefore, that the teachings of child psychiatry tend to go unheeded by medical trainees in other disciplines.

The child psychiatrist has a tradition of study in psychopathology and the management of the disturbed child. The pediatrician, on the other hand, has been concerned with the biological and psychological development of the normal and the sick child, because the physician must provide services to both. These differences in the frames of reference inhibit clear communication in interdisciplinary teaching. Both groups must work collaboratively toward a more lucid sharing of the rich backgrounds of each discipline.

Child development: A tool in diagnosis and treatment

Child health care professionals are concerned primarily with the developmental processes which have direct implications for intervention and prevention in practice. They are concerned with an understanding of the dynamic development of individual differences and behavior patterns of children, through observation of child-rearing practices and their consequences for the growth and development of the child. These professionals are concerned with the understanding of how curiosity and learning patterns emerge and how coping behavior of the child develops. Assessment of all these factors is important in understanding the personality development of the child as well as the capacities of children and their families to master adversities. The child health practitioners are able continuously to make such observations on their child patients. They are almost the only professionals who spend sufficient time with the child and mother to make such assessments on a continuous basis throughout the life cycle of childhood and adolescence. Therefore, the health care practitioner not only has a practical requirement for child developmental knowledge but also has a unique opportunity to contribute to research in areas of child development, with its implications for prevention and early intervention.

Research in child development from clinical practice

It is evident that the application of the techniques of social scientists and developmental biologists to clinical settings is certain to increase our knowledge of the development of children. There are rich opportunities for collaborative studies of patterns of child care which occur spontaneously in various clinical settings and in social agencies where children are being seen regularly by child health care professionals. In foster homes, adoptive institutions, and adoptive homes, as well as in various institutional placements, the impact of physical illness and various handicapping conditions provides a variety of challenging issues for continued clinical observation and study.

Training in developmental biology and the opportunities to watch the unfolding of psychological and social development place the physician in a unique position to raise clinical research questions and to participate in aspects of clinical research in child development. The health care professionals have an opportunity to observe closely and exactly, and from these observations to derive the hypotheses which ultimately lead to better intervention programs.

But medicine holds with great tenacity to its disease-oriented training and research rather than to a dynamic understanding of human development. The concepts that have been refined from developmental biology must become basic to all medical education. Human beings must be understood in terms of their total development—both the biological and psychosocial—in order to allow research and child care programs to keep pace with the swiftly changing environment, with its varying impact on the developing organism—the child.

Needed changes in child care education

In medical education today, child development is still taught as isolated bits of information related to the expected sequential development of specific physical and mental skills—i.e., sitting, standing, talking, etc. This is a shallow understanding of what is meant by "dynamic development."

Our teaching of child development must become considerably broader in scope. For example, ideas such as that of critical phases in development are important in understanding the impact of external factors on infant and child development. Critical periods are times of extremely rapid growth of the nervous system. During these critical periods of development the child is exceptionally vulnerable to adverse physical or psychosocial circumstances. These may seriously retard or hinder the normal developmental process.

The understanding of development in dynamic terms makes diagnosis, prevention, and treatment much more rational; it certainly means that many of the problems which now are crudely and poorly defined and understood would come under much closer scrutiny from a developmental standpoint. Teaching centers for the health professions must become attuned to the vital need of teaching child development in a clinical setting so that developmental assessment becomes part of the process of understanding each child's assets and handicaps as a consequence of disease and/or adaptation to a variety of social and ecological settings.

Developmental assessment is a practical evaluation of the total development of each child-patient, which gives the practitioner an understanding of the individual development of the child as it relates to the expectations, life-styles, and attitudes of the parents. All of these factors must be assessed and placed in perspective by the professional in order to permit a sophisticated approach to preventive and therapeutic intervention programs with the child and the family.

In order to teach growth and development adequately, training centers must provide their trainees with an opportunity to observe presumably well infants and children. Longitudinal studies of children being followed in intensive long-term medical care are also an important training experience, teaching the importance of continuity of child health care in helping a child and family achieve the maximum health possible. We know that chronic disease in a child affects not only the behavior of the child but the mental and physical health of the whole family. We need to learn to understand and work with the consequent health and mental health problems of all the family.

Health care professionals are probably best trained by combining clinical involvement with a setting in which child development research is in progress. A research orientation to assessment would encourage practitioners to appreciate all of the significant variables influencing a child's development. It would refine their powers of observation and discipline their thinking so that development would be seen as a total process involving all aspects of living that impinge on the physical and mental health of a child.

Keeping abreast of change: A new mandate

Society continues to look to physicians and other health care professionals for solutions to new problems. However, as the problems become increasingly complex, the professional must provide a more sophisticated yet broad-based approach. The health care field is faced with a new kind and a new dimension of problem solving. We can no longer isolate one factor and consider it as a separate entity to be dealt with by a single specific intervention. We must consider how biological and psychosocial factors interrelate and—from this understanding—plan our more complex interventions.

Thus, a preventive approach to the leading cause of death in children—accidents—becomes more of a social than a medical problem. It is also clear that further reductions in infant death will depend upon the improvement of the living conditions of individuals in poverty and improved general health care. Certainly, the problems of delinquency and addiction require intervention beyond the scope of medical and health care practice. New physical and mental health care patterns and partnerships must emerge to serve all of our nation's children.

In our very rapidly increasing urban society—with the kinds of tensions that come from crowding, segregation, poor schooling, pollution, and inadequate family income—we must approach the problems and disorders of children in more dynamic terms. Our planning for the well-being of children must consider health care in terms of the current urban and rural scene and the associated ecological problems. The understanding of these ecological problems will depend to a large extent upon the background of the professional workers involved in the health care of children and upon their collaborating with parents and other caretakers of children. They must begin to utilize their expertise in child development to understand the whole child and all the factors that influence developmental processes. For example, ecologically induced developmental attrition results in a large loss of human potential. Infants nurtured by hopeless, depressed, and apathetic mothers in all social classes manifest a variety of physical and psychological illnesses later in life. In recent years we have come to know much more about intervention programs for young children and their families.

Findings from developmental research emphasize that much of the retardation, brain damage, and poor learning that we now encounter could have been prevented. We know the kinds of attention and nurturance infants and young children require to develop curiosity and a hunger for learning and love of life. We must act now—in accordance with our knowledge. Health professionals and educators concerned with all children need to become aware that they have an important contribution to policy-making for health care in the community and nation.

I lay it down as a prime condition of sane society,
obvious as such to anyone but an idiot, that in any
decent community, children should find in every
part of their native country, food, clothing, lodging,
instruction, and parental kindness for the asking
. . . . the children must have them as if by magic,
with nothing to do but rub the lamp, like
Aladdin, and have their needs satisfied.

GEORGE BERNARD SHAW in *Parents and
Children*, 1914

4

Parents as the Developmental Advocates of Children

IRVING N. BERLIN, M.D.
ROXIE BERLIN, M.S.W., PH.D.

Allan Chase,[2] in *The Biological Imperatives, Health, Politics,
and Human Survival,* states that to reduce the specters of physical
illness, overpopulation, environmental pollution, decay of the
cities, and other critical ills of society, it is first essential to eliminate poverty. It becomes obvious that to eliminate ghettos, one
must eliminate poverty. To eliminate physical and mental illness
and malnutrition for one-third of our population, one must eliminate poverty. For humanity to survive, one must eliminate
poverty.

Epidemiology and mental illness

In the area of severe mental illness, data indicate that the
greatest number of emotionally disturbed children come from the
lowest socioeconomic levels. These children, when hospitalized,

are cared for by the most poorly trained state hospital aides. Millions of moderately and severely disturbed children have no hope of being treated by competent mental health professionals or even by trained nonprofessionals. Therefore, any approach to the problems of these children cannot be primarily a psychotherapeutic one. Aside from the question of the efficacy of psychotherapy, we must, as child-caring professionals, become committed to a preventive and early interventive approach. Prevention and early intervention are therefore linked to a comprehensive health program.

One of the most important aspects of a comprehensive health program is the developmental orientation of the professionals who are working in that program. This orientation includes the understanding of the principle of critical periods in a child's development. This principle is derived from observations and experiments which show that there are optimal times during development for learning to walk and to talk, and much before that, for learning to become attached to a nurturant person who facilitates all other learning by his or her sensitive and responsive understanding of the infant's needs. We now know that when such optimal moments in time are missed, such learning is never as fully acquired again. Thus when, because of maternal depression or illness, the normal attachment or development of dependable, nurturant, mother-child relationships are long delayed, trusting other human beings and relating easily to them may be difficult for that child later. Similarly if there is failure to acquire certain physical or social skills when the human organism is ready to do so, those skills are never learned with the same ease or as completely.

Along with understanding about critical periods, other normal signposts of physical and psychological factors must be clearly understood to help assess the developmental level of the child. Biological factors such as malnutrition or premature birth which crucially interfere with development must also be understood to help plan the interventions required to make up for developmentally based disorders.

Prevention and early intervention depend upon effective training programs for large numbers of nonprofessionals in order that continuous contact may be maintained with all families in the program. The development of ongoing relations with families makes possible early detection of deviations in development so they can be worked with immediately. Such treatment must necessarily include working with the parents to involve them as active participants in the treatment process.

Family oriented programs are particularly effective in finding developmental problems which result from severe maternal depression, nutritional lacks, and birth difficulties. Epidemiological data indicate that maternal depression, like poor nutrition of pregnant mothers and infants as well as birth insults, can be found at all socioeconimic levels but is most prevalent and least frequently detected at the poverty level. Parental involvement by the nonprofessional not only reduces the depression and apathy of the mother as she becomes more effective with her child, but also reduces the developmental problem in the child. If problems which result from maternal depression are not resolved early in development, severe health, mental health, and learning problems are likely to occur at a later age. Thus, failure to thrive, social, physical, and nutritionally-caused retardation and psychoses of childhood, along with both apathy and hyperactivity and their attendant learning problems, have all been noted as results of severe developmental deficits.

A comprehensive program which focuses on prevention and early intervention is essential to reduce the incidence and severity of presently diagnosed emotional and mental illness.

To quote Chase again: [2]

> Biologically, since we can produce the bumper crops of all the known tools of prevention of the physical and mental disorders caused by hunger, there is no moral excuse for the staggeringly high infant mortality and childhood disease and death rates that prevail among our more than forty million urban and rural poor. Nor, for that matter, are the environmental, biological contributing causes of the socially costly, low scholastic achievement of the poorly nourished children of our urban and rural poor beyond the present technological and agricultural capacities of our society to correct and eliminate in less than a decade. But here, however, we are confronted with health conditions that must be prevented or cured by political, rather than medical actions.

The importance of parental involvement

Political action to eliminate poverty requires involvement by the poor themselves as participant and informed citizens. Concern of poor parents for the education of their children reflects their recognition that, without education, their children will remain in poverty and thus powerless. Therefore, any general approach to children's problems must take into account the large number of children who are failing to learn in school. Many children in special programs at junior high and high school levels or in dropout prevention programs could have been identified as nonlearners at kindergarten or early grade school levels. Educators have recognized that in our nation many children, particularly from poor families, enter school without having had the requisite experiences for being able to learn in school. Parents, mothers in particular, are the primary teachers of their children up to the time the children enter school.

Head Start was a national endeavor to use a school-like program to ameliorate the deficiencies of children brought up in poverty. The results of the Head Start program are well known. Although the four-year-olds in the program made considerable gains when compared with a non-Head Start group, the gains were not generally maintained over a period of years, except for that group of children whose parents became actively involved participants in the educational program.

One lesson learned from Head Start was that four years of age was too old to begin remediation. Programs aimed at preventing school failure need to be concerned with children younger than four years. A number of preschool and day care programs are presently attempting to evaluate the usefulness of these programs in influencing children's development.

A second important lesson which might be learned from Head Start is that parental involvement in an educational program may be *the critical factor* in preventing school failure.

Most programs which attempt to work with children at preschool ages give only lip service to the parental involvement component. Many program directors are quick to admit that it is difficult to involve parents by inviting them to appear at school and also difficult to keep them involved for the duration of the programs. Thus, after becoming discouraged about parent involvement, most program directors and staff members once again try to use their own roles as educators to make up for the deficiencies of mothers as educators of their own children.

There are a few research programs which involve parents and provide some basic data that offer hope for the establishment of feasible broad-scale programs that could benefit large numbers of preschool children and their families.

The Perry Pre-School Project [15] in Ypsilanti, Michigan, successfully involved parents of four-year-olds in their preschool program by supplementing their morning sessions with afternoon visits to the parents at home. These visits attempted to engage the mother in the process of educating her child. The visits were structured to augment and extend the preschool activities. Significant gains were made by the end of the first year, as measured by the Stanford-Binet.

Another significant study was made by Karnes [10] in Illinois. It demonstrated that mothers on Aid to Dependent Children can be taught to be effective teachers of their own preschool children. Mothers of the experimental group were invited to attend a training program where they made instructional materials and learned to use them to teach their children at home. The teachers encouraged the mothers to recognize that their assistance was very important to the development of their children's educational competence. The children of the teaching mothers made Binet IQ gains of 7.46 points, significantly greater than the .07 points gained by the control group.

We have already indicated that any comprehensive program dealing with children's problems must include the use of nonprofessional staff and must include a training program and supervision for that staff if its use is to be maximized.

A purely preventive programmatic approach would be one which used mothers of preschool-age children in poverty populations as nonprofessionals in child development programs. They would provide either day care or preschool experiences. Such an approach is the only economically feasible route for reducing the increasing numbers of children who are nonlearners in school. Any program involving the education of young children requires a high adult-to-child ratio and is therefore expensive. If the adults have to be hired at staff salaries, the cost of large preschool programs would be prohibitive. The current need is for programs which can be mounted on a large enough scale to have an impact on the present educational and poverty scene.

Bettye Caldwell [1] quotes some of the current research programs as costing between $2,000 and $9,000 per child. Even though these costs include a research component, the amount is formidable when generalized to include a fair share of the poverty population.

If mothers were considered an integral part of the staff, the cost of such programs would be drastically reduced. Obvious and immediate questions are asked: "What about working mothers?" "What do you do about mothers of young children who do not want to be involved?" These are real questions which come out of the experiences of all workers who have attempted to work with parents, particularly those parents who, themselves, have had unsatisfactory experiences in school.

There are clear answers to these questions. One is that although many mothers work for a living, a large population of ADC mothers exists who do not work, who have preschool children, and who could form the nucleus for such a program if it were carefully structured. Such a program would be attractive to ADC mothers if it offered a relatively small monetary incentive in addition to welfare grants and the practical and educational benefits of the program to their children. The program would offer opportunities to learn to work effectively with children in a supervised child care center, together with an educational component in child development, nutrition, teaching, and educational play techniques, etc.

The Aid to Dependent Children program was originally established to allow mothers to stay home with their young children because this was considered the best environment for the children. Research now indicates that poverty has become cyclical and that children of families who themselves have been brought up in poverty are unlikely to acquire the kind of education that will permit them to break the poverty cycle. Now it would seem that the intent of the ADC program would be better served by an educational program that would involve the parents in the educational process of their children.

Furthermore, another appreciable population of families living at the poverty level is made up of those mothers who work for low wages and seek day care services for their children. These are largely unskilled workers who have no investment in their jobs. They work outside the home in order to escape welfare and sometimes to escape the frustrations and depressions of coping with home problems and with young children in conditions of poverty.

Many of these families are eligible for day care services under Title IV of the Social Security Act. Quality day care services which meet federal interagency standards cost about $12.00 per day. The cost of hiring these mothers as child care workers and providing an effective and meaningful educational component to their jobs can be cost accounted against the cost of day care programs for their children which do not include these mothers' child care services and training and the resulting stimulation to learning about children which then motivates these mothers to become better informed, more community minded, and better educational models for their children.

To briefly summarize, two groups of parents form a population that is sufficient to begin a large-scale program for child development, using parents as the paraprofessional teachers. One group consists of those mothers currently on ADC; the second is that group of unskilled workers who qualify for Title IV day care as potential ADC mothers. A nuclear program begun on this scale could be expanded to meet any developing needs.

A program such as this would permit many mothers of preschool children to learn to be effective teachers of their children with the accompanying increased capacity of their children to learn. Such programs would require parent-child centers in each community. However, the primary cost of staffing would be the same as is presently being expended by welfare services (plus a relatively small increment as incentive) together with that money used for day care services for borderline or potential welfare families. Training programs are available locally in many community colleges through their Family Life Programs.

The present crisis in the mental health field cannot be met by professionals who are prepared to work only on a one-to-one basis with already disturbed children. Present needs are too great. Professionals in mental health fields need to use themselves as educators, consultants, and supervisors of paraprofessionals in order to maximize their effectiveness. Professionals can extend their effectiveness by training and supervising nonprofessionals to work with the large numbers of families needing their help. This may be one element of a neighborhood-based child advocate program.

In the final analysis, in our society, parents are the only ones who are wholly accountable for their children. Parents deserve a primary place in any program that claims to have an integrative or comprehensive approach to the solution of children's problems. The need to include effective use of nonprofessionals in comprehensive programs must go hand in hand with the need to consider parents of children in the programs as high-priority nonprofessionals.

We must approach the problems of two generations simultaneously. The effort to develop effective and competent paraprofessionals and to utilize parents in these roles not only enhances the sense of worth and competence of the adults, but also affects the learning, curiosity, and competence of the children. In order to become concerned and involved citizens who are able to join others in breaking the poverty cycle, both generations require the full commitment of the mental health professions. The professional commitment must be to use expertise in behavioral sciences to help awaken concern in the poor about the importance of prevention and early intervention and to work with the poor to implement programs for their children. Thus, professionals become committed to use themselves so that the poor or powerless can become potent and effective as adults and children through their own efforts.

REFERENCES

1. CALDWELL, B. M. What does research tell us about day care? *Children Today*, 1972, *1*: 1.
2. CHASE, A. *The Biological Imperatives, Health, Politics and Human Survival.* New York: Holt, Rhinehart, Winston, 1971.
3. COUGHLIN, B. J. The rights of children. *Child Welfare*, 1968, *47*, 133–142.
4. GARBER, M., & TOCCO, T. S. The measurement of environmental process characteristics in six follow-through communities. In

I. J. Gordon (Ed.), *Research Reports: Reaching the Child through Parent Education: The Florida Approach.* Gainsville, Florida: University of Florida, 1969. Pp. 76–86.

5. GORDON, I. J. Early child stimulation through parent education. In I. J. Gordon (Ed.), *Research Reports: Reaching the Child through Parent Education: The Florida Aproach.* Gainsville, Florida: University of Florida, 1969. Pp. 1–12.

6. GORDON, I. J. The Florida parent education model. In I. J. Gordon (Ed.), *Research Reports: Reaching the Child through Parent Education: The Florida Approach.* Gainsville, Florida: University of Florida, 1969. Pp. 68–75.

7. GREENWOOD, G. E. Parent educator as classroom aide. In I. J. Gordon (Ed.), *Research Reports: Reaching the Child through Parent Education: The Florida Approach.* Gainsville, Florida: University of Florida, 1969. Pp. 98–109.

8. JESTER, R. E., & BAILEY, J. P., JR. Hearing-speech scores on the Griffiths Mental Development Scale as a function of language usage in the home. In I. J. Gordon (Ed.), *Research Reports: Reaching the Child through Parent Education: The Florida Approach.* Gainsville, Florida: University of Florida, 1969. Pp. 21–31.

9. Joint Commission on Mental Health of Children. *Crisis in Child Mental Health: Challenge for the 1970s.* New York: Harper & Row, 1969.

10. KARNES, M., et al. An approach for working with mothers of disadvantaged preschool children. *Merrill-Palmer Quarterly,* 1968, 14, 173–184.

11. KATZ, A. H. *Parents of the Handicapped.* Springfield, Ill.: Charles C Thomas, 1961.

12. KOZOL, J. *Death at an Early Age.* Boston: Houghton Mifflin, 1967.

13. MAURELLI, J. A. A factor analytic study of a series of intellectual stimulation tasks for infants and toddlers. In I. J. Gordon (Ed.), *Research Reports: Reaching the Child through Parent Education: The Florida Approach.* Gainsville, Florida: University of Florida, 1969. Pp. 32–44.

14. SIEGEL, B. L. The parent educator as home visitor. In I. J. Gordon (Ed.), *Research Reports: Reaching the Child through Parent Education: The Florida Approach.* Gainsville, Florida: University of Florida, 1969. Pp. 87–97.

15. WEIKERT, D., & LAMBIE, D. Preschool intervention through a home teaching program. In J. Hellmuth (Ed.), *Disadvantaged Child.* Vol. 2. New York: Brunner/Mazel, 1968. Pp. 435–500.

16. ZIGLER, E. F. A national priority: Raising the quality of children's lives. *Children,* 1970, 17, 166–170.

17. ZIGLER, E. F. Project Head Start: Success or failure? *Children Today,* 1973, 2:6, 2–7.

... The vision that lies behind epidemiologic
inquiry is a world free from disease and suffering.
The field of medicine has a similar high purpose
and seeks to achieve it by treating sick people and
restoring them rapidly to health. The difference is
that an epidemiologist must view every sick person
as a failure, not an opportunity.

REUEL A. STALLONES

5

Epidemiology
and Disordered Learning

STANLEY WALZER, M.D.
JULIUS B. RICHMOND, M.D.
THEODORE DE BUNO, M.D.

Health professionals are concerned as never before with what
is to become of the lives which we help to preserve and nurture.
We no longer define health as the mere absence of disease but
seek to ensure that every child's potential for optimal functioning
is realized. As diseases have been brought increasingly under control, our attention has gradually shifted to more subtle problems.
We are now focusing our investigations on the prevention and
treatment of those disorders which, although not life threatening,
do result in serious loss of human potential. Of these handicapping disorders, learning impairment is the most pervasive.

Learning is the primary activity of childhood and represents
the central developmental task for the school-age child. Erikson [20] has characterized this period of life as the time of "industry"—the child "learns to win recognition by producing things"
and the "wider society becomes significant in its ways of admit-
ting the child to an understanding of meaningful roles in the total

46

economy." How "industry" becomes translated into daily learning activities is a function of the culture in which the child lives.

It is estimated that "about ten per cent of all American children of average intelligence read so badly that their total adjustment is impaired." [14] Many more children can read but are so impaired in their learning skills that as adults they are unable to function in jobs in our technological society.

Bruner [9] has pointed out that "as our technology grows increasingly complex in both machinery and human organization, the role of school becomes more central in the society, not simply as an agent of socialization, but as a transmitter of basic skills." In such a technological society there is great emphasis on academic achievements; learning becomes equated with the acquisition of academic skills. Children who do not demonstrate early mastery of these skills are viewed with concern.

In other cultures (and in some subcultures within our own society) the same premium is not yet placed upon academic learning, and the mastery of alternate skills is acceptable and appropriate. Nevertheless, our concern must be for *all* children since, inevitably, those with academic skills will be better equipped to function in whatever roles they choose within their own society. Therefore, there has been considerable interest in the study of disordered learning, employing the same basic epidemiological methods that have proved of value in controlling disease and solving other social problems.

Definitions of learning disorders

Some definitions of learning disorders exclude the organically impaired, some the intellectually deficient. Some include the physically handicapped but do not recognize the socially deprived or maladjusted.

Would we, for instance, all agree that the child suffering impairment of neurosensory integration due to protein insufficiency has a learning disorder? Would we agree that the socially disadvantaged child, deprived environmentally (and perhaps biologically), has a learning disorder? Does the child with "average" endowment who is failing in an upper-middle-class educational environment have a learning disorder? Shall we include the

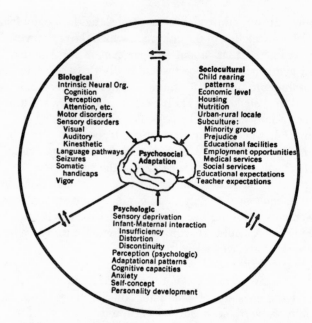

Figure 1. **MULTIPLE FACTORS AFFECTING**
PSYCHOSOCIAL ADAPTATION
From: S. Walzer and J. B. Richmond, The epidemiology of learning disorders, *Pediatric Clinics of North America*, 20, August 1973.

autistic child or the retarded child? Does the "slow-blooming child" represent an example of disordered learning?

Perhaps all of these children should be excluded and only children with specific types of deficits should be included within the category of learning disabilities.

In order to bypass the difficulties introduced by inconsistent definition, we will approach the problem of disordered learning in a more global way. We are concerned ultimately with the child's psychosocial adaptation—the capacity to use his or her internal and external resources to the fullest in order to function optimally within the existing circumstances. The factors that shape the total development of the child are complex but intimately related, and are presented in Figure 1. Successful adaptation is only possible when some degree of homeostasis exists among the many variables.

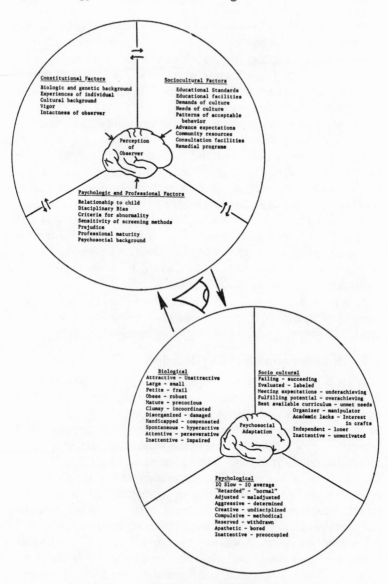

**Figure 2. OBSERVER PERCEPTION OF
ADAPTIVE BEHAVIORS**

From: S. Walzer and J. B. Richmond, The epidemiology of learning disorders, *Pediatric Clinics of North America*, 20, August 1973.

With this model, learning can be viewed as a complex adaptive phenomenon influenced by any or all of the factors presented. Because this conceptual framework emphasizes the interaction of a variety of significant factors as they affect learning, it will accommodate and relate the extensive data on disordered learning within an overall perspective.

We must be cautious about observer variability when employing such a model. We are dealing not only with multiple factors operating within a child, but also with multiple disciplines. The view we have of the child is influenced in no small measure by the observer's perception, professional background, and personal psychology, including his or her individual biases. Evaluation of the child's adaptation is, in reality, a synthesis of the observer's own personal expectations and the actual adaptive behaviors exhibited by the child. The observer's perceptions are, in fact, shaped by the same factors which influence the psychosocial adaptation of the child (Figure 2).

This phenomenon helps to explain the difficulties we experience in comparing our perceptions and evaluations across cultural, interpersonal, and interdisciplinary boundaries.

Epidemiology and learning disorders

What is the contribution that epidemiology can make in clarifying the complex interactions involved in disordered learning? In most diseases and disorders of childhood, epidemiology has provided an important framework for planning corrective and preventive programs to decrease the severity of handicaps and reduce the numbers of individuals affected. Epidemiology is more than a "study of causes of illnesses existent in a population . . . it not only studies the distribution of prevalence rates in different populations, but also seeks to understand the forces which make the prevalence rates higher in one population than in another." [27]

Epidemiological methods can be applied to the problem of learning disability only with difficulty. In order to study the prevalence or etiology of a disease or condition, we must be able to define it, using widely accepted criteria. Learning disorders, however, do not form a generic group but, rather, reflect an interplay of factors affecting the child's capacity for psychosocial adaptation. Estimates of the prevalence of learning disabilities are, therefore, clouded by problems of semantic confusion and inconsistent definition. On this basis alone we would expect that the application of traditional epidemiological principles and methods would result in epidemiological chaos.

However, learning disorders are so prevalent and take such a toll of human potential that we must pursue the epidemiological investigation, which could lead to effective treatment and prevention programs. In attempting to discover which children are most often affected by which predominant factors and how these factors work to produce learning disorders, two investigative approaches are basically possible. We can develop epidemiological strategies on specific problems and relate these meaningfully to the overall phenomena of learning impairment. If we accept the concept that a complex interaction of factors may be involved etiologically, then programs organized from a comprehensive multifactorial approach would have great appeal. Thus, a large number of underachievers would be studied relative to a large number of variables in order to determine the etiological significance of each variable in the general population of underachievers.

PRESENT FINDINGS. The existing epidemiological data on learning disorders emphasize the difficulties we have had in approaching the problem. This is surprising in view of the practical importance of epidemiological data in this area; it is not surprising when one thinks of the fragmentation of effort which has occurred in gathering the data. Thus, numerous subgroup studies are found in widely scattered professional journals and publications, with few attempts at pulling together of pertinent material. As a consequence we find numerous "estimates" of the numbers of children with specific disorders affecting learning, but these are often poorly documented. Furthermore, little is ever presented regarding the overall incidence of learning disabilities or the characteristics of children who are not learning.

We do have documentation of the numbers of exceptional children already enrolled in special education programs, but few data regarding the children who do not meet the formal criteria for inclusion in special programs. Despite this paucity of data, one has only to enter a regular class in any metropolitan school system to become impressed with the fact that very few pupils appear to be learning optimally and, to pursue our theme, that maladaptation to the learning situation is resulting daily in serious loss of the children's potential. Even in the well-structured, stable environments that exist in some "model" schools, it is readily apparent that a sizable number of children are not being reached or are not reaching out. Who are these children and why are they functioning below their potential? These are the questions we are trying to approach and answer. But we are still in great need of strategies and tools as well as the commitment of human and material resources to convert our qualitative observations into meaningful data.

METHODS FOR EPIDEMIOLOGIC STUDY. Comprehensive multidimensional studies attempt to define which of the many interacting variables are etiologically or developmentally significant for a broad group of children who manifest the symptom of disordered learning. We place a high value-judgment on comprehensiveness because this approach closely approximates our hypothesis that it is a complex interplay of variables, rather than the specific variables themselves, that affects learning.

The interplay of variables can have complicated ramifications affecting not only etiological issues but also the ability to recognize the presence of the disorder. This phenomenon can best be demonstrated by considering the problem of mental retardation. If we look only for reflections of intellectual impairment in any group, we may overlook some crucial dynamics of the group situation that critically affect our ascertainment. We may be misled into accepting impairment where none exists or fail to recognize it when it is there.

It would be unthinkable today to report the incidence of mental retardation in a community without carefully correlating social class factors. A large number of investigations have confirmed that a disproportionate number of mentally retarded and suspected mentally retarded come from the lower socioeconomic groups. This observation suggests that, although children in all social classes may be vulnerable to the biological and social factors contributing to retardation, children of lower economic families experience the greatest clustering of factors and therefore the greatest vulnerability.

The issues, however, are more complex. In a study of retardation in Onondaga County, New York, Gruenberg[26] noted that there was a considerable discrepancy between numbers of children referred because of behavior leading to a *social suspicion* of "mental retardation" and those who were referred with specific psychological testing data substantiating retardation. Out of a total of 3.5 percent of the population reported as being "possibly retarded," only one percent had the retardation documented on the basis of a *measured* IQ below 75. This led Gruenberg to conclude that "behavior leading to the social suspicion of 'mental retardation' is not necessarily a fixed characteristic of individual children but is rather a complex set of manifestations of some children's relationship to their immediate environment."

Birch and Richardson[5] similarly reported disproportionately high overall incidences of retardation in the low economic groups. However, of those considered to be retarded by the community, only 25 percent of the children in the least privileged economic class had IQs under 60, while 100 percent of the children in the highest privileged groups had IQs under 60.

The data from such studies suggest that:

1. Socioeconomic class and retardation are related.

2. Many children are viewed as being retarded as a result of misinterpretations of social behaviors.

3. Misinterpretation about the degree of retardation occurs more often in children of the lower economic groups; children of the higher economic groups tends to be more accurately identified through diagnostic evaluation and, as a group, to be more seriously impaired.

4. Privileged children with mild or moderate degrees of impairment (unlike the disadvantaged children) may go unnoticed or may be given enough advantages to enable them to get by.

It is evident, therefore, that the interaction of variables affects both etiologic and ascertainment issues. On this basis comprehensiveness is a critical factor for epidemiological strategies. It also allows for a high degree of generalization to the broad category of children with learning disorders. At times, however, such studies have the limitation of lacking the specificity to define fully a particular facet of the problem.

A second investigative method focuses more specifically on certain relevant variables. A group of children may be studied because they are predisposed to learning disorders by virtue of specifically defined etiological factors. Thus, there exists an extensive literature on the developmental consequences of prematurity, low birth weight, various prenatal and perinatal disorders, and early exposures to environmental pollutants. Alternatively, a group of children with learning disorders may be studied relative to a specific variable of interest to the investigator. Specific studies provide a large body of information about etiological factors and the pathogenetic sequences that ensue. They offer us the possibility of identifying learning-disordered children early in their lives, by focusing our detection on populations most at risk for developing these disorders.

However, an obvious dilemma exists. Epidemiological studies that are undertaken with very specific criteria do not provide comprehensive data. We are limited in the generalizations that can be made to the broad group of children categorized as underachievers. These limitations can be demonstrated by considering specific studies.

Brenner and her colleagues [8] have reported the results of a study of children with disordered learning. Employing a test battery of visuomotor abilities, they surveyed 810 healthy school children eight to nine years of age. Of the 54 children identified as having a significantly deficient performance, 14 were matched with an equal number of visuomotor adequate children and followed for three years. Subsequently, the children with visuomotor impairment were found to perform less adequately than the controls on the tests of spatial judgment and manual skills; the visuomotor impaired children also manifested a variety of educational and emotional problems.

By employing specific criteria, these investigators identified a unique population which subsequently was shown to be at risk for learning disorders. Not only *how*, but even some of the reasons *why* they were different were suggested. However, since the original study screened *only* for visuomotor differences, the most valid piece of epidemiological data that resulted was the provocative conclusion that 6.7 percent of the original "healthy" sample were actually impaired by the investigators' criteria and were at risk for developing learning problems. In the original group of 810, there may have been children who subsequently were underachievers for reasons other than visuomotor difficulties. This study ignores these children for the sake of clarifying the relationship existing between a specific handicap and subsequent learning. The specific criteria employed in selecting the children to be followed limit the generalizations that can be made about the broad category of children with disordered learning.

It is evident that both styles of investigative procedures are important and yield different types of information relative to epidemiological issues. Any study, single or multifactorial, that helps clarify the processes at work in producing learning disorders is a valuable contribution to the epidemiological literature.

From our interactional model it is evident that any attempt to isolate individual etiological variables is fraught with difficulties and represents an artificial categorization of etiological factors. We might better present the epidemiological data by emphasizing the types of investigative strategies that have been employed to obtain the information and the types of data that emerge from such studies.

BIOLOGICAL FACTORS. Although specific experimental and clinical observations have limitations, they do isolate important aspects of the problem of disordered learning. Thus, the question is raised as to whether organicity (i.e., minimal brain damage) and learning disability frequently coexist. Although there is no justification for the assumption that all learning-disordered children demonstrate evidence of brain damage, there is mounting evidence that signs of neurological instability are more common in children with learning disorders than in the normal population.

Wolff and Hurwitz [59] have recently demonstrated a significant increase in choreiform twitches in children with learning disabilities; these short motor jerks of brief duration were previously reported by Prechtl and Stemmer [45] in children exhibiting behavioral disorders such as hyperkinesis, defects in concentration, and learning disorders. They were felt to represent signs of minor neurological instability. In a subsequent study, Hurwitz et al.[30] found that boys with learning disabilities were significantly retarded in sensorimotor tapping and automatization tasks, both of which require competence in sequencing repetitive actions. These findings suggest the presence of neuropsychologic deficits in this group. Several other investigators have also emphasized that equivocal or "soft" neurological signs are more common among children with behavior disorders than in control subjects.[28,32,35,55]

Electroencephalographic abnormalities (i.e., excessive slow activity) frequently have been reported among children with behavioral disorders, most commonly those diagnosed as "hyperactive." [1,15,22,25,33,36,49,55] Several investigators have also reported an increased incidence of electroencephalographic abnormalities in children identified specifically as underachievers when compared with control populations.[29,39]

Specific approaches to the consideration of etiology have emphasized the relevance of prenatal and neonatal factors in the subsequent appearance of disordered learning. More common perinatal factors (such as hypoxia) have been of interest as possible causes of minimal brain damage and associated learning disorder.

Pertinent animal experiments indicating the role of asphyxia neonatorum in brain damage have been undertaken by Sechzer, Faro, and Windle.[50] Developmental studies done on monkeys asphyxiated for fifteen minutes after birth revealed the survival and normal functioning of "adaptive behaviors" (i.e., visual depth perception, visual placing, independent locomotion) although they were significantly delayed in their appearance. In contrast, however, behaviors that were considered to be "acquired" (i.e., memory, learning) remained severely impaired throughout the life of the animal. Comparisons of other behaviors of significance in children with minimal brain damage, such as hyperactivity, incoordination, decreased attention span, and difficulties with impulse control, revealed striking similarities to those observed in the asphyxiated monkeys. Although these investigators do not as yet have developmental information on monkeys asphyxiated for shorter periods, it is evident that animal models and experiments such as these will yield much important information about the relevance of neonatal factors in developmental issues.

Other biological factors have recently been shown to be related to certain aspects of learning function. For example, a relationship between errors in sex chromosome number and learning has been demonstrated in two groups of individuals. There is considerable evidence that a specific cognitive deficit is associated with Turner's syndrome (usually 45 chromosomes instead of the normal 46, with only one X chromosome).[38,51] These individuals suffer a neurocognitional deficit in space-form perception; they have difficulty with visuoconstructional recognition and performance. They have considerable difficulty in copying the variety of designs presented in many of the standard psychological tests (Benton Visual Retention Test, Bender Visual Motor Gestalt Test). When asked to draw a human person (the Draw-a-Person Test), they produce a figure often grossly distorted because of their space-form disorientation.

Other research has recently suggested the possibility of a learning deficit in phenotypic males whose chromosomal abnormality consists of an extra X chromosome (having a complement of 47, XXY instead of the expected 46, XY). In one systematic study, boys with this chromosome constitution were identified at birth and followed developmentally throughout their childhood.[53] Of the six boys over four years of age, four have demonstrated difficulties with language function. Three of these have undergone formal speech and language evaluation, in which an articulatory defect and a dysnomia have been demonstrated. Despite normal or superior intelligence, all four have subsequently shown significant difficulty with early learning, including reading and arithmetic skills. It is of interest that early speech disorders are commonly reported in children with learning disorders who have normal chromosomal complements. The relationship between language disorders and subsequent learning disability has been described by several investigators.[14]

Since comprehensiveness of the investigative procedure adds data that define better the general population of disordered learners, such studies are extremely desirable. More recent technological thrusts have brought us to the point where broad approaches to the study of learning disorders may now be feasible. Myklebust and his colleagues[39] have recently reported the results of a comprehensive and complex interdisciplinary psychoneurological study of children with disordered learning. Using specific screening tests, they identified 15 percent of a population of 2,704 children as underachievers. Ophthalmological, neurologic, electroencephalographic, educational, and psychological evaluations were done on these children and their paired controls to determine the reasons for their failure to learn at the expected level. The psychoeducational evaluations revealed that these children were most disturbed in cognitive functions pertaining to converting auditory information into visual equivalents. Thus, syllabication tests, in which letters and word parts must be matched with sounds they make, were the most effective discriminators between the learning-disordered children and the controls. Although the ophthalmologic findings were negative, the electroencephalographic and neurological studies revealed a higher incidence of abnormal signs.

BIOSOCIAL FACTORS. The interplay of factors in the etiology of learning disorders is most evident when we consider biological and social factors as they affect learning. It is difficult to study the selective effects of social factors on learning, since the same population of underprivileged children at high risk for a pathological environment is also at highest risk for a biological insult.

A number of well-documented studies have associated complications of pregnancy and birth (especially prematurity) with later neurological, intellectual, educational, and behavioral deficiencies.[2,16,17,18,24,34,37,43,52,54] At the same time, the relationship of prematurity and low birth weight to social class has been emphasized. Chase[12] has reported that between 1950 and 1967 the most outstanding nationwide trend in prematurity has been the increasing proportion of low-birth-weight infants in nonwhite populations at the same time that the rate for white infants remained relatively stable. The proportion of low-birth-weight infants increased from 10 to 14 percent for nonwhite populations while the incidence among white infants remained at about seven percent. Thus, prematurity and low birth weight are more frequently the problems of the disadvantaged. With the observation that infants of low birth weight are subject to excessive morbidity, particularly of the central nervous system, it is obvious that children in lower income areas are at risk for developmental impairment.

Other research has been directed to studying the influence of environmental pollution on the developing fetus and the young child. Again, the child of the inner city area, more frequently the underprivileged, is at greater risk than the child of the suburbs.

It has recently been demonstrated that increasing concentrations of environmental carbon monoxide are associated with a decrease in the oxygen-carrying capacity of hemoglobin in healthy newborn infants.[3] The implications of this observation for subsequent behavioral development are still unknown.

Current interest has also been directed to environmental lead and its influence on central nervous system development. Among the potential sources for toxic amounts of lead in the inner city atmosphere are lead accumulation from the combustion of leaded gasolines and lead from flaking paint which may be ingested (pica). Extensive follow-up studies of children who have had lead poisoning have indicated a high incidence (as much as 50 percent) of neurologic sequelae, particularly after encephalopathy.[10,13,31,44,48]

The pervasive aspect of the problem presented by excessive environmental lead has recently been emphasized. Oberle [42] reported that five to ten percent of ghetto children between one and six have elevated blood levels of lead. Needleman [40,41] demonstrated a significantly increased lead content in the deciduous teeth in a population of supposedly asymptomatic children from high risk urban areas, as compared to a suburban low risk area. The relevance of this finding for minimal brain dysfunction and learning disabilities is still unclear. Further systematic studies employing sensitive measures of development and learning are necessary to determine whether this group of children might be at risk for minimal cerebral dysfunction and its behavioral correlates.

Birch [4] has aptly summarized the plight of the disadvantaged child. He notes that the nonwhite, socially disadvantaged infant is subject to an "excessive continuum of risk reflected at the extremes by perinatal, neonatal, and infant death and in the survivors by a reduced functional potential."

PSYCHOSOCIAL FACTORS. The role of psychological factors in

the etiology of learning disorders is an issue clouded by ambiguity. It is well known that psychological problems and learning disorders are commonly found in association.[6,7,21,23,46,56] What still remains unanswered, however, is whether the emotional disorders are a consequence of school failure, or a cause of it.

In recent years many investigators have studied the impact of unfavorable environment in urban and rural poverty areas on child development. There has been much recent interest in the effects of social and cultural factors on the psychological development and educational achievement of children.

Reading retardation has been shown by Eisenberg[19] and others to be related directly to social class. There are now abundant data illustrating the early developmental decline that takes place in children of disadvantaged background. Caldwell and Richmond[11,47] have demonstrated a downward drift in the developmental performance of young children of lower economic backgrounds. These children enter elementary school with considerable developmental disadvantage, and the discrepancy in performance between the two groups continues to widen rather than diminish during the early school years.

When the inner-city children of the poor attend school, too often they meet with a teaching system geared to promote failure. Surrounded by pessimistic attitudes about their intellectual potential, they often find overcrowded schools, ill-qualified teachers who spend more time coping with disciplinary problems than teaching, and a curriculum attuned more to the needs of the middle class than to the special educational needs of the disadvantaged. Children of the lower socioeconomic groups all too frequently find the abstract educational model of the middle-class school system to be meaningless and nonproductive, leaving them feeling discouraged and frustrated with school. Their response may be to "drop out" in order to avoid the painful learning situation.

The relationship between a disruptive life in urban ghettos and cognitive growth has been emphasized by Wolff.[57,58] Cognitive development in general depends upon the ability to attend selectively to relevant novelties against a background of unobtrusively familiar surroundings. Children living in social disruption suffer, not from a lack of sensory input, but rather from

Table 1

Causative Factors	Preventive Corollary
Nutritional deprivation	Provision of adequate diet: Economic improvement.
Emotional deprivation	Provision of comfortable and stimulating psychological environment.
Cultural deprivation	Cultural enrichment.
Reproductive casualty	Favorable prenatal and perinatal environment and medical care.
Developmental abnormalities	Genetic counselling; prevention of fetal insults. Developmental assessment for early recognition.
Physical handicaps	Preventive health care and early remediation of defects.
Mental retardation	Early developmental assessment. Early medical, psychological and educational intervention.
Psychiatric disturbance	Favorable environment; preventive child guidance.
Specific educational handicaps	Early identification; special educational and psychological services.

inappropriate or excessive stimulation, which prevents the selective attention necessary for adequate cognitive growth.

It becomes evident that learning disorders can be viewed as maladaptive phenomena resulting from a complex interplay of variables, which can best be evaluated by comprehensive strategies.

Intervention and prevention: Needs and programs

A primary aim of epidemiological investigation is to provide a framework for introducing meaningful intervention and prevention programs. As studies define etiological factors, we must be swift to postulate preventive corollaries and devise therapeutic methods to render the disorders less handicapping (Table 1).

Critical to all programs for prevention and intervention is the need for early developmental assessment. Much research has been directed to designing early developmental evaluation tests and more sophisticated methods for early neurological assessment. Attention has been directed to the role of repeated screening examinations for both physical abnormalities and developmental retardation in order to identify remediable conditions.

Equally important for program development is an improved taxonomy of learning disorders. Semantic chaos so surrounds this group of disorders that there is, in effect, considerable fragmentation of the available knowledge in this area. A variety of etiologic and descriptive terms have been used somewhat interchangeably to describe these children: minimal brain damage, minimal cerebral dysfunction, clumsy child syndrome, visual-motor disability, hyperkinetic syndrome, dyslexia, specific reading disability, congenital word blindness, perceptual motor handicaps, production or acquisition learning problems, and strephosymbolia are just some of the terms applied to the disorders and utilized by clinicians to describe or study the problem. When the data from the literature are compiled, we are left with a chaotic array of terms and are unable to group the data or use them in a comparable way to answer questions about prevalence or etiology.

Prevention and intervention programs must be directed not only to the educational and social needs, but also to the total health and welfare needs of the child. It is evident that children who are malnourished, chronically ill, or suffering from a physical impairment, given the same objective conditions for learning as children not impaired, will derive less from the learning experiences than the unimpaired children. Programs involving total health care are therefore directly related to the issue of decreasing the incidence and handicap of learning disabilities.

During the last decade, considerable interest has been directed toward reversing the developmental decline induced through environmental deprivation. In the mid-1960's, the health, educational, and welfare programs for young children were brought together in a national effort—Project Head Start. This is a comprehensive program offering health, social service, and educational opportunities to preschool children of disadvantaged groups. The results obtained from developmentally oriented enrichment programs reveal that early intervention can stimulate the intellectual, emotional, and social development in children from deprived backgrounds (Figure 3).[47]

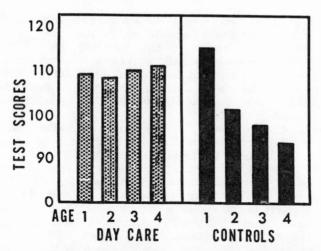

Figure 3. CROSS-SECTIONAL MEAN DEVELOPMENTAL
TEST SCORES FOR DAY CARE AND CONTROL
CHILDREN TESTED AT AGES 1, 2, 3, and 4
From: S. Walzer and J. B. Richmond, The epidemiology of learn-
ing disorders, *Pediatric Clinics of North America*, 20, August 1973.

Since programs designed to foster growth and development of
young children cannot be presumed to sustain their impact in-
definitely, there also has been interest in "follow through" programs for school-age children in order to extend the benefits
derived from day care and Head Start programs.

Prevention of learning impairment is more than just a theo-
retic possibility even though, to date, relatively few specific preventive programs have been implemented. This is directly
related to the fact that these measures go beyond the resources
of subgroups and require a concerted effort on a societal level.
It is clearly a responsibility shared by everyone concerned with
the welfare of children—and one which deserves the highest
priority of our attention and resources.

REFERENCES

1. ANDERSON, W. W. The hyperkinetic child: A neurological appraisal.
   Neurology, 1963, *13*, 968.
2. BAUMGARTNER, L. The public health significance of low birth
   weight in the U.S.A. with special reference to varying practices

in providing special care to infants of low birth weights. *Bulletin of the World Health Organization,* 1962, *26,* 175.

3. BEHRMAN, R. E., FISCHER, D. E., & PATON, J. Air pollution in nurseries: Correlation with a decrease in oxygen-carrying capacity of hemoglobin. *Journal of Pediatrics,* 1971, *78,* 1050.

4. BIRCH, H. G. Health and the education of socially disadvantaged children. *Developmental Medicine and Child Neurology,* 1968, *10,* 580.

5. BIRCH, H., & RICHARDSON, S. A. The relation of handicaps to social and obstetrical factors in all children living in one city. Presented at the American Academy of Cerebral Palsy, December, 1965.

6. BLANCHARD, P. Psychogenic factors in some cases of reading disability. *American Journal of Orthopsychiatry,* 1935, *5,* 361.

7. BOWER, E. M. The education of emotionally handicapped children. A report to the California legislature prepared pursuant to Section 1 of Chapter 2385, Statutes of 1957. Sacramento: California State Department of Education, 1961.

8. BRENNER, M. W., GILLMAN, S., ZANGWILL, O. L., et al. Visuo-motor disability in school children. *British Medical Journal,* 1967, *4,* 259.

9. BRUNER, J. S. *Toward a Theory of Instruction.* Washington, D.C.: Howard University Press, 1966.

10. BYERS, R. K. Lead poisoning: Review and report of 45 cases. *Pediatrics,* 1959, *23,* 585.

11. CALDWELL, B. M., & RICHMOND, J. B. The Children's Center in Syracuse, N.Y. In L. L. Dittman (Ed.), *Early Child Care: The New Perspectives.* New York: Atherton Press, 1968.

12. CHASE, H. C., & BYRNES, M. E. Trends in "prematurity": United States, 1950–1967. *American Journal of Public Health,* 1970, *60,* 1967.

13. CHISHOLM, J. J., & HARRISON, H. E. Treatment of acute lead encephalopathy. *Pediatrics,* 1957, *19,* 2.

14. CRITCHLEY, M. *Developmental Dyslexia.* London: William Heinemann Medical Books, 1964.

15. DAVEAU, M. The EEG of 150 children with behavior disorders. *Electroencephalography and Clinical Neurophysiology,* 1958, *10,* 198.

16. DOUGLAS, J. W. B. Mental ability and school achievement of premature children at eight years of age. *British Medical Journal,* 1956, *1,* 1210.

17. DRILLEN, C. M. *The Growth and Development of Prematurely Born Children.* Baltimore: Williams and Wilkins, 1964.

18. DRILLEN, C. M. The incidence of mental and physical handicaps in school-age children of very low birth weight. *Pediatrics,* 1967, *39,* 238.

19. EISENBERG, L. The epidemiology of reading retardation and a

program for preventative intervention. In J. Money (Ed.), *The Disabled Reader*. Baltimore: Johns Hopkins Press, 1966.

20. ERIKSON, E. H. *Childhood and Society*. New York: W. W. Norton, 1937.

21. FABIAN, A. A. Clinical and experimental studies of school children who are retarded in reading. *Quarterly Journal of Child Behavior*, 1951, *3*, 15.

22. FORSMANN, H., & FREY, T. S. Electroencephalograms of boys with behavior disorders. *Acta Psychiatrica et Neurologica Scandinavica*, 1953, *28*, 61.

23. GATES, A. The role of personality maladjustment in reading disability. *Journal of Genetic Psychology*, 1941, *59*, 77.

24. GOLDBERG, I. D., GOLDSTEIN, H., QUADE, D., & ROGOT, E. Association of perinatal factors with blindness in children. *Public Health Reports*, 1967, *82*, 519.

25. GROSS, M. D., & WILSON, W. C. Behavior disorders of children with cerebral dysrhythmias. *Archives of General Psychiatry*, 1964, *11*, 610.

26. GRUENBERG, E. M. *Technical Report of the Mental Health Research Unit, New York State Department of Mental Hygiene*. Syracuse: Syracuse University Press, 1955.

27. GRUENBERG, E. M. Epidemiologic aspects of brain damage. In H. G. Birch (Ed.), *Brain Damage in Children: The Biologic and Social Aspects*. Baltimore: Williams and Wilkins, 1964.

28. HERTZIG, M. E., BORTNER, M., & BIRCH, H. G. Neurologic findings in children educationally designated as "brain-damaged." *American Journal of Orthopsychiatry*, 1969, *39*, 437.

29. HUGHES, J. F. Electroencephalography and learning disabilities. In H. R. Myklebust (Ed.), *Progress in Learning Disabilities*. Vol. II. New York: Grune and Stratton, 1971.

30. HURWITZ, I., BIBACE, R. M. A., WOLFF, P. H., & ROWBOTHAM, B. M. The neuropsychological function of normal boys, delinquent boys and boys with learning problems. *Perceptual and Motor Skills*, 1972, *35*, 387.

31. JACOBZINER, H. Lead poisoning in children. *Clinical Pediatrics*, 1966, *5*, 277.

32. KENNARD, M. A. Value of equivocal signs in neurologic diagnosis. *Neurology*, 1960, *10*, 753.

33. KLINKERFUSS, G. H., LANGE, P. H., WEINBERG, W. A., et al. Electroencephalographic abnormalities of children with hyperkinetic behavior. *Neurology*, 1965, *15*, 883.

34. KNOBLOCH, H., RIDER, R., HARPER, P., & PASAMANICK, B. Neuropsychiatric sequelae of prematurity. *Journal of the American Medical Association*, 1956, *161*, 581.

35. LARSEN, V. L. Physical characteristics of disturbed adolescents. *Archives of General Psychiatry*, 1964, *10*, 55.

36. LAUFER, M. S., DENHOFF, E., & SOLOMONS, G. Hyperkinetic impulse disorder in children's behavior problems. *Psychosomatic Medicine*, 1957, *19*, 38.

37. LILIENFELD, A. M., PASAMANICK, B., & ROGERS, M. Relationship between pregnancy experience and the development of certain neuropsychiatric disorders in childhood. *American Journal of Public Health*, 1955, *45*, 637.

38. MONEY, J., & ALEXANDER, D. Turner's syndrome: Further demonstration of the presence of specific cognitional deficits. *Journal of Medical Genetics*, 1966, *3*, 47.

39. MYKLEBUST, H. R. Identification and diagnosis of children with learning disabilities: An interdisciplinary study of criteria. In S. Walzer and P. H. Wolff (Eds.), *Minimal Cerebral Dysfunction in Children*. New York: Grune and Stratton, 1973.

40. NEEDLEMAN, H. L. Lead poisoning in children: Neurologic implications of widespread subclinical intoxication. In S. Walzer and P. H. Wolff (Eds.), *Minimal Cerebral Dysfunction in Children*. New York: Grune and Stratton, 1973.

41. NEEDLEMAN, H. L., & TUNCAY, O. C. Lead levels in deciduous teeth of urban and suburban American children. *Nature*, 1972, *235* (No. 5333), 111.

42. OBERLE, M. W. Lead poisoning: A preventable childhood disease of the slums. *Science*, 1969, *165*, 991.

43. PASAMANICK, B., & LILIENFELD, A.M. Association of maternal and fetal factors with development of mental deficiency. I. Abnormalities in the prenatal and perinatal periods. *Journal of the American Medical Association*, 1955, *159*, 155.

44. PERLSTEIN, M. A., & ATTALA, R. Neurologic sequelae of plumbism in children. *Clinical Pediatrics*, 1966, *5*, 292.

45. PRECHTL, H. F. R., & STEMMER, C. J. The choreiform syndrome in children. *Developmental Medicine and Child Neurology*, 1962, *4*, 119.

46. RAINES, S., & TAIT, A. T. Emotional factors in reading retardation. *Journal of Educational Research*, 1951, *2*, 51.

47. RICHMOND, J. B. Disadvantaged children: What have they compelled us to learn? *Yale Journal of Biology and Medicine*, 1970, *43*, 127.

48. SACHS, H. K., BLANKSMA, L.A., MURRAY, E. F., & O'CONNELL, M. J. Ambulatory treatment of lead poisoning: Report of 1,155 cases. *Pediatrics*, 1970, *46*, 389.

49. SATTERFIELD, J. H. EEG issues in children with minimal brain dysfunction. In S. Walzer and P. H. Wolff (Eds.), *Minimal Cerebral Dysfunction in Children*. New York: Grune and Stratton, 1973.

50. SECHZER, J. A., FARO, M. D., & WINDLE, W. F. Studies of monkeys asphyxiated at birth: Implications for minimal cerebral dysfunction. In S. Walzer and P. H. Wolff (Eds.), *Minimal*

Cerebral Dysfunction in Children. New York: Grune and Stratton, 1973.

51. SHAFFER, J. W. A specific cognitive deficit observed in gonadal aplasia (Turner's syndrome). *Journal of Clinical Psychology,* 1962, *18,* 403.
52. VERNON, M. Prematurity and deafness: The magnitude and nature of the problem among deaf children. *Exceptional Children,* 1967, *33,* 289.
53. WALZER, S. Unpublished data.
54. WEINER, G. Scholastic achievement at age 12-13 for prematurely born infants. *Journal of Special Education,* 1968, *2,* 237–250.
55. WIKLER, A., DIXON, J. F., & PARKER, J. B., JR. Brain function in problem children and controls: Psychometric, neurological and electroencephalographic comparisons. *American Journal of Psychiatry,* 1970, *127,* 634.
56. WITTY, P. Reading success and emotional adjustment. *Elementary English Review,* 1950, *27,* 281.
57. WOLFF, P. H. What we must and must not teach our young children from what we know about early cognitive development. In P. H. Wolff and R. MacKeith (Eds.), *Planning for Better Learning.* London: Spastics International Medical Publications in association with William Heinemann Medical Books, 1969. P. 7.
58. WOLFF, P. H., & FEINBLOOM, R. I. Critical periods and cognitive development in the first two years. *Pediatrics,* 1969, *44,* 999.
59. WOLFF, P. H., & HURWITZ, I. The choreiform syndrome. *Developmental Medicine and Child Neurology,* 1966, *8,* 160.

MADMAN
He was caged up—
Caged like a mad bull.
He had no friends
Except
The cold touch
Of steel
On the bars.

He was kept
Alive
By the warm touch
Of sunlight
Through the bars.

BILL O'SHEA, Age 10, Australia

_____ 6

The Many Faces
of Advocacy

NORMAN V. LOURIE, A.C.S.W.

The Joint Commission on the Mental Health of Children concluded that we must seek a new national commitment to children.
To achieve such a commitment, to ensure it, the Commission proposed a process and a system of child advocacy. This
chapter explores the meaning of such advocacy.

Multiple meanings of advocacy

The term *advocacy* is generally used to mean "raising a fuss"
in behalf of a cause, usually resulting in a planned effort, seeking
to achieve an objective. Advocacy is as complex and diverse as
man's problems and his attempts to deal with them. Clothed in
wide acceptance at a particular time, ideas or concepts become
popular, striking, or expressive of a general desire; they gain
prominence and wide use. Advocacy, specifically child advocacy,

seems to be such an idea today. The term is coming to be used widely; the concept is as yet carried out poorly.

Advocacy, advocate and *child advocacy* are increasingly popular words. Overused, they have many diverse and legitimate meanings. The lawyer, for instance, has long been known as an advocate. The terms came into recent prominence as a result of the report of the Joint Commission on the Mental Health of Children (1969). The 1970 White House Conference on Children was highly concerned with the unmet, critical needs of children and with the concepts of advocacy as they related to prevention of disease and disorder and provision of health, mental health, and social services. Recommendations were made calling for advocacy in behalf of children of many ages and related to many critical needs.

The concept of advocacy, a term long known primarily to lawyers and courts, has lately been embraced by the consumer and professional as a device for increasing pressures against the social structure to achieve social equity and justice. This happened before the report of the Joint Commission, but the report acted as a clarion call to persons concerned with the fate of America's children to find a new way of advocating for them.

Many recent congressional and federal agency actions reflect new initiatives in behalf of children. The Office of Child Development in the U.S. Department of Health, Education, and Welfare (H.E.W.) came into being, in part, as a result of the Joint Commission's recommendations for a high level children's policy unit in H.E.W. Recently, the Office of Child Development announced that one of its organizational units would have "child advocacy" as its main function. The U.S. Office of Education and the National Institute of Mental Health are offering jointly funded grants for child advocacy projects. Congress is seriously considering major legislation which is a move toward universal child development programs, another form of advocacy. The Administration's welfare reform legislation contains substantially expanded federal benefits for children and families and calls for a federal income floor for all families with children. Social Security legislation, with special provisions for children, is broadened periodically. Congress has enacted major family planning legislation and provided substantial new funding in this field.

The Secretary of H.E.W. has been interested in service delivery coordination. Within H.E.W., legislative planning is under way for an Allied Services Bill mentioned by the President in a message to Congress early in 1972, a bill designed to improve ways in which services are delivered.

The 1970s opened with considerable discussion about integrating social services and improving service delivery. Such positive moves were recommended by the Joint Commission as representing one aspect of child advocacy. One of the child development bills (S. 2007) contained a specific proposal made by the Joint Commission for local councils to initiate and monitor needed children's programs.* Several proposals, even though not passed, vetoed, or not funded, indicate positive interest. However, no activity yet shows the capacity to carry out what was the Joint Commission's main thrust when it called for a system at every level of government to assure effective carrying out of clearly agreed-upon national goals for children.

Problems in social aspects of advocacy

Correction of any social problem or of any injustice is always complicated by the fact that social solutions take place in changing social situations and require constant updating. The rate of

---

* The bill, an extension of the Economic Opportunity Act, passed both houses of Congress and was vetoed by President Nixon on December 9, 1971. The President gave eight reasons for vetoing the child development legislation:

1. Immediate need or desirability for such programs not demonstrated.
2. Some duplication of present federal programs and provisions of H.R. 1.
3. Prospect of a $20 billion program unjustified for program whose effectiveness is yet to be demonstrated.
4. The program might tend to basically alter family relationships in the United States and, before moving in this direction, the American people should be fully consulted.
5. Good social policy requires that we enhance rather than diminish parental authority particularly in early years of life.
6. There is yet no adequate answer to the crucial question of who are qualified staff and where they would come from.
7. Would create a new army of bureaucrats; 7000 communities eligible to ask for direct federal grants. Head Start experience, with fewer than 1200 grantees, is a difficult management problem.
8. The state would be relegated to an insignificant role. Initiative for preschool education would shift from state to federal government. Only eight (8) states now require kindergarten. Federal level would retain an excessive measure of operational control for preschool education.

social change is accelerating faster than ever. However, our inability to cope with it has made it seem more frightening. As a result we rarely encounter positive social change that will really enhance the well-being of children and their families.

Approaches to making social change orderly and useful, with a minimum of pain and suffering, range from the simple to the complex. Mounting a drive to advocate a better life for America's children is indeed a complex task.

ADVOCACY AND ACTION. In the human services fields, what used to be marked as charity and benevolence is in fact a right. Advocacy has many faces. Every action taken in behalf of a cause is an advocate action. Jane Addams, one of the social work pioneers, once said that action was the one medium man had for appropriating and expressing the truth. Advocacy may thus mean action to achieve a better life for children from infancy to adulthood.

Compassion of professionals and citizens interested in human services usually has outpaced the means and social policies created in the nation to cope with social change. The knowledge-practice gap has always been wide. We know a great deal more than we use. We do not invest our resources in children at a level that matches our rhetoric about children being our most precious resource. Often the people working in the human services are blamed. They are, in fact, no more to blame than the physician who knows that only kidney dialysis can cure his patient but is frustrated by its unavailability. The unavailability is not a matter of lack of knowledge or technology, it is simply a matter of *social policy values and priority decisions with respect to how resources are spread and assigned.* The importance of children and youth to our nation is measured not by words but by provision of services.

One might be critical of human service workers, the social and helping professions, and human services establishments in respect to techniques used to express their beliefs and carry out their social action objectives. They have usually associated themselves with the poor and served as they could, within the constraints society has placed and keeping pace with the values that society has established. Their raised voices in behalf of the poor and unserved were lonely, long before the poor themselves organized. The concepts of the guaranteed minimum income, of higher assistance grants, of rights to treatment, and of more appropriate distribution of wealth have been the stated objectives of professional societies, guilds, and agencies long before the present surge of broad interest in these subjects.

THE NEEDS OF THE POOR AND POWERLESS. Until recent years, the legal system did not traditionally work for or listen to the dispossessed and the poor. In fact, for the legal system, as well as for society as a whole, the poor were beyond the pale, ineligible for and unentitled to rights and benefits guaranteed every other citizen.

In respect to income maintenance, to poverty and public assistance, the dilemma we face is rooted in the basic concepts of the Elizabethan Poor Law and the special pauper status it created. When assistance was given, no matter how limited, the individual gave up his claim to full citizenship. He became the proper objective of public regulations and restraints different from any used in providing other public benefits—a strange and illogical circumstance in a society which placed so much stress on due process and whose Constitution used welfare as a beautiful word, not associated with financial help to the poor.

Although in recent years we have removed many categories of individuals from the Poor Law stigma, we have not faced squarely the question: "Is public assistance a legal right or is it still a form of public largesse given conditionally, dependent on the behavior of the recipient?"

As a matter of national public policy, we cannot avoid answering the question, for the situation has changed. It changed, as many things have changed, primarily because the civil rights revolution brought us, as a nation, to face the issues more clearly and the legal system, including the courts, intervened and forcefully addressed itself to the matter of affording due process and access of the law to poor people. In the fields of health, mental health, and mental retardation, the issue of whether adequate services are rights has also been coming to the fore and is receiving major attention.

Advocating and advocacy generally mean action in support of one's beliefs in a cause, engaging in social action. Action can take many forms and be carried out at various levels in a society involving individuals, groups, organizations, or institutions.

Action, in effect, is the one medium that man has for consolidating his convictions by seeking their realization. In the human service fields, therefore, almost any action toward realizing a goal yet unrealized could be called advocacy.

Social action and political advocacy

Social action and political advocacy, which represent embracing of a cause, take place at many levels. The National Associations of Mental Health and Mental Retardation are advocates, for instance. So are the American Civil Liberties Union, the Welfare Rights Organization, and proponents of community control. Sometimes, an advocacy group is a transitory one or one with a single cause. The Committee of One Hundred and the Committee for National Health Security, which work for national health insurance legislation, are such groups. Some of the activities of trade unions, professional societies, and citizen groups fit the category of advocates. Sometimes, social welfare agencies and individuals "lobby" for a cause as part of their normal activity. Industries and businesses pursue political advocacy in their own interests and sometimes broaden their concerns to social issues. Associations of health and welfare agencies and civic groups of all types engage in advocacy, as do churches and church-related groups and boards of trustees of social and health agencies.

The motives for advocacy are countless. Groups described by sociologists as the powerless and disenfranchised, the lower socioeconomic groups, carry out social action advocacy activities in their own behalf. Often we find coalitions of the powerful and the powerless, although the latter often question the motives of the former. New emphasis in law and regulation on maximum participation of the consumer highlight the legitimate role of social action advocacy and maximum participation of citizens in a democratic society. In recent years, governmental support of citizen advocacy has increased. However, it is important to recognize that recent government-supported advocacy by citizens and government employees (Community Action Agencies, consumer and human relations official agencies, etc.) is a new or expanded form of long cherished government responsibility to its constituents in the United States. More often, advocacy is translated in government by protection of the powerful rather than the powerless; there is, nevertheless, a long history of citizen advocacy by government in many fields. In the wake of the civil rights revolution we find a seeking, in the human services field, to reverse the processes of human services benevolence wherein the *haves* provided services to the *have nots* in order to balance the market place and maintain stability in which affluence of the majority could prosper. This is, of course, by itself, a most complex socioeconomic, political area which should not be overlooked. The new thrust reaches for a condition wherein services are provided to all, based on need and equity rather than on a charitable base.

ADVOCACY FOR ALL CHILDREN A NECESSITY. The Joint Commission was clear on rights of children and families, and advocacy to obtain them. It recognized the need for immediate concentration on the most suffering, in order to relieve mental and physical distress and to achieve health, equality, and justice for all. It also emphasized equal concern for all children and all families. Services for the poor alone traditionally become poor, unpopular services. Services available to the nonpoor have often been denied to the poor. Neither is a substitute for universality. So with advocacy. While there are powerless people, they need to be helped to have equal power. Some try to achieve power through their own efforts while others seek coalitions.

Advocacy used in this sense is an extension of philosophy and values underlying all social welfare activity. It implies concern for the dignity and rights of the individual—rights to self-realization in every aspect of living, to reasonable self-determination, and to compassionate attention to achieve the benefits of a technological and wealthy society and to relieve suffering for all people. It defends the powerless and seeks equal opportunity for them.

ADVOCACY FOR THE INDIVIDUAL, CLINICAL ADVOCACY: PROBLEMS OF DEFINITION. Another type of advocacy is that used by practically all agencies that deal with people problems—intervening with another agency on behalf of a client, urging an agency to change policies, practices, or regulations. This is activity to secure a better chance for an individual or sometimes for a group.

Some ascribe advocacy to more detailed agency operations,

for instance, an agency's keeping a good resource file so staff members can make better referrals; doing research which will result in improving help to people; providing transportation services to get someone to another service; or acting as broker to get a service or change in service and policy.

The problem with these definitions is that they, in effect, could stretch so that everything one does, including bedside or deskside treatment, could be described as advocacy—except that advocacy in reality requires taking a stand on someone's behalf.

Some professionals contend that too much advocacy can encourage dependency. Some emphasize the person's own role in his treatment and adjustment, and the importance of choice. Many still believe that agencies are not giving adult and youth clients enough say in choice of alternatives for themselves. Self-help groups and community control movements have clinical, social, and political implications, but all express the desire for participation in advocating for themselves, rather than being advocated for by what they consider to be benevolent persons.

Medical and social work case management models contain elements related to this usage of the advocacy concept. Should the agency be the advocate as part of a treatment process? Does this type of advocacy on the part of an agency contain reminder or remnant of the benevolent, philanthropic motives where the *haves* were gingerly adjusting the *have nots* to the acceptance of their role in the market place? *

---

* While social work literature calls for universality of social services, historically, in function, by broad structure of agencies and through laws and regulation, social services have concentrated on low income groups except in a few areas, primarily in agencies providing family services and services for the handicapped. The war on poverty brought many social agencies to a new concentration on the poor. It did not fundamentally change program structures or methods. The war on poverty brought many new publicly funded agencies for the poor, with the poor (or their representatives) as the management groups. Some of these will last, some will not remain. New child development legislation growing out of the Head Start-OEO experience calls for maximum consumer participation. Many regulations of federal agencies call for consumer representation on management bodies. Some of the new forms are really not new. Community Action Agencies, generated by the Economic Opportunity Act, are reminders of the settlement house and of action forms generated in the depression of the 1930s. They often resemble activities carried out within Works Progress Administration projects.

ADVOCACY FOR BETTER HEALTH AND MENTAL HEALTH PROGRAMS.
Each argument holds elements of truth. Sick people need skillful treatment. Society needs better conditions for humans to prevent sickness, suffering, and inequalities. We can speculate on
what is an optimal set of social circumstances but we must also
act on what can be done *now* to help bring about more optimal
situations. Evidence is mounting that financial and social well-
being is no guarantee of protection from either physical or emotional stress in this society. However, the correlation between
poverty and severe health and mental health problems is very
clear.

A high value of the community mental health center movement, like the thrust of the public education system, is that it is,
presumably, an agent for all comers, not only for lower economic
and social classes. This is the social welfare, the human services
utility concept which underlies the Joint Commission's recommendations. While recognizing that the most needy require more
attention at a specific time, the notion is that useful services
must be universal.

The recent drive of human service agencies is that they be
resources for helping the individual as well as advocates for
the general cause or issue that a person represents. Settlement
houses, for instance, saw social betterment as both their cause
and their function. Porter Lee, one of the early social work pioneers, in 1937 described social work as both cause and function.
Other early social work leaders were primarily activists. Today,
many helping organizations with case treatment responsibilities
as tradition are changing their style.

That part of the community mental health movement which
both reaches out to persons in need of services and involves the
community is reminiscent of the settlement house and is different from the traditional mental hospital or clinic.

Communes and self-help movements, like cooperatives, are
efforts toward self-determination and advocacy of certain individual solutions to problems. The rise of such movements suggests to us that social helping institutions cannot fully serve
unless they literally join with the stockholders and give them a
participating voice in the entire process, including advocacy.
The development of outreach programs, seeking out those in

need and helping them to obtain services, is another expression of this type of advocacy.

Advocacy and the law

Another major *use* of the advocacy concept is the *use* of law to achieve social purposes and redress current social wrongs. The Federal Legal Services Program created by the Economic Opportunity Act of 1964 could be characterized as the legal profession's 20th century version of the Hippocratic Oath. Legal services for the poor under this program and similar services available under the social services titles of the Social Security Act are now widespread and have had significant effect on social law. Use of the law to challenge is not new. Decisions by courts are subject to attitudes and conditions of the time. In recent years, legal advocacy, supported by public funds, in legal services offices for the poor throughout the nation, has taken individual and class action cases through the highest courts to establish entitlements of citizens for a variety of public services, challenging restrictions by administrators of social law and regulation. These expressions of legal advocacy have ranged over civil rights, mental health, mental retardation, education, and public assistance residency and entitlement questions. The courts have made many decisions with people-oriented direction in the changing social atmosphere.

The legal advocacy idea and machinery are now accepted in some areas of the country, with public legal services established as independent agencies, not controlled by another executive branch agency. Social services funds provided in the Social Security Act (75 per cent federal matching funds) are increasingly being used for legal services for the poor.

An attempt to forbid use of Social Security Act social services funds for legal services that would challenge federal law was recently struck down during debate on HR 1 in the 92nd Congress. While HR 1 put a $2.5 billion ceiling on social services (Titles I, IV, X, XIV, XVI, Social Security Act) which were previously open ended, these funds continue to be available for legal services.

Designed primarily for those who cannot afford to purchase legal assistance, the new agencies follow a course seen previously. Regulatory functions of governments, such as public utility, licensing, consumer protection, and human relations commissions are not new. Although often ineffective, the flavor of concentration is new, as is the constituency served, but the goals and objectives are universal in time.

CONFLICTS OF INTEREST. As science and technology advance in knowledge and techniques for solving human services, matters of decision and questions of social policy proliferate. The more science and technology produce in solutions for human problems, the greater the number of dilemmas that confront society.

It is natural that we turn to the law for answers. Conflicting social interests in our society use the law and the courts to seek answers. Law and courts have not always responded quickly enough to social issues. Conducted by humans, courts, like any human institution, make human errors and are subject to pressures of environmental, cultural, and social values and tones.

What is significant for the human services field today is that new groups of advocates are reaching out to the courts, and the courts are often responding in humanistic terms reflective of the times. Issues previously never brought to courts or considered in different times with different interpretations are being decided today with people-oriented values. Interpretations of law in recent years have guaranteed rights of people to economic assistance when they are poverty striken, to protection as consumers, and to health and education services. However, the law in some states remains nonresponsive to human needs.

Recent court decisions have guaranteed that all mentally retarded children in a state have the right to education and that all mentally ill in state institutions have the right to a level of care and treatment prescribed by the court. One can assume that, in time, the right of all children to quality health care, for instance, may be court directed. However, as in civil rights cases, the question of advocacy comes face to face with the issue of implementation. Court directives may not be carried out or may be undermined by lack of funds for implementation. Advocacy has a role in pushing for implementation.

Official and unofficial civil rights groups, government and private legal service bodies, and consumer oriented agents like Ralph Nader, by their successful legal approaches to social problems, have encouraged others to use the legal system. Groups like the National Association for Retarded Children have successfully taken their concerns to court. This trend is proliferating. It is logical to predict that issues of entitlements to more effective human services will increasingly be brought to court for airing and adjudicating.

In our fluid and pluralistic political situation, legislative response is often too slow. Solutions to human needs usually lag behind. Bureaucracies often are insensitive and sometimes are not given enough dollars to carry out their mandates effectively. It is likely that new faith in legal approaches to social solutions will escalate. People, through their organizations or coalitions of organizations, will increasingly go to the courts to address government agencies which they believe are not carrying out the intent of law in respect to a human service, including the quality of the service. Public "social utility" agencies designed to protect consumers of social welfare services have been less effective than necessary in reacting to pressure of public interest groups. Government in the future may be induced to create more effective consumer protection agencies. This is already happening in some fields.

Legal advocacy has potentials close to the goals of the Joint Commission and useful in their achievement. Increasingly, as they seek to assure entitlements, legal service advocacy agents are beginning to observe and evaluate human services systems to see whether the practice conforms with the rhetoric of law, regulations, institutional and professional expressions. A fair prediction is that individuals and organizations will move to use the legal advocacy process, through legal and court procedures, to seek restructuring of delivery systems and assurances that people get services to which they are entitled. However, as one of our leading jurists and a Joint Commission member has repeatedly pointed out, no court can assure adequate resources for services it rules are necessary for the protection of legal rights of individuals. These are essentially legislative and executive branch matters.

The issue of entitlement, of course, is by itself a vital question. Are a guaranteed income, a guaranteed job, health care, etc., entitlements? What about quality? On what criteria shall a service be judged? Who owns the system? What are the rights of consumers and professionals? What are the lines between professional and public interests? What obligations do professionals have to the society which sanctions their professional prerogatives? Can a profession have a monopoly? The long established but often ineffective laws and controls over economic monopolies bring this question to mind. Also involved in legal approaches to synthesis of systems and rights are such matters as definitions of problems and goals for solution.

Human service advocacy

For the human services fields—that is, the delivery of human services to persons with physical, social, and mental disabilities —advocacy has a separate and special meaning. All types of advocacy previously mentioned have relevance. However, the key to solving the problems of inadequate delivery of human services to families and children, of guaranteeing needed services, has to do, among other things, with presence of rational systems of service delivery. Such systems are not present today. Delivery system problems are so serious that inundation of a community with services would, by itself, not be a guarantee that children would be adequately served. Given the highest expressions of all of the advocacy techniques discussed above, people's needs will still remain unmet if delivery systems are not corrected.

This leads to another type of advocacy, operational advocacy, which will be discussed in the following chapter.

Human dignity, economic freedom, individual
responsibility, these are the characteristics
that distinguish democracy from all other forms
devised by man.

DWIGHT D. EISENHOWER

7

Operational Advocacy:
Objectives and Obstacles

NORMAN V. LOURIE, A.C.S.W.

Framework of operational advocacy

The term *advocacy* is used in many legitimate ways. Each
needs examination in context to understand its boundaries and
limitations. The Joint Commission used a variety of terms, but
its most significant contribution was its *concept* of operational
advocacy. It did not use the term, but in describing the needs
for a more rational set of human service delivery systems, it
described what this author and others have come to call "operational advocacy." It also described a model system at the neighborhood level capable of evaluating local needs and setting in
motion action to generate services to meet them. The model is
not a substitute for a total planning and systems effort. The
Commission looked upon it as an activist advocacy device, potentially useful in its continued thrust at planners at all levels
toward a reality-oriented major overhaul of service delivery
arrangements.

Operational advocacy is best defined as presence of a system
or systems of delivering human services focusing on ease of access at local, neighborhood levels. Such systems know the vulnerable children and families, especially those at risk, and know
their needs and assure that they are met. Different from cause-

oriented advocacy, operational advocacy exists when human service resources are so ordered that vital preventive and remedial
requirements are met.

No such arrangements exist in the United States today. In
fact, our arrangements for delivering services are more often
characterized as chaotic and fragmented and not designed to
guarantee that needs are either known or met. Certainly, some
excellent programs and services exist. None are universal enough
to represent guarantees of providing services where and when
required. The Commission found, just as have other studies, including the White House Conferences on Children (held each
decade since 1912), that there are too many poor, unhealthy,
unhappy, malnourished, and poorly educated children, as Berlin
points out in his discussion of the rights of children.

Even the presence of a strong commitment to advocacy for
children translated into law and resources would not by itself
be a guarantee, the Commission concluded. It is possible, hypo-
thetically, to overwhelm a community with human services and
still have unmet needs if the systems of delivery are not arranged effectively. This would be true in any field. Electricity,
water, and telephone service need tremendous systematization
to flow evenly in and out of dwellings and offices. Without the
regulation we impose on these systems, there could easily be a
situation in which some homes, offices, and plants were unserved
or underserved. In fact, there could be a hopeless jumble of wires
and pipes making efficient delivery of utilities impossible. Environmental pollution, for instance, is an example of the need
for operational advocacy in the physical field. It requires the
same coalition of aroused community citizens, experts, legislators, and informed, accountable executives.

The Commission detailed its recommendations and called for
comprehensive, systematic approaches to meeting children's
needs. The Commission called for replacement of fragmented
systems. The Commission concluded that even a strong commitment could be empty rhetoric unless it was translated into implementation through effective delivery arrangements.

This concept of operational advocacy, when examined together with the total Joint Commission body of findings and

recommendations, ascribes to advocacy and children's-advocate concepts their most forceful and complete meanings.

Some will hold that operational advocacy appears to be a substitute for the concepts and acts of sound social planning. It is not an attempt to redefine or substitute for social planning. Indeed it is a major support of and a major advocate for planning. Its use is important because it is the final, ultimate result of planning applied in reality. It holds that the final translation of planning is assuring that agreed-upon needs are met. In this sense the highest expression of advocacy includes support of sound planning not as an end in itself but as a means to human value achievement.

United States social services have a good deal of planning now. In fact each major federal program sets up separate planning machinery. At state and local levels the provider and consumer are faced with what often appear to be incomprehensible comprehensive planning efforts. The present human services planning systems, like the delivery systems, are disjointed and competitive.

Without operational advocacy, with its local, accessible character, all other forms of advocacy could be futile, resulting in absence of ultimate expression in terms of adequate, specific descriptions of need and effective delivery of services to children and their families.

Present service delivery problems

The concept of operational advocacy is best viewed against present service delivery realities.

The interactional processes among national, state, and local human service programs, agencies (public and voluntary), professionals, governments, and legislatures are numerous and complex. Currently between 400 and 500 categorical federal grant programs flow downward to state and local governments and to private vendors of human services. Of these, 280 are in H.E.W. alone.

Thousands of programs have produced tremendous results. Some have also produced serious questions. A few questions are concerned with narrowness and specificity of the program, some with selection of priorities, some with administrative deficiencies, and some with the undue weight of special interests.

Individual categorical programs have had tremendous impact on production and growth of systems and services. However, they have also produced conditions of duplication, overlapping, fragmentation, and considerable confusion. Systems and programs result in concentric operational arrangements which interfere with objectives of comprehensiveness and guarantee of human services delivery to those who need services.

INDIVIDUAL VS. FAMILY NEEDS. The specialized services developed in many communities are a potential aid to families and children. However, some such services have become so overly specialized, frequently so expensive, so poorly coordinated, or so centered on individuals rather than families, that few parents or even agencies have the resources needed to mobilize these services for the well-being of each family member or for the family as a unit. Specialized but splintered services must be coordinated. The social, physical, and economic structures of communities must be better adapted to fostering the health and mental health of individuals and families. The planning and administration of services and programs should be directed toward strengthening the family through family involvement as part of the community with the nature and effectiveness of required services. The family as part of the community can adapt more readily to today's society and carry out its important functions.

PROBLEMS OF SPECIALIZED SERVICES. Specialization is important, but, as one views the constant proliferation of new systems for delivery, one is impressed that each seeks to become the generalist, the case manager, the core service. One suspects that the important specialties are hindered in doing their best because each is caught up in trying to become everything to everybody.

Thus, as one views the community mental health center, the public or voluntary generalized social services agency, the vocational rehabilitation agency, the community action agency, the settlement house, the neighborhood health center, or one of the special children's health programs, etc., one is impressed with the increasing similarity of their functions despite their claimed differences. A similar situation exists in the training of professionals. Examination of curricula reveals that, across disciplinary lines, several of the helping professions are increasingly being taught about the primacy of their profession in solving human service needs. Collaborative work with specialized emphasis to better serve children and their families more fully is rarely taught.

Ample evidence exists that present service arrangements lead to poor and fragmented help. Often they suffer from the following characteristics:

1. Service arrangements tend to be oriented to the needs of professionals, guilds, agencies, interest groups, or others who provide or support service rather than to join with those served to assure meeting the needs of these families and children.

2. Service tends to be oriented to crisis and symptoms rather than to getting at fundamental problems and environmental determinants of crisis. Even when fundamental environmental problems are recognized by professionals associated with programs, fear of controversy or lack of resources often results in program planners' and administrators' failure to publicize or attempt to solve underlying problems.

3. Only a small fraction of those in need are served.

4. Hard core populations are screened out or fall out. Some agencies deliberately serve safe risks. Fads and fashions, rather than sound research findings, often dictate what are service risks. Methods of effective work with hard core populations are not utilized.

5. Available funds are spread over a large number of programs; no one program has enough "critical mass" to be very effective. Programs and systems compete with each other for categorical legislation and funds. New delivery forms are created with little reference to what exists. A frenetic concentric circle of activities results. Service traditions, competitive professional loyalties, and nonfunctional professional service arrangements are impediments to complete services.

6. Little follow-up or evaluation takes place, even though both are critical in establishing what works and what doesn't.

7. There is absence of real horizontal and vertical coordination and too little real planning, particularly across program lines, to meet needs. Objectives often conflict or overlap.

8. Innovations are often only marginal upgradings of existing

systems or updated recreations of old forms. Faddism replaces planning and evaluation.

9. When formal service systems fail to meet needs, compensatory "underground" systems arise, which the formal system ignores or represses. Absence of service by a logical source induces service development by an illogical source, further compounding confusion.

Surrounding present service delivery systems are problems of management and policy-making at all levels:

1. Data are inconsistently reported, confused, and unusable. Management information systems are not informative and are usually too cumbersome to be helpful.

2. Difficulty persists in defining priorities and problems.

3. Absence of a central overview for coordination of service delivery and needs results in little or no long-term planning.

4. Separation of research from operations has not been achieved.

PROBLEMS OF CHANGING SERVICE PATTERNS. No simple set of cause and effect relationships can be identified and used in solving service delivery problems. Nor can problems be solved in a crisis atmosphere or by short-term imperatives. Long-term approaches to solutions are needed. Congressional committees with their political and financing considerations, constituent groups of all types and at all levels, universities, professional societies, guilds, voluntary and public agencies, including their professional personnel, are all concerned. Their interactions, relationships, objectives, stances, attitudes, perspectives, and positions alone and together ultimately govern outcome.

The consequences of the present arrangements tend to arrest forward movement at all levels. If we are to approach realization of objectives—specifically, more effective articulation of existing and future programs as they effect service delivery—all of these groups, forces, and individuals will need to examine and modify their points of view and practice. They will need to communicate, think together, and reach consensus on the nature of change needed on many fronts.

Needed are a series of interdisciplinary activities directed to long-range solutions and designed to effect system and service delivery change.

Efforts to effect change

Operational advocacy proposes an approach to affect the concerns and practices of appropriate individuals and groups of various legislative and human service interests and viewpoints. It seeks to find ways to integrate and coordinate planning and services by interdisciplinary, intergroup, intersystem communication. The purpose is to produce more effective approaches to implementation of the many objectives inherent in human service.

Several congressional committees, though well meaning, make decisions and recommend legislation on the same subject often without knowledge of each others' actions. The results produce competing and overlapping local operational programs, which are extremely difficult to administer. Agencies and professionals, state and local governments must employ experts in grantsmanship—creative packagers of money and methods—in order to fund any of their programs. A specialty has developed, resulting in a person who is skilled at putting program monies together and winding through the complex of difficult legal, regulatory, and funding mechanisms. People presumably engaged in helping others are preoccupied with "working the system." This is a poor substitute for sound planning to meet people's requirements for a healthier, more effective life. We seem to have achieved a triumph of *technique* over *purpose*.

Operational advocacy, fully translated, would require considerable restructuring and coalescing of resources, forces, and systems. It would mean rearranging delivery systems so that the present "farmer's market" set of services is converted to a "supermarket," a rational flow of goods and services to the customer rather than a set of stalls from which he chooses at random.

WHOSE RESPONSIBILITY ARE HUMAN SERVICES? A key issue is the point of responsibility. In most human service fields now, no one is really responsible for solving particular problems. Even where such responsibility is legally determined, the translation is usually incomplete.

The task is a vast one. It has to begin at a national level with analysis of law, policy, and regulation, in which legislators and policymakers would join with a view to better solutions. Nationally, professionals, guilds, interest groups, consumers, and service agencies would need to join in a truly ecumenical movement. For congressmen, citizens, consumers, and particularly professionals, constituent groups, and service organizations (governmental and nongovernmental), a basic question is whether they can cope with the problem of reaching common ground.

How ready are we at all of these levels to give up territorial prerogatives in order to join in a move toward operational advocacy, through operational coalitions which guarantee to children and families that their needs will be known and met?

Operational advocacy, then, is the ultimate instrument for translating all other advocacy efforts into reality. While all expressions of advocacy are important, their successes could well be futile exercises without the fundamental rearrangements which are a prerequisite for successful operational advocacy.

Methods of bringing about operational advocacy

While achievement of operational advocacy must proceed at all levels, the governmental level is the most vital because human services in the United States today are primarily a product of law and public appropriations. The voluntary dollar is miniscule by comparison, and no voluntary service agency can function without public sanction. Thus, federal and state governments first need to establish legal policy and organizational frameworks with executive authority for coordinating services for children and families. As a beginning, we should attempt to overcome the present fragmented federal legislative authorities. Some legislation for joint funding now exists, particularly through the Intergovernmental Cooperation Act. However, this is only permissive legislation and has not been very effective.

The present Secretary of Health, Education, and Welfare has shown a marked interest in operational advocacy. His office has developed an Allied Services Bill which provides incentives to states in the directions of both joint funding and interprogram coordination. The Secretary and members of his staff responsible for major H.E.W. human services programs have spent considerable energy on the issues of service delivery improvement. Together with representatives of the Joint Commission, they have been exploring various options for realistically approaching achievement of operational advocacy through improvement of federal approaches in law, policy, training, and technical assistance in the field.

In our political system, constituencies must lend their convictions to such efforts. Government, no matter how correct in its goals, cannot achieve them without constituent support. Groups concerned, including professionals and consumers, must go together to government with unified convictions on social policy and comprehensive human services approaches. This requires education of citizens, especially parents and professionals.

This is unlikely to happen until the groups come together in ways that change atmosphere and practice. Individuals and groups of various viewpoints and interests bury individual objectives in larger goals. The joint motives are to produce more effective approaches to implement human services, goals, and objectives through sound laws and plans for operational advocacy, plans designed to assure that needs are known and met.

There can be no national commitment without such collaboration of voluntary and public sectors. Social policy and law, geared to putting more of the nation's resources into meeting needs of children and families, would be one outcome; appropriate social planning would be another.

Like coordination, social planning is a much misused term. Essentially, it is a mobilization of principles into action. Comprehensive human services planning includes defining what is important and what is superfluous, and how the elements should operationally fit together.

Operational advocacy does not discard other advocacy forms; it does not discard planning. It encourages them all. Ultimately, it puts them together in the interest of each family and child needing help and relief from suffering.

Operational advocacy is impossible to achieve in the present atmosphere. Too many obstacles exist. Laws, priorities, and lack of funds stand in the way. But if our objectives are clear, we know what the obstacles are. We know what must be done. We need strong advocates from the community, the professions, and the Congress, as well as a responsive executive branch, to achieve operational advocacy.

The New Federalism: Old problems

The problems of nonintegration and noncoordination of federal categorical grants are attacked by the present national administration using its New Federalism approach. The New Federalism concept suggests that the alternative to running things from Washington through the categorical grants system is to return funds to states and localities on a less categorical basis and to give these governments power to plan and spend. The theory is that costs will be lower and that funds will be used more effectively than under present arrangements.

The General Revenue Sharing Act was a first move. The administration's Special Revenue Sharing proposals, not acted on by Congress, will be resubmitted. Decentralization of federal agency powers to regional offices, regrouping of federal agencies into new combinations, and breaking up old alliances among bureaucracies, special interest groups, and congressional committees are all devices in the New Federalism approach. Without assessing these New Federalism moves, it is obvious that they, too, will not meet our human services delivery objectives unless they result in the type of situation spelled out in our operational advocacy definitions.

The New Federalism idea is rooted in the conviction that the federal government is too big and unwieldy. This may be. Perhaps more state and local government power over dollars and plans for service could produce a better result. However, decentralizing decision, power, and fiscal controls alone will not improve human service delivery unless there is a strong national child and family policy demanding that needs be met and service delivery improved. Indeed, unless this is accomplished, decentralization could merely result in more loci for confusion similar to the present ones.

Two other thoughts are important. One is the issue of whether state and local governments have the capacity to competently develop policy and administer major programs without federal overview and help. Many believe that, with few exceptions, they do not. Secondly, categorical programs have been crucial in getting massive attention, including citizen and legislative interest and funds. It is questionable whether advances could have been made without them. Eliminating some categories could hurt progress.

Finally, advocates of the New Federalism have not always been consistent on decentralization and decategorization. The new Cancer Institute and the National Institute of Education are examples of activity the administration believes is legitimately federal. The administration moved to centralize rather than decentralize welfare in these instances.

The Family Assistance Plan did not pass. (States will continue to administer the AFDC program.) However, the President's proposal for national administration of cash assistance to the aged, blind, and disabled did pass. Effective January 1974 the Federal Social Security Administration began to administer a new Supplemental Security Income Program. It replaces state and local cash assistance programs for the aged, blind, and disabled. While most are reluctant to use the term, it is a fully federally funded, guaranteed minimum social and economic program for these groups. Thus the rationale of the New Federalism is neither consistent nor logical. Although it may reduce some bureaucracies, it will encourage others.

Vigilance and massive support for federal children and family programs may develop new models of federal-state-local collaboration where aims and ends are more clearly viewed, periodically reexamined, and realistically reformulated as necessary.

Operational advocacy is a major step in that direction.

. . . and this is the crime of which I accuse
my country and my countrymen, and for which
neither I nor time nor history will ever
forgive them, that they have destroyed thousands
of lives and do not know it and do not want to
know it.

JAMES BALDWIN in *The Fire Next Time*

_____8

Poverty and Racism
as They Affect Children

CHESTER M. PIERCE, M.D.

The charge for this chapter was to discuss reasons why so little
action has been taken on urgent child problems over the years.
Most recently, why have the efforts of the Joint Commission on
Mental Health of Children, especially as they relate to poverty
and racism, had so little notice or impact?

Such a charge of course defies certitude. Nevertheless, in my
opinion there are two primary reasons why action has been relatively minimal. On the one hand, from the very beginning, the
Joint Commission included poverty and racism only as afterthoughts. As this chapter will demonstrate, such afterthoughts
had ongoing built-in designs to keep them from being too im-
pactful or significant. Such procedural unconcern reflects the
historical position of the society with regard to the minority poor.
On the other hand, since completion of the study, persistent and
powerful advocacy has been lacking for programs which affect
children of the poor and especially minorities. With few notable
exceptions, those multiple sources which must and should alert
and guide the public in consideration of the proposals have been
silent. This position likewise typifies the usual positions of society
in regard to the minority poor.

History

Let us start with some historical comments about the functioning of the Joint Commission on Mental Health of Children, which reflect the positions of the society in regard to one area of urgent concern to children.

For purposes of contrast, one can view the life histories of the Children's Television Workshop (producers of Sesame Street and Electric Company) and the Joint Commission on Mental Health of Children. Both groups were planning during the same period. Indeed some of the same persons worked with both groups. The major point to be made is that *from the beginning* the Children's Television Workshop planned for and included the participating perspective of Blacks and "community" persons. Despite whatever success or failure one ascribes to the television shows, it is incontestable history that Blacks and traditionally powerless groups had a voice in the planning.

On October 23, 1967, Dr. Joseph Bobbitt, Executive Director of the Commission, could write: "The work of the Commission has progressed well during its first year, but it has become increasingly apparent that if we are going to come up with a report which speaks for all the nation's children, we must have consultants who are knowledgeable with respect to some of the special problems faced by children of minority groups in the mental health and mental illness area." [1] As a result, a "committee" consisting of three whites, one Black, one Chicano, one Asian-American, and one native American Indian was formed and was to be expanded by its second meeting which would be held on November 20, 1967. This group was designated the Committee on Minority Group Children.

It should be noted that even the designation "committee," if not less prestigious, was at least different from most of the planned sub-groups working for the Commission which were called "task forces." It should be noted further that, although the Commission had numerous minority persons on its Board of Directors, the very fact that the Board consisted of so many persons assured that critical policy decisions would have to be made by a relative handful. In the actual functioning of the Board, most members of the Committee on Minority Group Children believed (whether it was true or not) that no minority member served in a significant decision-making capacity. Nor did it seem that any important administrative post on the full-time staff was occupied by a Black, a member of the Spanish-speaking ethnos, an American Indian, or an Asian-American. Such was the historical context when the Minority Committee began its labors about one year after the Commission had been in operation. The Commission's life as established by Congress was for about two years.

Once the Minority Committee began its deliberations, it proceeded with remarkable cohesiveness of purpose and a distinctive joy of work despite the demand for immediate action. The first and never-ending task of the committee was to make white professional colleagues *aware* of special minority concerns which demanded special and sometimes different considerations. The final report of the Commission indicates that such an awareness did, in time, become manifest.

COMMITTEE PROBLEMS. In answer to the question posed by this chapter, however, three events were critical. Each of these events indicated to the Minority Committee, in ever more harsh terms, that their expertise and engagement in their task would not persuade or prevail when their ideas failed to match those of the policy makers. Since almost all of the committee members were minority persons, this experience neither surprised nor discouraged them, for it paralleled the knowledge of a lifetime in dealing with the majority. Such knowledge could be translated to mean that, unless pushed continuously, the majority would be unresponsive to the needs of the poverty-stricken minority.

The first of these episodes seemingly was innocuous. In a casual manner, the committee learned that a "task force" had suggested, and may have persuaded the policy makers, that it would be an excellent idea to propose to Congress that all welfare mothers be given opportunity to get training so they could get jobs. Incidentally, a recurrent difficulty in minority relations is the fact that minority members nearly always are closed out from essential information sources. And when they do get information, it is perforce not only late but screened, selected, and fractionated.

In this instance, the Minority Committee acted quickly and

forced a meeting with the advocates of this plan for welfare mothers. Our concerns were many. We knew that what was offered as an "opportunity" could soon be read as "obligation." We believed the evidence flimsy or nonexistent that Black and Spanish-speaking welfare mothers gave less adequate mothering to their children during the preschool years. We worried about what it would mean in terms of self-image to mothers and children of all colors, in poverty and on welfare, when they recognized, as we thought they would, that society considered these mothers inept and inadequate. Yet, paradoxically, it was suggested that the mother surrogates for the children left at home would be neighborhood mothers, presumably just as ill fit for the maternal vocation. The psychological sequelae to self-image and family life could be monumental. The vital issue was whether or not all women would be obliged to leave the home and whether or not true safeguards could be guaranteed to make it an elective process.

As a result of expressed concerns, attitudes softened, but the Minority Group knew that they had heard merely the first stanza of a recurrent chorus. This same theme would reappear in various guises throughout the tenure of the deliberations. We knew, as indeed it turned out, that in the 1970s congressmen and executives in the federal branch would be singing more refrains of this chorus. Now the chorus includes a political slogan, "workfare" for the poor.

The next contest centered about whether or not the Committee should make public its views about racism prior to release of the Commission's report. We believed that few whites were aware of the magnitude of the despair and the mounting impatience of minority people concerning the racial issues of our time. We hoped to mobilize a more massive and concerted and immediate effort to dilute these rising and potentially explosive dissatisfactions. We believed that separate release of our findings would give the matter a different impetus and visualization than if they were buried in a complete commission report.

Without going into detail, it is sufficient to say that the Commission decided to abide by its own rules (decided upon prior to inclusion of a minority focus) which forbade release of any part of its findings on a segmental basis. The reasons for this decision seem good and appropriate when viewed from the perspective of the history of commissions. To the Commission's credit, it did in fact say that we as a group could do what we as a group could have done without its consent. Namely, we were advised that we could release as our own opinions whatever we wished but these would not, of course, have official endorsement. Thus, the findings and deliberations of the Committee, while it was in action, could not have impact and pave the way for the final report.

This frustration wasn't all bitter despite the necessary unpleasantness it generated (such as when the two Black psychiatrists on the Committee called the senior members of the Commission "racists"). The position of the Committee on the effects of racism were given to Senator Fred Harris of Oklahoma, the husband of a Committee member who was a Comanche Indian. Senator Harris was then a member of the Kerner Commission whose report had yet to be released.* The findings and assertions about racism by the Committee on Minority Group Children confirmed the findings that the Kerner Commission later published, to the amazement and/or chagrin of the nation. Hence, the Committee as early as 1967 was talking about the need for America to realize that perhaps its most important domestic issue was white racism.

The final blow, which indicated a less than supportive role by the Commission establishment relative to what we felt to be the most important domestic crisis of our time, came about in the spring of 1968. This incident above all may indicate why actions called for by the Commission Report have received so little backing. Again it is illustrative of attitudes held about just what minority people could say about their own perception of things.

For several years, some Black psychiatrists had taken the view that: (1) racism was a mental illness; and (2) the federal government should take steps to eliminate it. On the basis of these views, it was believed that the federal government agency most responsible for treatment and prevention of racism was the National Institute of Mental Health. From the vantage point of Black professionals, this Institute itself, though liberal by any

---

* Report of National Advisory Commission on Civil Disorders. New York: Bantam Books, 1968.

standard applied to other federal agencies, was objectionably and functionally racist in its operation. Thus, it had to decontaminate itself before taking on more extensive and fundamental responsibilities concerning racism.[2]

As one of a large number of recommendations to be presented to the Board of Directors for its consideration, the Committee voted to include some statements about the National Institute of Mental Health. Without Committee knowledge, this recommendation was withdrawn before presentation to the Board. In essence, the Board, despite protests, sustained the removal of this recommendation. It was said to us later that it was unfair to single out any one agency. Yet the crux of the matter was that a recommendation could be removed without our knowledge or consent. It brought up knotty problems such as censorship and thwarting of inquiry. Furthermore, the Committee agonized about whether or not any other group's recommendations would be deleted without prior consultation. Basically, it came to this: why ask minority persons to come from all over the country, with prepared assignments, if in fact what they recommend can be controlled by censorship? The *actuality in behavior* is that a single white censor could decide better than a group of minority people what they should say and what they should want.

This action led to some upheaval. A majority of the Committee verbalized that they would join the two Black psychiatrists who actually submitted resignations.* The Black psychiatrists counseled their peers that they should not resign but should try to get the group's recommendations into the final report.

Many readers will be unconvinced that racism is an illness. They will believe the unilateral actions by the white censor were correct and obligatory. This was also the opinion of many majority participants at the time of the incident. Thus, it is pertinent to digress in order to clarify how Black psychiatrists and other mental health colleagues on the Committee reason that racism is a mental illness.

RACISM AS MENTAL ILLNESS. Manifest racist behavior by a white in the U.S. occurs toward any person who has a dark skin

---

* The two Black psychiatrists were Dr. Price Cobbs, then co-authoring the book, *Black Rage*, and this author. A third Black psychiatrist present throughout as liaison from the National Institute of Mental Health was Dr. James Comer, now Associate Dean of Yale Medical School.

color, but is perhaps most glaring in behavior toward Blacks. The behavior is based on the false assumption, born of contagious social illness, that dark skin color means inferiority and that the possession of white skin color means superiority. No matter what attributes of status, education, or affluence an individual possesses, the skin color indicates how he is treated (and often regarded) in any interracial transaction. Since this false belief is unshakable in the face of contrary evidence, it is, by definition, a delusion. As an operating delusion which would require attitudinal-emotional changes and modification, it is clearly to some extent within the province of psychiatry.

Besides being a mental illness, it is a public health illness of immense, virtually limitless, magnitude. Everyone in the U.S. is handicapped by racism. In other articles, the author has expanded on why racism is a mental health and public health illness of perception which is both contagious and lethal.[2,3,4,5]

NO MINORITY UTILIZATION AND DISCUSSION OF JOINT COMMISSION REPORT. A year after the censorship (in May 1969) in Miami, the Chairman and Vice Chairman of the Black Psychiatrists of America left an organizing meeting in order to attend an open session at which the Joint Commission's child advocacy recommendations were being discussed. We were concerned about the general reaction to the proposals of the Joint Commission on Mental Health of Children. The Black Psychiatrists of America dwelled on the impact of the Joint Commission on Mental Health of Children and the National Institute of Mental Health as related to minority issues. The success was greater with N.I.M.H., since more extensive employment of Blacks is now evident at all levels; Blacks are on review committees advising about fund dispersion, and a minority center has been established within the Institute. However, Black America and, probably, other ethnic minorities have failed to understand and debate the issues and recommendations brought forth by the Joint Commission. In all likelihood, most of these findings and recommendations would be endorsed by most thoughtful people. However, there is a need for keener attention to the proposals since, if attended to, they commit the future via their influence on children.

It is my opinion that one reason such debate has not materialized is that the problems of minorities and poor were not "truly" included even after they finally were acknowledged. There was no dissemination of findings to minority groups or organizations for their use or their efforts to help secure implementation of important child mental health research. As a result, there was never an impetus to actualize recommendations, since the recommendations were really not welcomed or expected. This is one component of why there has been so little action. The other component deals with the consideration of why powerful organizations of the majority have failed to be more vigorous in popularizing the Commission's recommendations. This may be due to the tenor of the recommendations, which were prevention-oriented and not, as most majority organizations wanted, primarily treatment-directed.

The demand for institutionalized child care

Evidence is increasing that during the coming decade demands for institutionalized child care will be intensified. Some studies indicate that perhaps half the children under age six already are given care outside their homes.[6] Yet this growing demand may be characterized by a plethora of doubts which prevent the country from too precipitous an embrace with the unknown. These doubts seem to originate in various sociocultural phenomena and they brake the plunge into total institutionalized nursery schools and day centers. Hence, few organizations and agencies in the society have been outspoken about the type of, and the extent to which we should move toward, child day care.

Perhaps as with universal grade school education, which gained great impetus in the 1890s, our society will adopt something which has enormous and probably more positive than negative ramifications without knowing what it is doing or why it is being done. In the 1890s, compulsory school attendance seemed to grow out of demands to keep children off the streets. Of course, those few who seem to be present in all ages regarded the need for education in terms of more lofty aspirations.

Today some of the major generative power for the movement toward compulsory nursery care also may be coming from the great masses with less than total altruism or inspired philosophy. In our country it is a truism that nothing can happen unless the white middle class wills it to happen. In a real sense, it occurs not infrequently that whatever bends the will of the white middle-class female (the true purveyor and vehicle of American culture) will result in social application. Currently, the American white middle-class female is of a mind to share, if not abandon, the job of child care.

Such a state of mind has evolved slowly, from a multitude of necessities. Nevertheless, especially since World War I, women have found their way more and more into the work force. As such, they are now not only welcomed but vital to the economy of our nation, particularly in the "urban" reaches of the society. More and more, also, women need to work in order to sustain living planes that the society makes appear appropriate for their families.

In the same period of time there have been other sweeping social changes far too numerous to elaborate. Key ones include: (1) lengthening and broadening the educative opportunities for females; (2) technological advances which have brought increasing leisure time, including less obligation for time to do housework; (3) the effect of mass media, particularly movies, television, and women's magazines, which portray and emphasize glamorous/interesting lives outside the home; and (4) the advent of easily available and convenient contraceptives which, among other effects, permit women (especially educated, well-paid, middle-class females) to determine their sexual activity without fear of pregnancy.

In such a climate, it is not difficult to understand the wide acceptance of and sympathy for the women's liberation movement. Nor is it surprising that as women leave the house, with less ambivalence and more marketable skills, there are trends toward blurring of sexual distinctions. At the same time, along with the increasing unisexual identity, unistandard morality is developing. From this base we contemplate the disruptions to traditional family organization as well as the statistically staggering divorce rates.

So it is that survival of the species demands some social controls to aid the middle-class mother in rearing her young. The root of Judeo-Christian ethic is so deep however, that such a demand, if voiced too openly, might cause excessive guilt and shame. Hence, it is necessary to take two pathways which are germane to our inquiry. Pathway One urges some conservatism about the rapid change. It might be augmented by conscious and unconscious male feelings which express rebellion by passive aggressive maneuvers such as not energizing strident and vigorous organizational support for the demand for universal child care.

Pathway Two is more relevant to this chapter. Pathway Two is one the society finds ever useful. Namely, it can accomplish simultaneously what it wishes, build in some conservative time restraints, insure a quality standard, and continue in the ego-syntonic position of grateful master to the oppressed minorities. That is, Pathway Two says that one should make it look as though the demand for universal child care is created by minorities. Then, if they are trained over a period of time, while they are being grateful at being controlled and given to, they will be molded to our tastes in terms of quality control. To work best, this maneuver can't be negotiated with unseemly and awkward urgency. Hence, we have the second major reason, in my opinion, for the relatively slow actualization of the Commission's work. Although universal day care was not an actual recommendation, day care for many children was recommended.

Let us look a bit more, however, at some of the assumptions and arguments about training Black or other minority mothers to do what so many have done for decades in this country, namely, care for their children and white children as well. If some of the motivating power for child care programs stems from liberal, middle-class, white females who are sympathetic toward or are members of women's liberation groups, it is easy to understand that such women would not view themselves as exploiting their Black, Red, and Brown sisters. Yet in actual behavior, in order for white females to be freed from some of the numerous and boring burdens of child care, someone else must care for the children. The available and maneuverable woman power (for first it must be female child care agents) is found in the demographic pool in which swim the Blacks, Browns, Reds, and poor whites. Thus, they are the ones who can be mobilized for this task. The prototypical white female will feel easier philosophically and psychologically if, in the 1970s, the child-care giver at least superficially is a far different creature from the unqualified Black mammy who was idealized as generous and all-loving in her care for the whites, who were all-exploiting in their regard for her.

But Blacks, Browns, Reds, and oppressed Yellows have, like the white female, been exposed to all sorts of educational and social influences in the passage of time. They possess a resolve, both expressed and unexpressed, not to be blinded by the superficial. They know that unless strict precautions are instituted and observed, the 1970s caregiver will be basically no different than the romanticized Black mammy. They realize too that they must watch carefully for and dilute the virtually inevitable maneuvers that whites will utilize in Black-white interactions.[3] These offensive maneuvers attempt to make the Black and other poor minority women feel guilty, inadequate, fearful, ashamed, passively accepting, grateful, etc.

Now we return to the recurrent theme. It should be recalled that there is no incontrovertible evidence to indicate that Black mother-child or Black family-child interactions are inferior. In fact, one could argue that they have been marvelously adaptive in sustaining Blacks in America despite the terrible outrages which have been suffered. Also it should be mentioned that actually Black child-care givers have been much in demand by whites at all levels throughout the history of this country. Further, countless Black mothers have left their children in the care of Black neighbors, friends, and relatives while they went out to earn a living. Thus, even without training opportunities, many Black women have functioned at very satisfactory levels as mother surrogates. For example, most psychiatrists have observed that a white adult who had such a Black mammy oftentimes (if not usually) will believe that his or her untrained Black mammy embodied more of the precious and essential attributes of mothering than did the designated and/or biological mother.

However, as the ancients realized, reason stands ready at all times to persuade necessity. Therefore, offensive maneuvers are called for to make a virtue of necessity. It is reasonable, we are told, to teach Black women how to be mothers. This will give them an increase in self-esteem and at the same instance, permit them to get jobs taking care of children. Thus, they won't have to be on welfare. This, it is said, will aid the self-image of the Black child. We are told that we should observe the positive benefits that occurred to the children of Israel reared in a kibbutz or the children of the U.S.S.R. who had institutionalized nursery care.

These arguments cannot be divorced from specific cultural, historical, social, and political events. Indeed, if we were a small, new country with a nationalized common religion, surrounded by enemies, and if we made *every* child subject to the same upbringing, then we might imagine that our children would grow up with the strengths (and weaknesses) of the children reared in a kibbutz. Or if the country were in the midst of financial and political crises where again every mother's child was subjected to similar upbringing because mothers were deployed to help sustain the economy, then we should expect the same strengths (and weaknesses) of the children reared in the '30s and '40s in the U.S.S.R. However, when the refrain is sung, there has been little mention that what would befall the minority mother and child would befall every mother and child. This is not spelled out forcefully, even though in proposed legislation the design appears to be to give relief to middle-class white women who wish to leave their homes without concern about the welfare of their children.

As a result, most effort by organizations or spokesmen focuses on the poor minority people. We need this legislation to help us rid ourselves of "the problem." So goes the rhetoric. The implication, as always, is that the poor have invited their affliction. Understandably, in times of stiffening sentiment against the poor and the minorities, it isn't polite or easy to speak up with just the right word and volume to move the society to compulsory nursery care. And at the same time, the harried spokesman must do it in a way which blames the poor yet produces a way to make them more grateful and passive without making it appear that the bounds of generosity for an essentially undeserving group are being exceeded. This accounts for some of the trouble in actualizing some of the Commission's efforts. People see it perhaps as another poverty program, when, in fact, as pointed out in this paper, such concerns were not prominent in the work of the Commission nor indeed (and probably properly so) in the overall emphasis of its recommendations. To come to grips with this component of why there has been so little action, one can conclude that much study is needed. Public opinion must be sampled. This would then lead to complementing the other component part. For, once opinion has been sampled, ideas for debate can be presented and action can be energized, guided of course by as sophisticated and careful research as can be accomplished.

It is true that data indicate that in ghettos, generations of poverty and inhumanity have created problems. It is also true that the positive values of inner city culture and its survival functions are not researched. This limits utilization of these values for the enhancement of the self-image of the children born into such generational problems.

But at this point in history, many problems should be anticipated in order to make the process of opinion sampling, public education, debate, and research more meaningful.

Some problems to anticipate

1. WHO WILL MAKE A PROFIT? Unhappily, this question is posed first, for its solution will determine the outcome of all other problems, including the overriding one of how to improve the quality of life for children and thereby help to commit humankind to a future where all people live better and longer.

When billions of dollars will be made available for child care programs, the profit and power motives will be paramount. Currently, many people are concerned that power considerations will leave them even more impotent in the task of shaping their children's lives. Additionally, profit-making factors may become crucial in deciding who is contracted to design care. Hence, it is not improbable that minority children may come to spend the bulk of their nursery years in programs designed with major inputs by say, an engineer assigned by his company to plan a profit-making contract in the area of child care. Perhaps such skills can be applied usefully and wisely. However, even if such were the case, many parents would feel that at least they should be consulted.

Acceptance does not necessarily mean a good program. One grim caveat needs to be aired. Undoubtedly many minority parents would accept without challenge any plan offered as long as it provided convenience and relief. The reason for this uncritical attitude is that such parents have been educated and conditioned to accept whatever is offered, since the function of effective racism is to make minority citizens docile, passive, and gratefully accepting of any and all abuse. Up to this time, racism by this definition has enjoyed matchless effectiveness in the United States. Thus, a projected concern by the society should be, will any preschool program be accepted with such avidity by the defeated, demoralized poor that it will, in final analysis, speed the process toward greater passivity and increasing alienation by minority members? If such a situation were to take place on a gigantic and national scale, the multiplier effect could be unimaginably disastrous from the viewpoint of how each new generation's views about itself, about family, about color, about hope are shaped.

The possibility of large profits being made, particularly by manipulating the hopeless, makes such a gruesome possibility very plausible. This plausibility is not heard much in the refrain that poor mothers will be able to go to work if they elect to do so. Some mothers will be able to and they should have the opportunity to work if they elect to do so. Other poor mothers will not be able to work for a variety of reasons. But all poor mothers and their children can be affected if such devices are used as that of local authorities granting privileges only on the basis of who collaborates (such as going to work as very, very cheap labor). The profit motive will require much attention and thought in order to diminish unwholesome developments. This sort of material must be part of the public consciousness as program issues are debated and resolved. A basic issue concerns a decent, living wage for those in poverty working in these programs. Cheap labor means poor programs.

2. WHO WILL EXERT CONTROL? In this context control is spoken of not as influence or profit but as to quality of care. Obviously no one is so sagacious and so able as to be qualified to monitor all the various programs that the Commission hoped would be enacted.

Many issues should be part of the public awareness when such programs are actualized. For instance, in the area of preschool education, a curriculum that might be laudatory for a child in Beverly Hills might be less advantageous to a child in Appalachia. Yet there might be a common overlapping core. Hopefully the child and the teacher from either situation could make a graceful horizontal transfer to the other situation. But how is that to be accomplished? And how is it to be assessed? And who should design and evaluate the assessment? Perfect answers will never be known. However, should the society decide to work in this area, a diversity of programs, each designed to be helpful to particular groups of children, can make large inroads. This brings up the last of the major problem areas.

3. HOW SERIOUS IS THE COMMITMENT OF SOCIETY? The society in its deliberations about the Joint Commission ideas must allocate sufficient resources to bring about desired ends. This means that generous amounts of time, money, effort, and good will must be exercised to achieve goals. If what is required demands expensive technology, such as computer assisted instruction, then society must pay and decide that something else equally valid is less urgent at the present time. In order to make such decisions, the public will need to have knowledge of long-range plans, alternative possibilities, and suggested priority listings. It would seem nearly impossible to mobilize sufficient commitment unless the public, particularly white middle-class America, comes to the belief that the future of children is our most precious resource and as such must be given highest, most immediate, and sustained priority.

A program to combat the effect of racism on minorities

At this point, the logical questions are: What must be done and how can it be done? The author proposes as a first step a nationwide psychological training program designed and conducted by, for example, Blacks. This program should be the result of multidisciplinary and interdisciplinary research effort. The effort would have to have both community input and monitoring. It would have to be carefully evaluated so that the investigation results would modify the various psychological training packages being used by specially trained social innovators who were invited into communities. These innovators would operate in formal as well as parallel education systems: in commonplace

Black institutions, e.g., the church, the lodge; in inner city community agencies, etc. They would have at their disposal various training devices, literature, and information for persons of different ages, sex, and socioeconomic status in the Black community. Basic use of material would result from careful research and development by the coordinated, interdisciplinary, multidisciplinary effort. This effort as indicated would be ongoing and flexibly adaptive. As of 1973, critical areas of coordination which should form training packages are: (1) Black child development; (2) reading; (3) Black group dynamics; (4) the positive and negative features for Blacks of behavioral modification, including biofeedback alterations; and (5) understanding and critical awareness of the effects of mass media.

Training would be available for all who chose to enter into it. However, its very design would force any participant to be highly cognizant of the special needs of the Black child. Black children themselves would constitute a primary group of participants. The effort would be to move all Black citizens to attitudes of hope, toughness, and group unity. Each individual citizen would leave his training as a functioning demographer, systems analyst, and propagandist. He would be aware of "parenting" models and would hope that the Black posterity produced persons who were both supergeneralists and supranationalists.

To some readers, the thought of psychological training will promote ethical uneasiness and sociopolitical anxieties. To such readers I would argue that a group of Blacks, acting in good faith, under community sanction, and with informed opinions, might do no worse in molding the psyches of Blacks than the networks, the movies, the chain newspapers, and national magazines. Nor could it be argued that such training per se would be necessarily any more sinister than much which goes on presently in our public school systems.

To other readers, the idea of psychological training "packages" and "community innovators" would seem to be unfeasible. To such readers I would suggest that the state of the art is such that, just as we use selection and training techniques to send men to hazardous situations or to prepare people to live in different cultures, we could elect, if we wished to commit the effort and resources, to ameliorate the lives of ghetto dwellers. Then they could take an active role in modifying the society. All of society would gain by such modifications.

The model is presented in terms of the subjects most in need of attention for Black children. But since Blacks are the social barometer of our society, the same sort of model could be patterned for other minority or majority children in poverty.

Conclusions

What has been argued here is the fact that there were and are significant sociocultural blocks as to why the report of the Joint Commission on Mental Health of Children has failed to garner more action for its minority group programs. In order to get the necessary support, a process of opinion sampling, informed public debate, and ongoing research must be launched. Then a coordinated research effort designed to produce psychological training packages would be the next step.

Any program to succeed must attend to the whole gamut of individual wants and needs and yet contain enough elasticity and flexibility to accommodate all sorts of demographic and cultural differences. All of this is made exceedingly difficult because of as yet unyielding social, political, and economic realities.

Nevertheless, the dream must remain that in order to preserve ourselves, our children must enjoy a better quality of life and must be moving toward the cosmopolite position.[7] As planetary citizens, they will exhibit a "protective curiosity" which will guard them against internal turmoil.

At present, almost all of our minority child population are living in segregated circumstances. Nearly 90 percent of Blacks live in segregated housing, so we are speaking of most Black children and probably most other "minority" children. Such circumstances are not likely to change during their formative years. What is predictable is that the awfulness of these circumstances will obliterate for many the will to accept any but second-class citizenship. A second-class citizen will find it even more arduous to become a planetary citizen. Yet, survival on this earth depends on the rapid development of global views and perspectives.

For second-class children, any massive program accepted and actualized should help banish depressive tendencies. The children must be freed from self-concepts of extraordinary ineffectiveness and minimal importance. They must pursue life as exciting, invigorating, in which it is possible for them to make a positive contribution, but without the need to encroach on others in order to attain fun. They must prize curiosity so that they will thrill to their imagination and locate zeal in adventure and find delight in mastery. As prosaic or remarkable as it may seem to some readers, there is at present a dearth of this sort of fun and curiosity in large numbers of our segregated children. The aim of programs envisioned by the Joint Commission on Mental Health of Children must make it a right to have fun and to be curious when one is a child. Failure to provide for such a right constitutes a crime against humanity. The magnitude and enormity of the crime should tug at the hearts of all adults as they admit that, in a country where people know how to walk on the moon, millions of second-class children still walk on ghetto streets.

REFERENCES

1. BOBBITT, J. Personal Communication to the Author.
2. PIERCE, C. M. The formation of the Black Psychiatrists of America. In C. Willie, B. Kramer and B. Brown (Eds.), *Mental Health and Racism*. Pittsburgh: University of Pittsburgh Press, 1973. Pp. 525–544.
3. PIERCE, C. M. Offensive mechanisms. In F. Barbour and P. Sargent (Eds.), *The Black Seventies*. Boston: Porter Sargent, 1970. Pp. 265–282.
4. PIERCE, C. M. Is bigotry the basis of the medical problems in the ghetto? In J. C. Norman (Ed.), *Medicine in the Ghetto*. New York: Appleton-Century-Crofts, 1969. Pp. 301–312.
5. PIERCE, C. M. Violence and counterviolence: The need for a children's domestic exchange. *American Journal of Orthopsychiatry*, 1969, 39, 553–568.
6. ROWE, R. (Ed.) Child care in Massachusetts. *The Public Responsibility Massachusetts Early Education Project*. Feb., 1972.
7. PIERCE, C. M. The Pre-Schooler and the Future. *Futurist*, 1972, 6, 13–15.

The law is the last result of human wisdom
acting upon human experience for the benefit
of the public.

SAMUEL JOHNSON

_____**9**

Courts and the Rights
of Human Beings,
Including Children

DAVID L. BAZELON

The courts and the adult criminal

Too many people need to believe that court reform and prison
reform will stem the tide of violent street crime. They do not
understand how life in the modern city can drive some people to
robbery and murder. They do not understand that hunger, cold,
filth, and a sense of inevitable failure are not conditions which
instill feelings of love and compassion. They do not understand
that these conditions produce self-hatred and apathy toward
others.

Courts and prisons are not the root of the problem. They are
merely withering branches. These branches can and should be
attended to, but we cannot allow that effort to distract us from
dealing with the decay in the roots. The roots of the problem are
poverty, racism, and the hopelessness that is their constant com-
panion.

By repairing the branches, of course, we can have the satisfaction of doing *something*. It is important to maintain a sense of
movement even if we aren't sure that the movement is really
forward. Violent street crime produces an enormous amount of

110

pain, not only in its victims but in all of us who must live with the fear that it will strike us or our loved ones. Maybe we don't have time to understand the problem and to find civilized and humane measures to end these senseless and horrible crimes. Maybe we have to do *something*, if only to divert our minds from the fear and pain.

THE SOCIAL SOURCES OF CRIME. Unless we understand, until we understand, we cannot make the sort of judgments and distinctions that will let us live with ourselves. If we succumb to the ugly and dangerous backlash that has already developed, we can only act like a lynch mob that searches out and destroys a scapegoat in order to abate its fury. There is already grave danger that our fundamental constitutional protections will be the scapegoat to appease an angry public that has been encouraged to believe that courts coddle criminals and thereby cause crime.

Certainly, many thoughtful persons recognize that courts don't cause crime. They admit that almost all violent street crime is nurtured by poverty, bitterness, ignorance, racism, and despair. But at issue is the proper role of the criminal courts in recognizing and coping with these conditions spawned by social injustice. The refrain we often hear is that, since social and economic problems raise questions of social justice, not criminal justice, and since criminal justice cannot solve these social problems, then the criminal justice system is necessarily left with the limited task of sorting out the guilty from the innocent by means of a fair trial.

INEQUALITY OF THE CRIMINAL PROCESS. It is questionable whether any system of criminal justice that pays no attention to social justice is worthy of respect or efforts to maintain it. The entire criminal process is pervaded by the malignant impact of social inequality. In the stationhouse, in the courtroom, on appeal, in prison, that process regularly accords different treatment to rich and poor, to white and nonwhite.

Little overt discrimination exists. In fact, rules that single out the poor or the nonwhite for differential treatment are usually not tolerated, at least not when they have become notorious. Covert discrimination results from rules that appear neutral but, when applied, impose great disadvantages on the poor, the nonwhite, and the uninformed. By hiding behind neutral rules, the system can ignore these practical disabilities and make sure that it doesn't learn anything about the persons who pass through.

As that function is carried out without protest, and a business-as-usual attitude is maintained in order to preserve the image and dignity of the courts, attention is diverted from the real problems and an imprimatur of respectability is provided that obscures the underlying chaos. The courts have no interest in serving as high-priced janitors, sweeping society's debris under the rug, thus making the solution of the problem even more difficult.

TO EXPOSE THE ISSUES. There is some direct action that the judicial system can take to strip away the cloak of unreality. For example, it can open its eyes to the inadequacies of legal representation in criminal cases, and to the difficult questions that plea bargaining systematically hides. It obviously cannot, single-handedly, put into effect the needed social and economic changes. No matter what is done in the courtroom, it cannot change schools, hospitals, and housing. It can, however, focus public attention on the real problems, by blowing the whistle on the effort to sweep them under the rug. It needs to be made clear that the problem of violent crime cannot be solved simply by increasing the efficiency of the courts, or making the prisons more humane, or by overruling *Miranda v. Arizona*.

Members of the judicial system accused of the crime of "activism" can give to their accusers the same reply as that given by a doctor who heads a community health center in a slum in New York. His center had established a far-flung reputation as an activist group. They attracted the greatest attention through their efforts to secure enactment and enforcement of legislation prohibiting the use or retention of lead paint in houses. They invested great effort and public funds. When asked what this activist and apparently political role had to do with a health center's responsibility to treat sick people, the director's reply was short and to the point. "For years," he said, "I have treated children suffering from lead paint poisoning. They come to my attention after it's too late to do much for them. I've lived with the problem and I've watched them suffer and die. It's been an unforgettable nightmare, and I have to speak out."

Like that doctor, those in the criminal justice system have seen the suffering of both the offender and the victim after it is too late to do anything to help either one. They have been forced to preside over a grim parade of pain and social injustice that has left its scars. Everyone who carries such a scar has a responsibility to speak out. This does not mean that our social institutions will be improved as soon as judges speak out, but if judges swallow their pride and suppress their anger, pretending they cannot see or hear suffering in the streets, the conscience of the public will be soothed. If judges remain silent, they will unwittingly lend comfort to the champions of the status quo, the enemies of social and economic change, who will point to their silence as a sign that nothing is really wrong. If judges hide behind the bulwark of the present system, then none of them should be surprised that the real problems remain unresolved.

Juvenile justice and the promise of treatment

As we turn from the ways the courts deal with criminal problems in adults, we find that the same social problems compound their effects on children.

While it is unnecessary to recount in detail the history of the juvenile courts, we may profit by reviewing the legal justifications for our juvenile court system. All of us have heard the two Latin words, *parens patriae.* But what does that phrase really mean? Black's Law Dictionary, the Noah Webster of the legal profession, tells us that *parens patriae* refers to "the sovereign power of guardianship (of the state) over persons under disability such as minors, and insane and incompetent persons." I suppose that is a good dictionary definition, although it does not help us solve any of the difficult problems in this area of law. Unfortunately, for 60 years, courts have been using that phrase as if it were the all-encompassing answer. The judge closes his eyes, waves his magic gavel, intones the magic phrase, and the problems are supposed to go away. Well, they don't!

THE VARIETY OF CHILDREN'S PROBLEMS REFERRED TO COURTS. A chief difficulty with discussing the justification for juvenile courts is that they deal with so many different kinds of children: children who have committed antisocial offenses; children who are neglected or abandoned; children who are disturbed or "beyond parental control"; and the like. For instance, nine different categories exist in the District of Columbia. Some jurisdictions provide different labels for similar categories. New York, for example, classifies children as "neglected," "delinquent," or "in need of supervision." The law of the District of Columbia makes no distinction whatever, although, in practice, the juvenile court classifies children as either "dependent" or "delinquent." It is understandable then that judges and scholars have suggested different justifications for society's right to deal with the child at all. At the risk of oversimplification, I will discuss three of the more prevalent justifications.

SOME PRESENT FUNCTIONS OF JUVENILE COURTS. First, there are those who think that the function of a juvenile court is to punish. According to these people, a child who commits an antisocial act, should, like an adult, be held responsible for it unless he can show that he has some kind of mental condition which excuses him from responsibility. This is the position taken by Justice Oliphant of the New Jersey Supreme Court. Quoting from one of his opinions:

> A peaceful citizen has the right to be protected by his government and to have a spade called a spade, and if young hoodlums are mentally incapable of a criminal intent they should be put to the burden of establishing that proposition in a court of law under established rules and are only entitled as a matter of right to the constitutional guarantees afforded to other citizens. (State v. Monahan, 15 N.J. 34, 104 A.2d 21, 40 [1954] [dissenting opinion]).

I do not say that a juvenile court cannot or should not ever undertake to "punish" children, although I think that is an extremely narrow view of the problem. And, of course, it completely ignores the neglected child or the child who is "beyond parental control." Such children may be deeply disturbed but surely are not "young hoodlums." But regardless of whether juvenile courts should sometimes punish children, it is evident that punishment is not the central justification for the juvenile courts as they exist today. If it were the central concern, we wouldn't need juvenile courts at all. We would need only a few more criminal court judges and some extra cells in the adult jails.

Others suggest that our juvenile courts exist to protect society. In the large view, I cannot quarrel with this concept. If we succeed in helping the child, we will also have made our society safer. Unfortunately, too much of the talk about protection ignores the element of treatment and rehabilitation. If treatment and rehabilitation are ignored, then protection of society means nothing more than getting the child out of the way, getting him off the streets. If we are going to follow Justice Oliphant's advice and call a spade a spade, I'd like to call this particular spade "preventive detention." Without discussing the constitutional or moral objections to preventive detention, I think I can assert with some confidence that it is not, nor does anyone claim it is, the only or even the primary purpose of our juvenile courts. Here again, if removal from the streets were the goal, the criminal courts could provide the solution just as quickly and perhaps more effectively than a juvenile court, which is restricted to essentially nonpunitive processes and whose jurisdiction is limited by the happenstance of the child's birthdate.

It is only when we turn to the treatment and rehabilitation of the child that we approach a satisfactory justification for our juvenile courts, at least as they exist today. I do not mean that punishment and safety are not factors to be considered, but I do claim that standing alone, they do not and cannot provide suitable underpinning for our present system. The central justification for assuming jurisdiction over a child in an informal, nonadversary proceeding is *the promise to treat him according to his needs.*

TREATMENT AND REHABILITATION: A FANTASY IN OUR TIME. In our juvenile court system, there is a promise of treatment. There was a time when we might have been proud of it. But now we know too much. We look around us and see the promise broken at every turn. It is full of cant and hypocrisy. And yet, it is made to do doubtle duty. It is used to justify the informal nonadversary procedures of the juvenile court; used again to justify the child's confinement.

THE GAULT CASE. The Supreme Court had a case dealing with a boy from Arizona, Gerald Gault. Gerald and a friend were supposed to have made a lewd telephone call to a neighbor. While his mother was at work, a probation officer took Gerald

into custody and questioned him. His mother returned home
that evening and neighbors told her that her son was "detained."
She went to the detention home where the officer told her that a
hearing would be held the following day. The hearing was held
in the judge's chambers and no record of the proceedings was
made. There was no lawyer. The neighbor did not testify, although seemingly Gerald admitted placing the call. When asked
what section of the law Gerald had violated, the officer stated,
"We set no specific charge in it, other than delinquency." There
is considerable doubt about the judge's ultimate determination.
At one point, he thought Gerald's phone call amounted to a
breach of the peace, elsewhere he said Gerald was "habitually
involved in immoral matters," a phrase used in Arizona's juvenile
court statute, and again he stated there was "probably another
ground, too."

Probably not a single justice of the peace in this country
would permit an adult to be convicted in such a proceeding.
According to the briefs and allegations in the Supreme Court,
almost every ingredient of the civilized procedures and safeguards which we refer to as due process of law was missing:
Gerald did not have adequate notice of the charges; he did not
have an opportunity to confront and cross-examine the witnesses
against him; he did not have counsel; he was not warned of any
privilege against self-incrimination; no appellate review was
provided; and the lack of a transcript made subsequent review
of what actually happened virtually impossible. I understand
that juvenile proceedings are not criminal proceedings and that
these procedures and safeguards are not necessarily applicable.
It is important to notice, though, that the Arizona Supreme
Court sought to justify these shortcuts because of the promise to
treat the child. This is from the Arizona Court:

> We are aware of the tide of criticism inundating juvenile
> proceedings. The major complaint deals with the informal,
> nonadversary procedure for determining delinquency rather
> than the treatment rendered after a finding of delinquency.
> On the other hand, juvenile courts do not exist to punish
> children for their transgressions against society. The juvenile
> court stands in the position of a protecting parent rather

than a prosecutor. It is an effort to substitute protection and guidance for punishment, to withdraw the child from criminal jurisdiction and use social sciences regarding the study of human behavior which permit flexibilities within the procedures. The aim of the court is to provide individualized justice for children. Whatever the formulation, the purpose is to provide authoritative treatment for those who are no longer responding to the normal restraints the child should receive at the hands of his parents. (In re: *Gault* 387 U. S. 1 [1967])

I do not find it objectionable to deprive the child of some procedural safeguards if the "individualized" treatment he is supposed to get requires the sacrifice and if the new procedures are reasonably fair. We should not blind ourselves, though, to what "individualized" treatment in our juvenile courts really is.

In the District of Columbia, for example, the juvenile justice system is still overloaded with work. We have too few judges, too few supporting personnel, too few dollars. In 1971, over 6,000 children in trouble had their cases heard by juvenile court judges in Washington, D.C. This averaged approximately five cases per day per judge. What is more disturbing is that while counsel is guaranteed to juveniles, pro forma representation by counsel lacking either time or resources to become familiar with the case is all too frequent. For juveniles above all, counsel must be sensitive to the child's needs, aware of available resources, and an advocate for bringing those resources to the client.

POVERTY, RACISM AND DIFFERENTIAL TREATMENT. In fact, blindness and insensitivity pervade the whole system. Some time ago, a Black girl named Betty Jean from the slums of Washington was brought before the Juvenile Court. Her attorney asked for a psychiatric examination. He submitted the following facts: his client had commenced sexual relations at the age of ten; she was the mother of an illegitimate child; she was raped by a neighborhood boy at the age of sixteen; she had nightmares and saw people staring at her when the lights were out. A physician who had treated her from time to time added the opinion that Betty Jean was "known . . . to have been a disturbed child since early childhood" and that she needed "nothing short of a complete psychiatric study." The juvenile judge recognized that, under the law, he had discretion to provide for such an examination and that the community had hospitals available for this purpose. But he did not. Here is why (these are his own words):

> Such experiences are far from being uncommon among children in her socioeconomic situation with the result that the traumatic effect may be expected to be far less than it would be in the case of a child raised by parents and relatives with different habits and customs.

So, sexual activity at the age of ten and rape at sixteen are "far from being uncommon" in the slums, and Betty Jean's experiences would not touch her as deeply as they would others, and on this basis the judge can refuse her access to a psychiatrist.

I do not deny that different people may be affected differently by the same experiences. But the judge's statement and similar statements amaze me. And the statement contains an internal contradiction which wrenches the whole system.

This young girl comes from the slums, a subculture which, according to the judge, insensitizes and makes it impossible for her to respond to experiences which would traumatize the rest of us. Yet, if Betty Jean could not respond to the rape, why the assumption that she could respond to other external stimuli, for example, the rules of behavior in our society. The judge never asked the question and with good reason. Its answer would undermine his confidence in the system which incarcerates Betty Jean.

For the purpose of denying her a psychiatrist, the judge saw that Betty Jean was a Black from the slums; but for the purpose of putting her away, he did not, or would not, see the same thing. For that purpose, Betty Jean might as well have been a white, middle-class child from the suburbs, for it was white, middle-class suburban values to which the judge was asking her to respond. We know that suburban children do not appear regularly before our juvenile courts. It is not that there is no delinquency in the suburbs, or that these children have no problems. But they have families and communities which have the time and money to be interested. And effective or not, they at least make the attempt. They know where the child psychiatry clinics are in this country.

Betty Jean is the kind of girl we must deal with in the courts. And if we recognize for some purposes that she is what she is, how can we ignore the fact for other purposes? It has always seemed to me that this kind of compartmentalization is a sign of deep and serious illness in the system.

The illusory promise of treatment

There are questions and problems, serious ones, and we are presently refusing to face them because we are soothed by juvenile courts' implied promise of treatment, a promise which is consistently being broken, in case after case.

I do not know how to make that promise a reality, and perhaps nobody does. But I do know that the first step is to awaken our consciousness to the fact that there is a promise. We must first know that there is a moral and legal obligation. As it is now, citizens, mental health professionals, lawyers, and judges are confused about what our obligations are. The people who are on the inside, running our receiving homes, training schools, prisons, and hospitals, know that things are radically wrong, but they will not speak out. And the people on the outside do not want to see the truth, so they go through elaborate rituals in order to blind themselves.

In California recently, I listened to a number of officials involved in the correctional process complain about the inadequacy of their facilities. And yet, not one of these people had ever spoken publicly of this problem. It is as if they thought that they were required to accept what was given to them. Everyone, from the guards to the psychologists, had become society's janitors, fixing a pipe here and there, sweeping the floor, making sure the heat was on, but never once suggesting that the structure was faulty. I know it is not easy to call one's own usefulness into question. But the structure *is* faulty.

I don't mean to sound supercilious about workers in the helping professions, for I believe they are attempting to do their jobs honestly and sincerely. And in any event, it ill-becomes me to criticize another profession on this score, since my profession is undoubtedly the worst offender. Judges are a resourceful lot, and there are numerous legal doctrines we can use, and do use, every day to avoid seeing what is before us. Some time ago, a severely disturbed 17-year-old sought a judicial hearing on his claim that he was being illegally held in our District of Columbia Receiving Home for Children without receiving any psychiatric assistance. He had been at the Home for eight months awaiting disposition of a pending charge in the juvenile court. The judge did not hold a hearing to learn what the facts were, because, in his opinion, whether or not the child was receiving psychiatric assistance "was not germane to the lawfulness of [the juvenile's] confinement." I can scarcely imagine anything more "germane" to the "lawfulness" of the child's confinement than a claim, a claim incidentally which the attorney for the superintendent of the institution candidly conceded was true, that he was receiving no treatment at all, although he was desperately in need of it, and although the promise of treatment was the justification for holding the boy.

FACING THE FACTS OR THE RITUAL. As judges, our deliberate blindness makes this situation even more serious. A child comes before us and claims that he is being held illegally. The society asks us to say whether or not he is correct. There are some judges who think they need only approve the way in which the juvenile home got custody of the child; that is, were the proceedings proper, was the order of confinement signed by the right person, and so forth. Even if this were the extent of our duty, and I do not think it is, society perceives that we are doing much more, namely deciding, in fact, that everything about the child's confinement is legal, the proceedings, the place of confinement, and the conditions of the confinement. The appearance becomes the reality and, in fact, we are putting our stamp of approval on his confinement and on the whole system under which he is held. When we refuse to discover the facts, we are participating in society's fraud; worse, we are the high priests in black robes who soothe society into thinking there is no fraud.

These comments apply to all judges but most particularly to the juvenile court judges themselves since they are the ones charged with administering the statutes. I say "administering the statutes" advisedly. I do not mean administering the juvenile homes. The juvenile court judges need not muckrake by going into the homes and telling the administrators how to do their jobs. However, before the judge approves the system, he should know what the system is.

Within the past three years, as attacks on the conditions of juvenile detention have mounted, judges have necessarily recognized the validity of the claims of unconstitutional confinement. In *Wyatt v. Stickney*, the court held that if the state of Alabama were going to maintain institutions which it calls "hospitals" or treatment facilities, it had to maintain humane and decent physical living conditions and make bona fide efforts to care for its charges (325 F. Supp. 781, M.D. Ala. 1972). In *Lollis v. New York State Department of Social Services*, confinement of a girl in her nightclothes for two weeks in a stripped room with no reading material was branded cruel and unusual punishment (322 F. Supp. 473, S.D.N.Y. 1970).

The results which such judicial actions can obtain will never solve all the problems of providing treatment to all who are being denied their rights. For one thing, judges are no more authorized or equipped to tell a detention center how to treat misbehaving juveniles than they are to tell the Federal Communications Commission to allocate a specific AM frequency. In both situations, they are only concerned whether the administrative officials have observed the constitutional and legislative mandates for assuring that the path to decision is trod deliberately and carefully, that appropriate alternatives have been considered, and that substantive results are not patently illegal. So, unless they are faced with conditions "so inadequate even a layman could determine that fact," judges are not going to be making treatment decisions.

I am fully willing to acknowledge that juvenile judges have a great deal of expertise in their area. Having discretion, of course, does not mean that it is being exercised. For example, suppose the juvenile court judge had before him 100 children, each with different needs and different problems. And suppose for each of the children the judge made only one of two decisions, either to release him or to send him to the one inadequate institution which the community provides. In a recent juvenile court record I studied, the disposition order was preprinted with two boxes— probation to the parents, or commitment to the Department of

Public Welfare. This means being held in a Department of Public Welfare Receiving Home until foster home or other placement is made. With so few good foster homes available, it may be many, many months of "temporary" care, a grave disservice to an already problem-ridden child. I would therefore, not call that an exercise in discretion. There are, after all, other things which can be done, ranging from provision of prompt foster care to more assistance for the child's parents, from community programs to sending the child to a private institution.

In January 1973, for example, the Chief Judge of the Superior Court for the District of Columbia ordered the Receiving Home for Children closed because it was not a suitable place of detention or acceptable home substitute. With the assistance of the Public Defender and the Department of Human Resources, the Court developed a plan whereby all current and future detainees would be housed in alternative settings, and at the same time initiated a plan for closely supervised "home" detention (In re: Savoy, Nos. J-4808-70, January 12, 1973). I believe imaginative juvenile court judges with an imaginative staff could borrow this example without further statutory authority. To be fair, I must say that it is not simply a failure of imagination which limits the search for alternatives. It is also a lack of staff, of time, of public understanding, and of money.

I think a court is justified in acting in this area simply on the basis of the most traditional notions of what a court must do when litigants come before it. However, I need not rely completely on the inherent responsibility of courts, for the legislature has not been silent. For example, our District of Columbia Code requires the Juvenile Court Act to be construed so that "the child shall receive such care and guidance, preferably in his own home, as will serve his welfare and the best interests of the District" and that, when a child must be removed from his home, the "court shall secure for him custody, care, and discipline as nearly as possible equivalent to that which should have been given him by his parents."

THE FAILURE OF THE TREATMENT MODEL. It is becoming increasingly apparent, however, that problems in fulfilling our promise of treatment exist beyond the obvious injustices of warehousing institutions and assembly-line courts. It doesn't take much exper-

tise to guess that children reared in the ghetto, where acknowledgment of one's own identity or worth is virtually impossible,
will develop at best a hard insensitivity to other humans. I sus-
pect that none of our providers of treatment services—psychiatrists, psychologists, or social workers—have the know-how to
implant middle-class sensibilities into youngsters who have been
neglected for 24 hours a day, every day. There is no magic
humanizing pill for these youths to swallow, and it is time we all
admitted it.

What is "treatment" anyway? Even the experts would agree
that the best nostrum is common sense and compassion. It is significant that most nonchemical breakthroughs in treating addiction to hard drugs and alcohol have been made by lay persons,
in the form of Alcoholics Anonymous, Synanon, therapeutic communities, supported work programs, and the like. Psychiatrists
admit their frustration and reluctance to treat alcoholics, addicts,
homosexuals, sociopaths. Why do we expect greater success with
juvenile misfits?

There is even a real danger in labeling our juvenile problems
"mental health" problems. In so doing, we erect a protective
medical shield around the same old harsh and punitive practices.
As a result, the disciplinary cells in a boys' institution are in the
infirmary and are called medical isolation.

If we want to make sure that our treatment efforts are really
constructive, we must examine our expectations much more
carefully. We must have a better understanding of what children really need; of whether specialists, and what *kind* of specialists, are needed at all; and of how we can improve and
extend services that are useful, and eliminate those that are useless or downright destructive. Such a reappraisal of what we are
attempting to do will cost money, and it will cause pain to admit
our well-intentioned mistakes.

Are the alternatives adequate treatment or punishment?

Where does this all lead? Suppose judges, psychiatrists, and
correction officials begin to see that the promise of treatment
cannot be completely fulfilled? In May 1966, the Juvenile Court
for the District of Columbia adopted a new policy memorandum
outlining the factors which must be considered before a juvenile

is waived to the adult court. It is now the Juvenile Court's stated policy that if treatment is not available, the child should be waived to the adult court. The question raised by this new policy is clear: Are we to punish someone because the community has not provided the means and facilities for this treatment and, perhaps, cure? Witness, too, the reduction of age limits from 18 to 16 for sending juveniles to the adult courts if rehabilitation efforts have failed or if their behavior is too serious. There is talk of lowering the age further to 14 or 15.

I have advocated, as the first step, learning the facts, on the assumption that once faced with reality, we would be jolted into action. Here we have a situation, though, in which the exposure of the lack of treatment prompts not treatment, but punishment. I am puzzled. Perhaps we have more deeply ingrained escape mechanisms than I had imagined. I must say that I have a certain amount of sympathy for the escape. None of us wants to be faced with the possibility of failure and none of us wants to have our usefulness called into question. Even if the juvenile court judges order treatment, they still have to face the possibility that the treatment itself is a ruse, at least when we are talking about mental and emotional disorders particularly associated with the slums. Why should juvenile court judges subject themselves to the frustration of impotence? This possibility of failure must prompt escape in this whole area, not only by judges, for if a judge feels threatened by the fact that treatment may be an illusion, how much more threatened must the doctors and social workers feel? If the courts and the legislature provided a psychiatrist for each disturbed child, then the burden of failure would shift to the psychiatric profession or the mental health clinics. The question of what is adequate treatment or rehabilitation for each child would still remain.

However, the error in the "lock 'em up" approach is obvious, I think. It is like cutting off a piece of leg in order to make the pants fit. It solves nothing except to provide an escape valve for the feelings of fear, outrage, and anger which have been aroused by the public's daily, escalating confrontation with violent crime. Since vengeance is a dirty word, these feelings are expressed in cries for punishment and deterrence. But whatever the deterrent effect which punishment may have on tax evaders or traffic violators, we know there is abundant evidence that punishment does not deter the very kind of street crime which puts us in such great fear. And even if punishment were a deterrent, there is a serious question whether it is *just* to punish the antisocial conduct of those who cannot enter society.

The role of racism

I have already described discriminatory actions against Black children and adults. However, the pervasiveness of the practice needs to be understood. The bigotry that infects the juvenile system is not strictly racial in character. Racism is too definite and too limited in its meaning and connotations. It implies a sort of conscious and malicious sense of superiority. The problem with using it to characterize a problem is that such language may obscure more subtle, but equally insidious, forms of discrimination.

We reject the family from the ghetto, and are insensitive or worse to their child's problems, not because of their color alone, but because they are poor, speak an uneducated dialect we do not understand, and perhaps fail to share our reverence for the majesty of the law that has oppressed them for centuries. We are unsympathetic to the deprived child's problems, or perhaps even unwilling to admit that these problems are a consequence of anything but incorrigible evil. Equally sad, it may lead us to believe that we cannot help such children.

When a well-to-do child offends, particularly in a vicious or violent way, we tend immediately to think of mental illness. After all, a nice child would not do such a thing unless he "wasn't right." When a ghetto child commits the same act, however, we may, much like the judge commenting on Betty Jean's problems, assume that such behavior is merely normal in view of his upbringing.

Even more sad, we may not be totally wrong. Poverty, fragmented families, and a neighborhood infested with violence may well lead children to believe that they cannot succeed within the system, and that criminal activity is an acceptable, or possibly the only, way to rise above the squalor that surrounds them.

Facing the issues

Faced with the impossible problems of juvenile offenders whose lives are already twisted by the effects of poverty, judges do little more than beat their judicial breasts and try at least to make the community realize what they are doing. This may serve some purpose. One of the causes of class prejudice is the success with which the rich can ignore the poor. We move to the suburbs, or to the upper floors of luxury apartment buildings, and refuse to worry about, let alone attempt to cure, what is happening downtown or down below. Perhaps judicial opinions, with the media coverage they sometimes receive, can do something to make the prosperous public and legislators realize what is happening in our cities and why.

Beyond that, there is a very real question what courts can do. At some point, just as English juries once refused to convict a man for stealing bread, American judges should perhaps study carefully the constitutionality of punishing children who have not had a chance in life. That would be a drastic step. But the law increasingly recognizes that every person has certain entitlements as a citizen. It is difficult to think what more basic entitlement there could be than a child's right to a fair start in life.

For too long we have ignored a preventive approach which concentrates on the first decade of a child's life. Yet we know that all children need certain fundamentals: nutritious food, safe housing, a stable family structure to provide personal affection and continual attention to health, learning, and emotional needs. It is time to realize that we must begin to take steps toward *preventing* a new generation of troubled children—rather than waiting for trouble and hoping to cure it. Our juvenile courts should be the last resort—not the front-line institution to deal with lives already scarred. Our first priority in distributing justice to children ought to be distributing income to their families, to allow them to create the type of home environment they may want for their children.

It may be that an adequate family income won't eradicate the effects of racism, won't stop crime cold, or solve all the problems of growing up in the ghetto, but I am increasingly convinced that nothing we do for children can *begin* to work without it.

All that is necessary for the triumph of evil is that
good men do nothing.

EDMUND BURKE

10

It Can Be Done:
Aspects of Delinquency
Treatment and Prevention

IRVING N. BERLIN, M.D.

The relationship between racism, poverty, and crime, now
well known, is described vividly in the Kerner Report. Despite
the many clear-cut studies which point to the environment and
impact of poverty in society as being ultimately causal in most
crime, thousands of children and adolescents are incarcerated
each year in a desperate effort to halt crime under the mistaken
illusion that current prison-like state schools or detention facilities can rehabilitate the young offender. The expense involved
in rehabilitation and the commitment to the rehabilitated youth,
once released, to help them find and maintain meaningful work
and a position in life are critical issues which need to be examined. We must also examine the right of the juvenile offender
to a treatment and rehabilitation program which at least increases his opportunities to be more fully participant in society.
Even more difficult to conceptualize is how one could prevent
juvenile crime. One such method is described in this chapter.

Crime in the suburbs vs. crime in the ghettos

Most crime occurs in the ghettos. However, it is also clear that
in our troubled society crime is on the increase in suburbia. Not
only drug addiction, but stealing, assault, sexual acting out

127

(rape), even murder, are increasing. The alienation within society, the depersonalization which is characteristic of our living, has not escaped our suburbs. Even child abuse, which is more prevalent in the ghetto and in low- and middle-income populations, is known to be increasing among the middle- and upper-middle-class populations.[13]

Closely associated with the increased number of disturbed and disturbing children in the upper middle class who will become delinquent are the increased numbers of depressed mothers and fathers who cannot relate to their children and nurture them. Thus, these youngsters are not too unlike their comrades from fragmented families living in ghetto poverty. Despite blue- and white-collar, as well as middle-class, affluence, these youngsters have usually not experienced the required early childhood intimacy and close, warm relationships. They, too, need to satisfy their pleasures immediately. They require substitute gratifications for the gratification and nurturance which they have not received in early interpersonal relationships.

Data clearly show that criminal incidents in our middle-class communities are growing, but the rate of apprehension for these crimes still remains low. Among recent statistics gathered by sociologists are those which show that a white child from a good family has a chance of 50-to-1 of being sent home with a reprimand or a warning by a police officer after commiting an assault or burglary or being caught with drugs. Sometimes such children are brought into detention and, after staying overnight, are released to their parents' custody.[16]

In the ghetto, chances are 9-to-1 that any Black, Chicano, or other minority child who is apprehended for any crime will be brought into custody and remain there until an investigation is conducted, that he or she will be charged with a crime, and that a disposition will be made in juvenile court. Thus, while offenders from the ghetto are the more usual occupants of our state schools and detention homes, characterologically they are not so different from their more affluent counterparts.

THE GHETTO OFFENDER. Crime is a way of life in the ghetto, not only because children throughout their development are constantly exposed to crime, but also because survival in a poverty environment depends on getting what one can when one can in order to exist. Several studies have shown that the strongest, the most effective, and the brightest youths in the ghetto are the leaders of the gangs. Frequently the followers are those especially vulnerable children who have had nutritional handicaps and other defects as a result of chronic poverty. Their leaders provide these more handicapped youngsters with the only models of successful coping in a ghetto environment.

The authoritarian institution and its authoritarian personnel

As a mental health consultant for a number of juvenile courts and state institutions for corrections, I have had an opportunity to observe and to try to understand the impact of an authoritarian institution and its authoritarian personnel upon children and adolescents.[3] I contrast it with one of the few institutions I know which is essentially authoritative (using authority relationship to promote learning) in its role and very clearly screens its personnel to find those young men and women who can be authoritative and firm without becoming authoritarian and punitive.

It is certainly clear that most of the offenders in the state schools are tough youngsters from poverty areas. Some are tough youngsters from suburbia. These children, because of their particular upbringing, have never experienced those relationships required to help them delay gratification and postpone acting on impulsive feelings until the appropriate moment and opportunity for attaining satisfaction actually occurs.

The "counselors" in the detention institutions are primarily lower-middle-class young men and women brought up in settings which demanded that they inhibit their impulsive behavior and postpone their gratification in order to maintain a comfortable relationship with relatively harsh, righteous and demanding parents. Such counselors find the unpredictable behavior of their counselees extremely frightening. They have been brought up in a setting in which fear and physical power were the factors which made delay of gratification and impulsive behavior possible. The anxiety provoked in them by these impulse-ridden youngsters finds them with no other methods of dealing with such situations except by harsh and punitive measures.

RULE BY UNHOLY ALLIANCES. The counselors' great fear of the

most impulsive and aggressive youngsters—who are often the brightest and who have learned to con their counselors—promotes both overt and covert alliances. The alliances are made between the counselors and the most aggressive and impulsive counselees to help rule the other detainees of the detention home in an aura of fear and punitiveness. Such alliances mean that the counselors often give up much of their power to the counselees, of whom they're afraid. It means, too, that the other children are victimized in a variety of ways; they are robbed of their possessions and often sexually as well as physically brutalized. Most lower-middle-class counselors, when questioned about the kinds of alliances they have utilized to maintain control, insist that these alliances are better for the counselees. Otherwise, they themselves might constantly lose their control and are fearful that they might be even more vicious and hurtful than the inmates to whom they have given over control. It is only when someone is badly hurt or killed by one of the inmates in control that the counselors I have known are even vaguely disturbed by such a situation. It is clear that their own overwhelming anxiety and fear of the impulse-ridden behavior of their counselees leaves them no recourse.

ISSUES IN GIRLS' STATE SCHOOLS. It is equally clear that in the girls' state schools or detention facilities the female counselors are also lower middle class. The girls are usually committed because of sexual acting out, prostitution, or involvement in the drug scene. The counselors are bound by a strict morality very common to their lower-middle-class upbringing, so they find themselves both terribly envious of and angry at their charges. While impulsive hostile acting out among girls is not as prominent, it still exists and also evokes anxiety and fear among the women counselors. There is a common punitive attitude toward their charges and an inability to behave toward counselees with any regard for their needs or with any human warmth or kindness. Their constant anger toward these girls also makes it difficult for them to work with them in any rehabilitative activities. These women are constantly fearful of being attacked and physically hurt by the girls who feel disliked, rebuffed, and retaliatory. Many girls seem to understand some of the envy and anger which are aimed at them for having dared to be sexually promiscuous and express in behavior the fantasies of their counselors.

An authoritative vs. an authoritarian detention facility

In the authoritarian detention facilities that I have worked with, the model of repression and punitiveness appears to flow from the director down to the counselors. In several instances, the directors I have known have themselves expressed enormous anger at the crimes of their counselees. At other times they have stated covert admiration for the agility, cleverness, intelligence of planning, etc., which enabled a counselee to get away with so many crimes.

In several instances it was clear that the director also was involved in many petty violations of state regulations in terms of using his state car and abusing other privileges. Most of these minor infractions of state rules were known to his subordinates. Since the director behaved illegally, subordinates also tended to act out. They were, thus, in many ways vulnerable to subtle blackmail on the part of some of the smarter counselees.

Another characteristic of the authoritarian institution was that the director's authority was often based on a coalition with the most violent and impulsive of his counselors who could, because of their physical strength and violence, maintain order. An occasional demonstration of their physical prowess and punitiveness was necessary, according to some directors, to maintain the kind of law and order required in such an institution, else it would become, and I quote, "a jungle without a king."

In contrast, in the most effective authoritative institution I have known, the director was a sociologist or criminologist who had spent many years in the criminal justice system working with youngsters. It was his philosophy that youngsters with criminal backgrounds required a rehabilitative experience. By that he meant they must be associated with adults who would behave toward the adolescent or the younger child with a nonpunitive firmness and consistency of concern for them. This behavior must be sufficiently prolonged for the adolescents to have the experience that there are adults who could not be provoked to behave toward them punitively; who had some belief in their capacity to learn to behave differently; and whom they would in time emulate as models for a new pattern of behavior that could work for them in daily living and prove satisfying.

THE CASE OF BENJIE. Benjamino, or Benjie, was a very large

Chicano boy, now age 14, who was sent to a detention home for assault. His three previous periods in state schools occurred for burglary. On each previous occasion, the fact that he was a very large boy for his age and extremely bright meant that he learned quickly to con the organization and to do exactly what was expected of him so he served a minimum sentence. As he himself said, he was usually better fed and was smarter because he learned so much from others during his period in the school.

In his ghetto home Benjie was feared because of his explosive temper and his enormous strength and agility; and he was the leader of his gang.

Paradoxically, Benjie was not a school dropout. Although he frequently skipped school, he nevertheless maintained himself in most of his classes and was smart enough to do fairly well in order to get by. That is, he could read well, could do basic mathematics fairly well, and was able to bluff in most other subjects. Benjie had his eye on the fact that without a high school diploma it was tough to get a job. It appeared to those of us who knew Benjie that the reasoning behind his staying in school was based on observation of his 18-year-o'd brother who had been a school dropout and, like Benjie, a gang leader, involved in drugs and various other criminal activities in the barrio. Now, because he could neither read nor write, Benjie's brother was not even effective as a gang leader in administrative tasks necessary to making deals and keeping any organization smoothly operational. Besides, as Benjie put it, "It's much easier to run an operation from the cover of a job, and in order to get a job you have to have a diploma."

Impact of authoritative attitudes. As his counselor, Benjie was assigned to Carlos. Carlos was a 26-year-old Chicano who had finished college with the help of more affluent relatives who hoped he would go into law. Instead he had decided to work with delinquent youngsters and was hoping at some point to become a social worker or psychologist. Carlos was 5′ 8″ tall, lithe, athletic, and strong, having played baseball in college. However, he was certainly no physical match for the 14-year-old Benjie.

Their initial relationship is perhaps best described by Benjie who often said, with great vehemence, how much he hated Carlos who "is an 'Uncle Tom', not even a Mexican because he'd gotten so much education." But mostly he hated Carlos because Carlos refused to be conned by his smiles and promises and because whenever he teased or tried to get Carlos angry with him, Carlos would very quickly tell him exactly how he, Carlos, was feeling. He would at no time try to bullshit Benjie or try to kid him into doing something for his, that is, for Carlos' sake. Neither could Benjie, with his vast experience in state institutions, find ways of bribing Carlos and getting on his good side. As Benjie would say to others, "That bastard Carlos is the same to all of these kids." Most of all he hated Carlos' patience and his capacity to flare up quickly in anger and to express his anger verbally, to take whatever action was necessary to restrain or detain Benjie, and stop any physical attack on other children or exploitation of them. Carlos kept strictly to his word in terms of the amount of time Benjie would have to spend in isolation for such activities, but also clearly stated his hope that Benjie would become interested in learning some of the skills to be learned at this institution and that he, Carlos, would try to help him.

For a time Benjie went around bragging that Carlos had said he was afraid of Benjie. Carlos had in fact once told him that. Benjie had threatened Carlos with a log and Carlos had said, "Look, you're big enough so that I couldn't take you on single-handed, and you might just lay me out and even knock me off. I'm scared as hell of you, but you know I can't let you do anything like that, so that no matter what happens, no matter what the circumstances, I would have to try to stop you. That's my job." What Benjie could not understand was why, if Carlos was afraid of him and knew that he might be so badly hurt by Benjie, he was nevertheless determined at all costs to stop him. That kind of craziness he had not encountered before.

The identification with counselors as models. Because most of the counselors in this setting were firm and consistent and mostly not punitive in how they behaved toward their counselees, there were no ruling cliques of counselees. Also, most of the counselors had been chosen because of their particular skill in various trades, or their capacities to teach various subjects in school.

The identification of Benjie with Carlos was first evident on the baseball field. Benjie, a very powerful hitter in sandlot baseball, had learned very little about the art of fielding. It was there that his first acceptance of Carlos as a teacher occurred. He later developed relationships with several other counselors, especially one who was an expert auto mechanic and another whom all the boys envied because his drag racer had the greatest motor around.

In a variety of ways his counselors were able to provide models of how men could live with some dignity without threat or punitiveness. They were concerned with learning and improving themselves without lording it over others and being superior or smug, and could express their feelings of not knowing or, as in Carlos' case, their anxiety or fear of being hurt without giving up on the job that they had to accomplish.

In this setting, for me, being authoritative came to mean that the counselors actually cared about the counselees as individual human beings. They hoped that through their own examples of behavior the counselees would learn self-control, be able to think for themselves, and that their challenges to the counselors would become not physical challenges but challenges to learn better and to outdo them in athletic or skill aspects of the program. I must say that in this rare setting the director was one of those people who also very clearly showed his willingness to learn from others, to do better, to accept criticism, and to try to learn from his mistakes.

Survival depends on help in the community

That Benjie came out of this experience a different kind of youngster should not be surprising. That he stayed a different kind of youngster is, indeed, surprising, because the temptation of the barrios was still there. It was, however, the continued interest of Carlos and other counselors in those youngsters who returned to the barrio, their efforts to help them gain jobs and to withstand the anxieties of working in regular jobs and the taunts and the temptations of their former associates, that finally made it possible for at least one youngster to make it. But such a possibility indicates that providing models which promote learning of skills and honest, forthright interactions has some promise. Providing opportunities for offenders to practice in the external world some of what they had learned in an authoritative institution becomes necessary. There is no question that this is an expensive experiment. The necessity of finding employment and keeping these youngsters in contact with their former counselors over a period of time is also expensive. However, these victims of our society have every right to that expense. There are certainly some experiments like this one which indicate that offenders can be, and have the right to be, rehabilitated.

Modeling techniques as help to delinquent youth

Another effort to alter behavior patterns in delinquent youth is the work in modeling by Dr. Irwin Sarason of the University of Washington. His work illustrates that delinquent youth are sensitive to models of behavior which are situation-related and presented to them to view, criticize, and react to. Dr. Sarason and his colleagues would first present typical enactments of situations found to be troublesome to youth about to be discharged from an institution. Thus the job interview situation, always difficult, is enacted for a group of potential parolees. The stress points in the interview are acted out with various responses possible by the job applicant to searching questions. Some of the feelings an applicant has when being questioned about his record or previous job performance, etc., are talked about. The best responses to questions are analyzed by the group. After several such demonstrations the youth are asked to play the various parts with comments from their peers. Sometimes the old, usual response and the better responses are both played out so that the models can be compared. The pleasure a youth has in saying "fuck you" to a hard-nosed, relentless personnel man's questions are then compared with the feelings of reducing the anger by an honest statement which has been previously rehearsed so the youth doesn't feel at a loss.

Many other difficult interpersonal situations are anticipated and played out until more successful models for coping with stress are evolved. Feelings when confronted by a supervisor who is antagonistic when one is late to work, or where one feels already judged and would tend to say "shove your job" and quit —the handling of such difficult situations is worked out and each one of the youths has a chance at the various roles. Preliminary data on this approach reveal a greater degree of success in previously frustrating and defeating efforts at obtaining and keeping a job.

Use of modeling techniques to deal with interpersonal prob-

lems and confrontations with authority in the institution is also
being tried to help the adolescents to experience firsthand more
successful handling of difficult and anxiety- or anger-producing
institutional situations. Peer critique of each modeling effort, the
authenticity of the modeling, and the effectiveness of the solution also lead to the use of group process to analyze both the inherent problems and pitfalls in each situation, permitting clearer
analysis of the origins of the usual or expected response, which
always come from previous unsuccessful experiences, and why
another response may be preferable and more effective. The vulnerability of delinquent youth to certain unknown situations and
how their response patterns have become habits are in some instances clarified.

The most seriously disturbed youth, psychiatrically, are the
slowest to adapt to role change and to learn to use modeling as
preparation for dealing with real life situations.

Some adolescents who are most skilled in conning the institution and handling institutional personnel for their own gain may
have difficulty in adapting to a new model required by new situations. These young people require a great deal of help and
practice to refrain from automatically enacting the old scenarios
when given a new script. However, some real change has occurred even with these "old timers."

Modeling as an aid to new behavior patterns both inside and
outside the institution requires an institutional administration
actively concerned with helping their counselees to change.

Delinquency prevention through participatory democracy

This leads us to the last issue I would like to raise—the implications of nonauthoritarian attitudes, in fact, participatory democracy in the schools as one tool to help youngsters feel less
vulnerable and helpless. Hopefully such learning will provide
real life alternatives to criminality and a vehicle for responsible
action in the communities. In school the use of democratic processes in learning, such as project methods of teaching indicated
in the Plowden Report in England, increases responsibility for
one's own behavior and that of others through student participation in decision-making in the classroom. It is based primarily on
teaching problem solving as a way of dealing first with educa-

tional problems, then problems of living in the classroom and in society. Using problem-solving methods as the vehicle for all teaching is one of the goals of such a curriculum. It is clearly geared to making problem-solving techniques a method of approaching all problems in living. The following pages describe the evolution of one such effort.

IMPACT ON JUNIOR HIGH SCHOOLS. An experimental elementary school had as its mission finding more effective ways of engaging students in learning. The large junior high school on the edge of the ghetto had many older, conservative teachers. A young progressive administrator had recently been appointed because of turmoil, in the classrooms and out, which distressed the teachers and many parents. When he learned about the efforts in project learning and participatory democracy in an elementary school, he asked several of his young and enterprising teachers to spend some time there and to report back.

They were enthused about the students' attitudes and wanted to try some of the project methods of learning and participatory democracy in their classrooms. They already had one such example in the arts and crafts teacher who never had any classroom problems because of her freedom in reacting to students' needs and desires and her all-out efforts to help them express themselves creatively. She did not get hung up on the issues of students' language, dress, or noise in the classroom, etc. As long as students were productively working, she was pleased. The students in her class made the rules and they worked. Other teachers and some parents saw this teacher as undermining discipline and student attitudes required for learning in other settings. Thus, the principal knew he had a battle on his hands, but the school problems were so great and the pressure from the central office and parents so continuous that he felt impelled to try something new, especially since, as a vice principal in a ghetto school, he had already experienced the effects of repression. In that school, though they drove overt rebellion and challenge underground, law and order efforts altered nothing but the dropout rate, which increased.

A CURRICULUM IN PARTICIPATORY DEMOCRACY. The principal and his young teachers devised a core curriculum in which several of them would teach classes in seventh, eighth, and ninth grades. In these core classes, students would spend a half day on projects which would include aspects of required subject matter. The other half day would be spent in physical education and other non-core electives. This required major rescheduling which affected other teachers who usually taught math, English, social studies, etc. Consequently, when the package was presented to the faculty, it aroused a good deal of hostility, especially when it became clear that the considerable team teaching to be done meant these several teachers would together have smaller than regular classes. The administrator stuck to his guns about the experimental effort and the need to involve students in determining what they would do, how it was to be done, and the effectiveness of their learning.

THE PARTICIPATORY PROCESS IN JUNIOR HIGH SCHOOL. Groups in the junior high school experimental classes were very difficult to get started. The process followed a particular pattern. The students, suspicious of the adults, vied with each other for leadership; several tried to cram their project ideas down the throats of their groups and were rebuffed. Project ideas, such as a sex education project using *Playboy* pictures, with the obvious purpose of testing the sincerity of the teachers were suggested. Also suggested was a study of what drugs gave the best high. A provocative girl suggested they study why male teachers were okay and female teachers were such stinkers. When each suggestion was carefully considered in terms of source material, tasks to be undertaken, and how classroom presentations could be made, suggestions became more reality-oriented. Thus, from this group came the idea of studying juvenile delinquency and the factors that lead to delinquency. At each step there was constant testing of project ownership. One teacher confronted his group with his right, like any other group member, to offer suggestions for consideration on their merits without special priority. When it became clear he was not pushing his ideas, but simply wanted them considered, the group began to look at his suggestions. One of the group who had been on juvenile probation offered his ex-caseworker as a resource for reading material on delinquency. After some preliminary reading, the group accepted the teacher's idea that many factors were related to delinquency.

Paired students then worked on the issues for which they had volunteered or chose from the remaining options. They asked their teacher to request data from the juvenile court which they felt they could not get. He suggested that he and several students write for the data and see what would happen. The students were correct. Only the teacher got the court's and probation department's last annual report.

In the junior high school the students used teachers' help with interpreting articles, in learning to use the periodical index, and in organizing their written and oral reports. Some students were eager to be in the spotlight and wanted to present lengthy reports; others were clearly anxious about making oral presentations and wanted minimal participation. The elected project chairmen dealt with the problem by full group discussion and final agreement on equal emphasis and time for each team member. In each project, history, English, and mathematics of some sort evolved as natural parts of the effort.

IMPACT OF PROJECT METHOD OF DATA GATHERING. To the dismay of the principal, one of the eighth-grade classes undertook a study of urban renewal and gathered a great deal of data about the intent and actual effect of such efforts. Especially telling were their detailed analyses which used the literature as a base followed by on-site visits to the housing projects in their area and the local urban renewal area. The urban renewal was intended to relocate poor people from ghetto and substandard, overcrowded housing. Instead it had turned into expensive middle-class housing and shopping centers, without providing new housing for the displaced poor or minorities, especially Blacks. Their surveys of ghetto apartment occupancy showed clearly that the result of urban renewal was increased crowding with profits for owners of ghetto buildings. Another group surveying delinquency in their area uncovered data about factors in the ghetto which increased delinquent behavior—overcrowding, unemployment, poverty, many families on welfare, lack of recreational facilities (except on the streets) and job opportunities for youth, and the hopelessness of most young adults and parents. The history behind each project and the collection and understanding of elementary statistics and preparing them for the report were part of everyone's experience.

These junior-high-school students, with their parents' help, turned the PTA into a Parent-Teacher-Student Association with students as voting members. Each project, with its remediation recommendations, was presented to the PTSA. Students were now fully participant in the PTA. From the urban renewal project presentation came recommendations of low cost housing and, to prevent further displacement and overcrowding in the ghetto, no demolition of existing housing until new housing was found for each family. Increased recreational facilities and 18-hour-use of all schools for community projects were also recommended. The delinquency project recommended special training of Black and white ghetto policemen who should also be involved in community recreation. Job training and jobs were essential. High interest, high impact classes with enthusiastic young teachers like those found in the one dropout academy, were recommended for all junior and senior high schools. The presentations were well received; however, a minority of parents and teachers were angered at the presumptuousness of the students in conducting investigations, gathering data, presenting their own statistics, and making recommendations as if they were adults in government.

OPPOSITION TO NEW TEACHING AND LEARNING METHODS. From other schools, students as well as a few teachers came to observe. In this junior high school, more students in regular classes wanted to participate in the experimental classes. When they couldn't officially get in, some of them simply stopped going to their regular classes and attended the new ones. Some teachers and parents viewed this as a break in discipline in the school rather than a desire of students to learn and participate in the curriculum decisions. Parents' and teachers' complaints were brought to the attention of the superintendent and the school board in an angry attack against the principal and his corps of young teachers.

Finally a hearing was scheduled. Students, and parents of experimental-class students, carefully presented their case. Most impressive was the comparison of dropouts from regular vs. experimental classes—approximately 28 percent vs. two percent. Supporting the enraged parents and teachers were several city councilmen. They had heard of the students' data collection in various projects, which reflected on them, their urban renewal office, the police, and juvenile authorities. This they felt could only be more divisive to the community. However, one councilman from the target school area was called on to speak and he commented angrily, "If finding out and facing the real facts are divisive, then there can be no real democracy." He called for the entire junior high school to become a learning and teaching center devoted to projects of community concern. The school board voted to sanction continuation of the experimental classes and asked the research division of the school to provide data on dropouts, learning as revealed by group tests, etc., to evaluate the effectiveness of the experimental classes. One of the mental health workers in the school, impressed with the new openness and freedom of expression of these students, as well as their increased ability to work together toward common objectives, offered to evaluate these variables using several interaction scales.

Conclusions

Throughout the country open schools, high schools, junior high schools, and the efforts in some elementary schools indicate that —given the opportunity and good models—young students will learn to use data gathering, hypothesis generation, and problem-solving efforts to their own integrative purposes. They first use these methods as participants in improving their school experience and then transfer these methods to informed citizen participation in the community. Participatory democracy can work in schools and probably, given good models, in other institutions in a democratic society.

It is clear that poverty and delinquency are linked. It is also clear that a society in trouble produces delinquents in all social classes, but most adolescent crime is committed against their own people by poor, minority youth in ghettos.

The abolition or reduction of poverty is essential for major reduction, not only of crime, but of mental retardation, developmental and learning disabilities, and some forms of mental illness, especially those forms resulting from lack of emotional sustenance to infants, which generational poverty with resulting depression and apathy in mothers makes widespread.

The evidence is clear that not only do we need to reduce and

VANDERBILT MEDICAL CENTER LIBRARY

eliminate poverty but that there are tools at hand to rehabilitate and treat the antisocial, delinquent youth: programs that require special people concerned with developing the potentials of others; programs that are expensive to run and maintain; programs which must extend into the community. Reduction of crime through meaningful work and the psychological support it provides requires a commitment of support in money and services which our society appears reluctant to make. Our commitment would cost less than the crimes and incarceration resulting from crimes. Such a societal commitment, however, clearly spells out an advocacy position for society in habilitating and helping children become effective citizens.

Such a commitment toward advocacy means a belief in the capacities of children and youth to learn how to think, and how to solve problems in school and out. Learning how to collect data for use in thinking about solutions to problems is the essence of a democratic education. It presupposes acquiring essential skills and knowledge that make data collection possible, and ability to use words and mathematics effectively.

The skills acquired in participatory democracy in school are the skills needed to communicate with others, not only to find facts, but to judge their value—not only to judge their value, but in the process to think about how these facts can be applied to solving specific problems. Such a process—thinking about how problems can be solved, communicating with others about them, and learning so that one can teach others how to think about problem solving—approaches the essence of participatory democracy.

We need to strongly advocate both the treatment and prevention of delinquency just as we advocate the treatment and prevention of physical and mental illness. In each process of advocacy we advance the general concern with children and their human rights.

REFERENCES

1. ALLEN, T. E. An innovation in treatment at a youth institution. *Federal Probation*, 1969, 33:1, 39–48.
2. BENDER, L. A psychiatrist looks at deviancy as a factor in juvenile delinquency. *Federal Probation*, 1968, 32:2, 35–42.

3. BERLIN, I. N. Mental health consultation with a juvenile probation department. *Crime and Delinquency*, 1964, *10*, 67–73.
4. BERLIN, I. N. The school's role in a participatory democracy. *American Journal of Orthopsychiatry*, 1972, *42*, 499–507.
5. BERNS, A. Juvenile detention: An eyewitness account. In Columbia Human Rights Law Review (Eds.), *Legal Rights of Children: Status, Progress and Proposals*. Fair Lawn, New Jersey: R. E. Burdick, 1972. Pp. 15–20.
6. CARSON, V. S. Case note: In the matter of Ella B.—A test for the right to assigned counsel in family court cases. In Columbia Human Rights Law Review (Eds.), *Legal Rights of Children: Status, Progress, and Proposals*. Fair Lawn, New Jersey: R. E. Burdick, 1972. Pp. 163–172.
7. CAYTON, C. E. Relationship of the probation officer and the defense attorney after Gault. *Federal Probation*, 1970, *34*:1, 8–13.
8. *The Challenge of Crime in a Free Society*. Report by the President's Commission on Law Enforcement and Administration of Justice. Washington, D.C.: U. S. Government Printing Office, 1967.
9. DEUTSCH, M. Conflicts: Productive and constructive. In *Kurt Lewin Memorial Address*. Washington, D.C.: American Psychological Association, September, 1968.
10. ELIAS, A. Innovations in correctional programs for juvenile delinquents. *Federal Probation*, 1968, *32*:4, 38–45.
11. FISHER, S. M. Life in a children's detention center: Strategies of survival. *American Journal of Orthopsychiatry*, 1972, *42*, 368–374.
12. FLANNERY, W. O. The applicability of the fourth amendment exclusionary rule to juveniles in delinquency proceedings. In Columbia Human Rights Law Review (Eds.) *Legal Rights of Children: Status, Progress and Proposals*. Fair lawn, New Jersey: R. E. Burdick, 1972. Pp. 129–162.
13. GIL, D. *Violence against Children, Physical Child Abuse in the United States*. Cambridge, Mass.: Harvard University Press, 1970.
14. HUGHES, T. R. Humanizing the detention setting. *Federal Probation*, 1971, *35*:3, 21–26.
15. HYNES, C. Discipline in a treatment-oriented school for delinquent boys. *Federal Probation*, 1969, *33*:4, 29–31.
16. *Juvenile Justice Confounded: Pretensions and Realities of Treatment Services*. Paramus, New Jersey: National Council on Crime and Delinquency, 1972.
17. KIRKPATRICK, A. M. Corporal punishment. *Federal Probation*, 1970, *34*:1, 41–44.
18. LONG, B. E. Behavioral science for elementary-school pupils. *Elementary School Journal*, 1970, *70*:5, 253–260.
19. MARK, J. I. Appellate review for juveniles: A "right" to a tran-

script. In Columbia Human Rights Law Review (Eds.), *Legal Rights of Children: Status, Progress and Proposals.* Fair Lawn, New Jersey: R. E. Burdick, 1972. Pp. 197–208.

20. MCCOLLUM, S. G. "Say, have you got anything around here for a dummy?" *Federal Probation,* 1971, 35:3, 37–42.

21. MOSHER, R. L., & SPRINTHALL, N. A. Psychological education in secondary schools: A program to promote individual and human development. *American Psychologist,* 1970, 25, 911–924.

22. POLSKY, H. W. *Cottage Six—The Social System of Delinquent Boys in Residential Treatment.* New York: Russell Sage Foundation, 1962.

23. RIVERA, G. *Willowbrook: A Report on How It Is and Why It Doesn't Have to Be That Way.* New York: Vintage Books, 1972.

24. SARASON, I. G., & GANZER, V. J. *Modeling: An Approach to the Rehabilitation of Juvenile Offenders.* Washington, D.C.: Department of Health, Education and Welfare, 1971.

25. STATSKY, W. P. The training of community judges: Rehabilitative adjudication. In Columbia Human Rights Law Review (Eds.), *Legal Rights of Children: Status, Progress and Proposals.* Fair Lawn, New Jersey: R. E. Burdick, 1972. Pp. 113–128.

26. STRINGER, L. A., & TAYLOR, R. M. *Project Summary: Mothers as Colleagues in School Mental Health Work.* Final Report, NIMH Grant MH-14793, 1970.

27. WEBER, G. H. Emotional and defensive reactions of cottage parents. In D. R. Cressey (Ed.), *The Prison: Studies in Institutional Organization and Change.* New York: Holt, Rinehart and Winston, 1961. Pp. 189–228.

28. WIZNER, S. The child and the state: Adversaries in the juvenile justice system. In Columbia Human Rights Law Review (Eds.), *Legal Rights of Children: Status, Progress and Proposals.* Fair Lawn, New Jersey: R. E. Burdick, 1972. Pp. 101–112.

CHILDREN LEARN WHAT THEY LIVE

If a child lives with criticism, he learns to condemn.
If a child lives with hostility, he learns to fight.
If a child lives with ridicule, he learns to be shy.
If a child lives with shame, he learns to feel guilty.
If a child lives with tolerance, he learns to be
patient.
If a child lives with encouragement, he learns
confidence.
If a child lives with praise, he learns to appreciate.
If a child lives with fairness, he learns justice.
If a child lives with security, he learns to have
faith.
If a child lives with approval, he learns to like
himself.
If a child lives with acceptance and friendship, he
learns to find love in the world.

DOROTHY LAW NOLTE

11

Parents' Advocate Role
in Education
as Primary Prevention

ROXIE BERLIN, M.S.W., PH.D.
IRVING N. BERLIN, M.D.

The past 25-year period has witnessed a trend of seeing the schools alienate themselves from the communities which they serve. Parents have increasingly been willing to leave their children's education completely to the schools, assuming that because education is the prerogative of educators, it is no longer that of the parents or family.

The schools seem to have accepted this responsibility. Since the number of nonlearners or low achievers has increased steadily, the schools, with the help of federal funds, have launched a number of remedial and enrichment programs, all of which have been largely ineffectual. Since the correlation between school achievement and socioeconomic level has been demonstrated to be high, the Head Start program was launched nationwide so that children of families in poverty could get special help in the schools to make up for deficiencies in experiences provided in the home. There is an increasing demand for day care services for working mothers that can, in effect, make up to the child for the attention and care he does not receive from a mother who is primarily concerned with earning a living.

Results from the Head Start program nationwide indicate that gains from this program are not lasting, except for those children whose mothers have become directly involved in the classroom process. Remedial and enrichment programs for school-age children have been largely ineffective. There is reason to accept the apparent fact that schools are not able to make up to a child for deficiencies in experience, evolving from his home life, which occur at preschool ages.

Seattle research

An Early Childhood Education Center, a school for children from kindergarten through second grade, was established in Seattle. Its purpose was to use every means possible to ensure that children would achieve the skills required for success in the third grade which is when most children with learning difficulties fail.

Since a strong emphasis was placed on the importance of learning to read, a variety of programs was considered. Members of a citizens' task force gave high priority to hiring a teacher whose sole job would be to teach parents how to help teach their own children. The teacher would work with parents who came to school, and would have a paraprofessional as an assistant who would make home visits to parents who did not come to school and whose children were underachievers. These two positions were funded the following year by the school district and this parent education program was implemented.

To demonstrate the usefulness of utilizing parent help to stimulate learning of underachievers, one of the authors (RB) worked with a group of parents in a study for a doctoral dissertation.

USE OF EDUCATIONAL GAMES: A VEHICLE FOR PARENTS TEACHING
THEIR CHILDREN. This program investigated the effect of helping
parents play educational games with their children to enhance
the concept development of these kindergarten children. Two
intact classrooms were used as experimental and control groups.
The control classroom was matched for racial balance and socioeconomic level with the experimental class. They were approximately the same in size and in the same geographic area.

Games were used as a means of involving parents in interaction with their children. The Boehm Test of Basic Concepts,
widely used to test conceptual readiness of children, was used in
both classes as a pre-test and again as a post-test, and was individually administered. The games used were developed from
the concepts tested for in the Boehm Test. Each game was specifically designed to teach a concept. Simple games, such as
those described below, were utilized.

Mothers of all children in one kindergarten class were invited
to participate in this program. They were to help in teaching age-
appropriate concepts through the use of games. Games were
chosen as a means of involving parents because we believed it to
be the easiest way to get parents to relate to their children. The
games were presented and demonstrated to the mothers at
weekly meetings held in the school. Simple instructions for the
use of each game accompanied each demonstration. Parents
were encouraged to play each game for 15 minutes at least once
a day for one week.

Home visits to those mothers who failed to attend the weekly
meetings were made with the help of a nonprofessional who had
been trained to demonstrate the games to the mothers and to
encourage the participation of the mothers in playing the games
with the children.

A series of ten games was used. The games were devised to
teach specific concepts and were assembled from simple materials at hand. For example, a game used to teach the meaning
of "pair" consisted of six pairs of cards having designs colored in
the shape of diamonds, circles, triangles, hearts, rectangles, and
clubs. The game was played by shuffling the cards and laying the
cards face down in three rows. The first player turns two cards
over. Any matching pair of cards is kept and placed in the play-

er's pile; the other cards are turned back face down. The object
is to remember where the cards are so that pairs can be obtained.
The game ends when all cards have been matched. The winner
has the most pairs of cards. Each pair counts as one point. In discussions around the use of this game, parents are urged to use
other examples of pairs with their children, such as shoes, socks,
mittens, salt and pepper shakers, as well as to use the same opportunities to teach related concepts such as "alike" or "different."

Another game used was a set of special dominoes. Each domino was made of two bright colored patterns. The concept to be
taught was "matching." The patterns had to be matched in order
to play a domino. The person who matched the most domino
patterns won.

One game designed to teach the concept of "separate" used a
string of pop-a-part beads and one die. The object of this game
was to separate every bead from every other bead. This may be
done by removing from the main segment of beads that number
of beads equal to the number on the die at each throw. Players
take turns until one player has separated all of his beads. Discussion around this game brings up ways of teaching related
concepts such as "each," "every," and "almost." Thus, *each* bead,
every bead, and "You *almost* separated all the beads" or "You
have *almost* won" are examples used.

The results of this experiment were that the children in the
experimental group, whose mothers were helped to play educational games with them, learned more concepts than the children
in the control group whose parents were not involved with them.
This result was statistically significant. In addition, a larger percentage of pupils in the experimental group made a greater than
average gain. Finally, the initially low achievers in the experimental group, those who knew the fewest concepts, benefited
more from this program than the middle and high achievers in
the experimental group and more than all groups in the control
classroom. This was also statistically significant. This study demonstrated that a program which involved mothers of low achieving pupils in kindergarten was effective in increasing concept
learning.

Another doctoral study in Seattle's inner-city schools investigated the effectiveness of using learning games with economically disadvantaged parents to increase the reading achievement of their second-grade children. In this study two classrooms with no significant differences in average reading scores were used and 30 children were randomly selected and assigned to three groups. Experimental and internal control groups were assigned from one classroom. The other classroom was used as an external control group. Individual IQ (Peabody Picture Vocabulary Test) and Form C of the Metropolitan Achievement Test were given to all subjects as pre-tests. Diagnostic reading tests were administered in order to establish the specific reading needs to be included in the first games.

Parents were invited to group meetings held once a week to learn to use each new game for the week and to discuss their reactions and their children's reactions to the previous games. Home visits were made to those parents who did not come to the group meetings. After the eight-week series of game playing, the subjects were tested using other forms of the previous tests. The results showed that children who had played learning games with their mothers achieved scores which resulted in significant improvement in vocabulary, composite reading, and IQ. Thus learning games used by these economically disadvantaged parents increased the reading achievement and IQ scores of their children. It indicates that these games may provide a technique useful to the school to involve parents in the learning process of their children.

In addition to these two recent studies in Seattle's inner-city area, a considerable number of other studies have reported significant success in increasing school achievement of children as a result of establishing programs to involve parents. There seem to be two essential elements of successful programs: (1) that the program have sufficient structure to provide the parents with specific techniques which they could learn to use with their children over a scheduled period of time, and (2) that the program provide for home visits to those parents who do not come to school. That is, most so-called unreachable parents were gradually reached and involved in working with their children.

A San Francisco program

In a program in San Francisco, 18 Black parents, whose children in a ghetto school were either failing academically or whose disruptive behavior had brought expulsion notices, were gathered by that school's mental health worker into a group to discuss what they as parents could do. Their first impulse was to complain to the superintendent of schools that their ghetto school had become a dumping ground for inadequate and hostile teachers and an ineffectual, tyrannical principal who would not be tolerated by parents in middle-class neighborhoods. After much discussion they agreed that all previous efforts to reach the superintendent and school board had resulted in lame excuses and no action.

After much deliberation and encouragement by the mental health worker they agreed they would have to gather data through regular and systematic classroom observations to convince the board of how poorly their children were being taught.

To gain entry into the school over the principal's objection these parents forced the community board to confront the superintendent and then a Black councilman to put pressure on the superintendent to allow the parents into the school as regular observers. The parent group also put two of their group up for election to the community board on the platform that an alert community board would not have allowed such a damaging school situation to exist or continue at their children's expense.

The first effects of having parents as regular observers in the elementary school classroom were that the teachers valiantly tried to teach better and that the children, aware that a parent in each classroom was watching and recording their behavior and the teacher's, tried to learn more and behave less disruptively. The supposition of poor teaching skills and inability to engage the children or to manage their behavior was effectively documented with many time-sample observations in most of the elementary school classes. The fact that the principal never made an appearance in even the most chaotic classes to help his teachers spoke eloquently of either his lack of concern with the teaching and learning in his school or his incapacity to help.

After several attempts, with the backing of the community

board and the Black city councilman, a hearing before the board occurred. The completeness of the documentation obviously disconcerted the board, which could find no way to wriggle out of the situation and ordered the superintendent to change administrators and teaching personnel in the schools.

Once in the school the parents, with the help of the mental health worker, documented the obvious changes in their own and other children in the classroom which their presence seemed to bring about. They were able, with these data, to obtain agreement from the new principal to continue their observations and, additionally, to be available to the teacher to help with specific teaching tasks that the teacher felt they might perform with those children who needed special attention. The teachers, after initial anxiety and distrust, came to value the parents' presence since it reduced disruptive behavior. They came to rely on their assistance in working with individual students and small groups in reading and elementary math. A few of the most talented parents, mostly mothers, became the first teachers' aides hired in that school. Unlike teachers' aides in other schools, having demonstrated their abilities to coach and teach children, they were not given housekeeping or record-keeping chores.

FINDINGS FROM THIS STUDY. Parents' presence in the classrooms as learning helpers made it clear to their own children that parents were interested in the child's learning. Perhaps as important, it demonstrated over time that their parents believed they could learn and that they as parents could help them learn. The achievement in reading and writing of these failing or about to be expelled students increased from year to year. Anecdotal records kept by the school mental health worker indicated that both the children and their parents began to feel more competent and effective. Their relationships at home also changed as parents learned new ways of involving themselves with their children and encouraging their learning. The often commented-upon apathy of Black parents and their children was not seen in this elementary school.

There can be no question that children headed toward academic failure, dropping out of school, and delinquency stayed in school and learned. Parents usually described as angry and unconcerned about their children became their active advocates. Moreover, many of the parents became active in helping other parents to recognize their importance to their kids' learning as manifested by their attendance in school and learning to work with their own and other children.

If positive mental health can be measured by positive and active involvement to change their life situations, these parents qualified. They became active not only in the community council but on behalf of their adolescents with the police and juvenile authorities, and more and more became a nucleus for parent involvement in other community activities which affected their children's and their own lives.

In retrospect it is clear that these parents' involvement in the school and in enhancing their own children's learning paid off with an enhanced sense of self-worth and competence of children and parents.

Many of these children became the first volunteer tutors of younger children when they entered junior high school. It seemed to us that having learned the benefits of learning, their altered attitudes toward feeling effective as young people led them to be eager to assist their classmates.

Some implications of the program

From these experimental efforts we can project the kind of program which might be helpful to primary school children who presently are doomed to failure in school and whose self-images as failures are difficult to alter later in their lives. While we did not evaluate the mental health of parents involved in these programs, it was clear from teachers' and observers' reports that the parents of low-achieving children also looked upon themselves as inadequate parents. Our work indicated that just as the lowest-achieving children make the greatest academic gains, so their parents' attitudes toward themselves and their children show the most marked alterations. Subjectively these parents were more pleased and proud of their children and could talk with teachers about their children more easily.

A MODEL ELEMENTARY SCHOOL PROGRAM. A school program that attempts to make full use of parent help to increase the school achievement of children would be based on the employment of

a teacher with expertise in the teaching of reading or other specific skills. That teacher's job would be to work with parents who
come into the school building for the express purpose of helping
their child learn. The teacher could work with parents singly or
in groups. The teacher would demonstrate to parents methods
of helping children learn to read which are appropriate for their
age or developmental level and would provide learning materials
for the parents' use. She would serve as a liaison with the child's
teacher and help identify areas where a child might need special
help. The teacher would then provide the parent with methods
and materials appropriate to the child's learning task and demonstrate their use, so the parent would know some ways of providing the help needed. The progress of the child could be
carefully monitored by both parent and teacher so that alternate
methods of learning might be used if those provided had not
been successful. The classroom teacher in this way, simply by
identifying the child who needs special help along with providing an assessment of the child's present level, could secure the
individualized help that child needed. The parent would be
used to provide the individual help. The teacher of parents
would serve as the intermediary in order that the classroom
teacher not be overburdened by working with parents while
managing a total classroom.

The nonprofessional staff members would work as assistants
to the teacher of parents and would make home visits to those
parents who did not come to school. These assistants would take
learning materials and would demonstrate their use to the parent. These materials would be designed by the parents' teacher
for a particular child needing to learn a particular task, as prescribed by the classroom teacher. The materials to be used with
the child would be left with the parents with instructions and
encouragement for their use. The assistants would make regular
follow-up visits.

An extension of this program would offer child care services to
enable parents of very young children to come to school. For
parents needing transportation in order to avail themselves of
this program, a volunteer program which involves other parents
in the school can be effective, particularly when parents meet in
groups.

Studies make clear that students who learn and are competent are obviously in better mental health than their fellows who fail in school and do not learn the basic skills necessary for employment in a technical society. Similarly we can, with some confidence, hypothesize that parents concerned with their children's learning and who have participated in helping their child learn have better mental health because their concern has actively enhanced their child's learning and thus, in our experience, enhanced the parent's sense of adequacy and worth as a parent. Such parental participation also reduces at least one aspect of conflict with the child, that of being successful in school.

Some effects of parental participation in the child's learning

In the process of parents playing learning games with their children several phenomena were observed.

First, the game-playing for a specified 15 minutes a day provided a vehicle for regular interaction in which the parents carried out a specific task which they had already learned with the child.

Second, in the process of the demonstration of the games parents were encouraged to practice how to overtly express their encouragement and approval to the child. Thus, often a new relationship evolved in which the parent was encouraging and approving of the child's success.

Third, most of the parents of the low achievers did not believe their children could learn. As they worked with their children using games to teach them they usually discovered, to their delight, that their children could learn and fairly rapidly. Many of these mothers for the first time became willing to go to school to discuss their child's progress. They also wanted to know how they could help their child. For these lower-class mothers, mostly Black, the fact that they could really help their nonlearning children to learn resulted in continued demand for materials to continue the work with their children beyond the duration of the program. The experience that their children could learn with their help altered most of the mother-child relationships markedly. The investigators found the mothers recounting other successes of the very children with whom they had previously had only a disappointed and angry involvement.

It was clear in each instance that the mothers were more interested, more giving, and proud of their children and clearly proud of themselves for having helped their youngsters to learn. As one mother put it, "I thought Georgia (a five-year-old) was a dummy and couldn't learn, but she's smart. She learns these games great and we have more fun playing them together. I've never seen her laugh and smile so much like when we do these games." These mothers and their children not only felt differently about themselves, but they had learned how to enhance their relationship so that they were more playful and warmer. Teachers commented that these poor learners were picking up and were among the most eager and responsive participants in the class.

Observers in the experiment and in school commented on the attitudinal and behavioral differences of these children and their mothers. Both children and parents showed enhanced capacity to cope, at least with school and, by anecdote, with other situations.

Conclusion

It is reasonable to expect that many parents, if offered assistance by the schools, would help in areas where they are needed. Parents are the primary teachers of their children up to the time their children enter school. Parent effectiveness may be enhanced through training programs for parents sponsored by school personnel who gain expertise in working with parents and teaching specific subjects to parents for them to use with children who need their help. The use of parent help may be an important financial consideration, perhaps the most important that may be used to reverse the trend toward nonlearning in the schools.

A variety of studies nationally have indicated success in involving parents in programs in such a way as to benefit academic achievement of their children. Gordon and Sally's work with infants in Florida,[6] Schaefer's work with 15-month- to three-year-old children in New York,[12,13,14] Weikert and Lambie's work,[16] and that of Hess and Shipman,[7] Karnes,[8] Levenstein,[9] and many others has indicated that work with parents leads to gains in achievement of children. In the states of California and Washington, several programs indicate that parent involvement programs may be particularly effective.[1,2,3]

Teachers currently at the end of their ropes in essentially non-rewarding jobs, just hanging on and not being productive as teachers, will initially be threatened by parents' presence in the classroom and involvement with children's learning. As they experience parents as allies in relevant learning they will feel rewarded because they can once again teach and feel competent and meaningful as human beings.

In the same way, parental efforts to help their children learn enhance the parent's and child's feelings of being effective and competent human beings, a critical attribute of positive mental health.

Parent involvement on a nationwide basis, as participant advocates in their child's learning, can improve the achievements of the child and the mental health of children, parents, and teachers.

REFERENCES

1. BERLIN, I. N. Professionals' participation in community activities: Is it part of the job? *American Journal of Orthopsychiatry*, 1971, *41*:3, 494–500.
2. BERLIN, I. N. The school's role in a participatory democracy. *American Journal of Orthopsychiatry*, 1972, *42*:3, 499–507.
3. BERLIN, R. The effect of playing educational games with parents on concept development of kindergarten children. Unpublished doctoral dissertation, University of Washington, 1971.
4. BOEHM, A. E. *Boehm Test of Basic Concepts*. New York: The Psychological Corporation, 1969.
5. CLEGG, B. E. The effectiveness of learning games used by economically disadvantaged parents to increase the reading achievement of their children. Unpublished doctoral dissertation, University of Washington, 1971.
6. GORDON, I. J., & SALLY, J. R. *Intellectual Stimulation for Infants and Toddlers*. University of Florida, Institute for Development of Human Resources, 1967.
7. HESS, R. D., & SHIPMAN, V. C. Early experience and the socialization of cognitive modes in children. *Child Development*, 1965, *36*, 869–886.

8. KARNES, M. An approach for working with mothers of disadvantaged pre-school children. *Merrill-Palmer Quarterly*, 1968, *14*, 173–184.
9. LEVENSTEIN, P. *Individual Narration among Preschoolers in a Cognitive Intervention Program in Low Income Families.* Freeport, New York: Council for Exceptional Children, 1969.
10. LONG, B. E. Behavioral science for elementary-school pupils. *Elementary School Journal*, 1970, 70:5, 253–260.
11. MOSHER, R. L., & SPRINTHALL, N. A. Psychological education in secondary schools: A program to promote individual and human development. *American Psychologist*, 1970, *25*, 911–924.
12. SCHAEFER, E. A home tutoring program. In children under three— Finding ways to stimulate and develop. *Children*, 1969, *16*, 49–61.
13. SCHAEFER, E. S., & BELL, R. Q. Development of a parental attitude research instrument. *Child Development*, 1958, *29*, 339–361.
14. SCHAEFER, E. S., & AARONSON, M. Infant education research project. Implementation and implications for a home tutoring program. In R. Parker (Ed.), *Conceptualization of Preschool Curriculum.* (In Press) 1973.
15. STRINGER, L. A., & TAYLOR, R. M. *Project Summary: Mothers as Colleagues in School Mental Health Work.* Final Report, NIMH Grant MH-14793, 1970. 8 pp.
16. WEIKERT, D., & LAMBIE, D. Preschool intervention through a home teaching program. In J. Hellmuth (Ed.), *Disadvantaged Child.* Vol. 2. New York: Brunner/Mazel, 1968. Pp. 435–500.

Man ultimately decides for himself! And in the end,
education must be education toward the ability
to decide.

VIKTOR FRANKL

The sources of educational science are any portions
of ascertained knowledge that enter into the heart,
head and hands of educators, and which, by
entering in, render the performance of the
educational function more enlightened, more
humane, more truly educational than it was before.

JOHN DEWEY

_____ **12**

The Schools and the
Mental Health of Children
and Adolescents

WILLIAM C. MORSE, PH.D.

The crisis in child mental health makes it most evident that
schools are only one of the many agencies involved in child mental health. However, the truth is, planned and unplanned, the
school does have a profound impact on the mental health of children and youth. And, in spite of the troubled children who confront us at every turn, there are still citizens, educators, and
professionals who would not include mental health in the school's
concerns.

School for all: New role in mental health

As we enter the mid-'70s, more and more is being asked of
schools. The schools have inherited a new and profound role in

This chapter has been prepared with the assistance of Beatrice Gustafson.

mental health. As states pass mandatory legislation, the demand is for schooling from age 0 to 25, including *all* children, disturbed, retarded, handicapped. The specific preventive mental health programs are one matter, but here is added the expectation of public school programs for *very* disturbed, autistic children. The "zero reject" policy, meaning no exclusions from school, also indicates a whole new clientele. Parents are demanding, by pressure through court cases, that schools attend to the welfare of all children.

It is one thing to indicate that schools have found themselves with a critical responsibility for providing mental health assistance. Do they have the potential for influence? Nearly all American children and youth between the ages of 5 and 17 spend from 25 to 40 percent of their waking time in school. Usually these school-age youngsters spend more time in the classroom than with their families. Although school is not solely responsible for the child's mental health, it is time to realize the great impact it has on the child's attitudes about himself and the world around him.

School's critical role at a critical time

School not only occupies a central position in the life of a child, but the educational enterprise has become a highly visible and costly "industry" impacting on a vast segment of our population in various ways at every moment. No enterprise touches so many lives so deeply. Youngsters are students; parents are ex-officio members; citizens pay supporting taxes; large numbers of adults are employed directly or in supportive roles; employers hire the product; and a significant number of others are engaged in contests of governance and control. Any institution which costs billions a year is a concern of all the people. What other institution is as potent in the social matrix?

Schools and education have been at the core of our swiftly changing society. For the most part, they have worked reasonably well in the transition from a frontier and rural society to a society primarily urban, highly complex, and based increasingly on new technological and scientific development. Indeed, it may be said that education, in part, has made possible that change. However, it is apparent that schools have not only served as a means for societal development, but that they are seen as the vehicle of social change and have become a sensitive index of fluctuations. Confusion comes easy at a time of social upheaval. The essential ambivalence about education today has an obvious genesis—schools at one and the same time are expected to mirror the present and draw a working sketch of the future.

Special demands are made of schools in areas of severe deprivation, whether Detroit or Appalachia. It is said there are still schools meeting in buildings of Civil War vintage. Like old wine in new bottles, building new schools is not enough if the content remains the same. The more desperate the problems of the community, the more meaningful should be the educational program. This is not to say that, interlinked as we are, the plight of one area is not the concern of others. There is clearly no suburbia except in relationship to cities. No institution can be tolerated in times of acute stress unless there is a direct relationship to confronting the problems of daily life.

New goals: New priorities

The role of the school is further confounded at present because the society which it reflects is experiencing a drastic reworking of goals and priorities. In the past, the universally accepted credo was that we were doing fine if the Gross National Product Index (GNP) was up—the more the better. The goal of increased production of goods and services was expected to bring every citizen, including the child citizen, into the promised land with a reasonable standard of living. On the average, we have made astonishing material gains of world renown. Yet, for significant segments of the population, we have not provided the minimal subsistence for life. When this happens, children are hardest hit.

Although we have not yet solved the GNP goal problem, a realignment is taking place. This is the adoption of the Quality of Life Index (QLI). This new set of priorities is sometimes pictured as in conflict with the GNP. It would be more accurate to say it is additive or complementary, for the vast majority of citizens are not about to follow the few who have given up the struggle for material things. Americans want material things but, increasingly, they want an equal attention to quality of life.

Thus, QLI is the matter of satisfaction with one's life condition. This focuses on the core of mental health: Is one's life satisfying, enjoyable, pleasant, meaningful, and worthwhile? Does it result in a feeling of well-being and self-esteem? At the low end, is life worth living? At the high end, is there a reasonable quota of satisfaction in living? Of course these are not new goals, but this articulation and prominence in present thinking represent a reordering of values. Attention to goodness of life often brings conflict and contention in a society which has concentrated on the GNP with great enthusiasm.

If there is no enjoyment in life, the "things index" becomes meaningless, which is not the same as saying that things are not important. Campbell [9] has been developing social survey methodology to assess the satisfaction with life, which is, of course, mental health. No social institution can escape the implications of this social evolution. Industry experiments with ways to get pride back into making things. Everywhere people have begun to question the affluent society as an adequate state. In reality, this is not a new concept, this right of all people to a satisfying and meaningful existence. The revolutionary aspect is in expecting the articulation to be matched with action. The shock of activation of these "accepted" values constitutes the current struggle.

Always, when a societal goal changes, the counterpart in the schools becomes obvious. Schools have had their GNP emphasis. Americans have traditionally seen education as a way to get ahead, to improve one's access to material goods. To do this, one learned to read and to solve problems in order to get a better job. Preoccupation with academic achievement, skills, and knowledge exists. Basic to this was learning to read, to understand, and to manipulate symbols. It would be false to say that these GNP-type objectives are not important or are not the responsibility of schools. Ample evidence exists identifying skills and knowledge as the criteria of success of a school program. State achievement testing programs report the school with the best scores. Commercial contracts are being let to guarantee achievement. Accountability, the learning disability movement, and efforts to make center-city pupils competitive are other examples of the intense concern the American public has with this aspect of the school function. However, as Coleman [12] and others point out, the school is no longer the single major source of skill and knowledge. With the expanding influence of the mass media, the role of the school has changed from the window to the world to the place where responsibilities affecting the welfare of others could be learned. Schools, however, still operate as if the child learned most of what he knows in the confines of the classroom.

NEW SOCIETAL GOALS AND NEW SCHOOL ROLES. Reflecting society's newly emerging goals and accepting the diminished importance of the school as the sole purveyor of knowledge, new priorities emerge for the school. To paraphrase Coleman, the goal of the school is to help make responsible, productive human beings who can lead in a task or follow responsibly and who can live with the consequences of their actions. This provides a positive antidote to the malaise which surrounds us, individual good over the commonwealth, fear of change, "cop-outs" by drugs and disillusion, and frantic cult searches with more exhibitionism than long-term values. The question becomes whether we can capitalize on this surge of hope which shows through in the desperate efforts to make overnight a society in which the quality of life is indeed better. And, can a change in the schools have an impact on the society? Can the schools really meet this challenge?

EDUCATION AND PERSONAL GROWTH: CHANGING VALUES. The proposal is not to jettison skills and knowledge as a vital school goal. However, it is not readily possible to separate either the content or the process of a young person's learning experience in school from his total growth as a person. All aspects of a child's development are crucial to a child's well-being. Each area of development interacts with others; a person functions as a whole. Schools need to reflect this balance in their educational goals. Educational institutions need to balance concern for achievement in knowledge and skills with a concern for the total development of the child. The close interrelationships of the intellectual, social, emotional, and physical development of young people and how these influence learning need to be taught in teacher education and practiced in schools. All too frequently, schools and teachers function as if the myth of the "disembodied intellect" were real.[40] It is widely believed that academic learning can be supplied in schools without regard for the feelings, actions, motivations, or social relationships of the learner. Whether or not the school does teach the "whole child," *the whole child, in fact, does come to school.*

The social change we are experiencing signifies for schools the acceptance of the parallel to the QLI as the schools' obligation. This is not the old mental health concept of the absence of illness, nor is it the romantic notion of some homogenized state of near nirvana. Without illusions, it is the quest for a vigorous, socially responsible, and personally satisfying life. As the country moves toward a more open and conscious concern with the affective aspects of life, matters of feelings, attitudes, and values take equal place with cognitive ones. It is not that schools have done nothing about such matters, it is, as Jersild [21] said some time ago, that "they do it so haphazardly and with so little perspective and often negative consequences." This is no longer enough when the quality of life becomes part of the national goal. The keystone of this chapter can be quite simply stated: The pupil has a right to a school which is humane in its nature and actively cultivates humaneness. Planned affective learning has equality with planned cognitive learning.

Throughout American educational history, however, considerable debate has taken place, not only about how schools can promote the development of young people, but about what the limits of their responsibilities are. As Rhodes [38] points out, we are, by national consensus, wary of organizing and regulating the social and personal aspects of learning. The result has been the lack of a clear basis for the schools to determine the extent of their responsibilities. Characteristically, lacking community consensus, the schools have responded on an erratic basis to the prominent ideas and concerns of the times. Worse, there has been a tendency to give lip service to principles which are not practiced. Although education can help young people achieve a satisfying life, it is not an opiate for all human problems. Popular belief in education as a potential cure-all for social ailments tends to place too much responsibility on the school and make it far too open to criticism for failing to accomplish things it was never designed to accomplish. For instance, education cannot, by itself, guarantee good mental health. However, rich educational experiences are one of the basic factors necessary for helping youngsters develop their maximum human potential and attain a satisfying life. As Silberman [42] has put it, schools have not really changed much because they have not faced up to the matter of goals, and goals are the implementation of values.

School mental health revisited

As the schools accept the responsibility and opportunity to improve the quality of life, the new focus of school mental health efforts becomes clear. It is not simply the absence of ill health, though the three percent of children with long-term and severe difficulties represent the extreme failure of society to safeguard their quality of life. It is not even only the concern for supportive assistance to the 10 to 12 percent who are floundering, though that, too, represents a deep concern. School mental health starts with concern for the well-being of the total pupil population.

All aspects of school life, particularly relationships of teachers and students and students with each other and the atmosphere, the culture, the climate and ethos of the school, in which these encounters occur, have potential for promoting positive human development. Schools can influence the growth of a person's capacity for establishing satisfying human relationships, for facing reality and coping with it, for experiencing joy in work and play, for using imagination and inventiveness for creative production, and for developing a personal identity. Or, schools can promote defeat, disillusionment, and despair which can be consolidated into patterns of cynicism, distrust, and alienation from the wider social community. The primary concern, therefore, is for the educational institution to support the total development of young people by providing the climate, content, and processes of learning compatible with those images of optimal human functioning, which we call basic principles of mental health. This is contemporary school mental health.

FEELINGS: A SUBJECT FOR EDUCATION. It is clear that the development of a new focus will require a great deal of work before the format is clear. While procedures are beginning to appear in the literature, the approach to total school mental health has a long way to go. Volumes exist on the research and methodology of teaching reading and other cognitive skills, yet so little on fostering adequate affect and feelings. The particular problems which underlie this lack of material, when it comes to helping children with feeling states, must be understood by those planning the next decade in school mental health. Otherwise, we run the risk of trying to imitate the idiosyncratic programs produced by charismatic leadership without the grounding to see the total. First, as Krathwohl [28] points out in his affective taxonomy, the affective terms are themselves elusive. While some experts may debate the definition of what reading really is, in a pragmatic sense teachers go about the business of teaching their pupils how to read. Not so with feelings. Kirsner [25] has worked to put a behavioral context on such terms as "awareness," but it goes hard. When it is a matter of self-esteem or a value, there is both the affective state and the substance to get clear. We are lost in the confusion of terms. As a practical actual example, say a school sets up a program to enhance empathic feelings of one youngster for another. But, in this day of accountability, how does one evaluate the result, given the state of psychological technology?

The result of the vague terminology is that schools, like other institutions, talk in motherhood-type generalities. Character education and citizenship training have always been problems for schools; retreat to structured courses or lectures about citizenship are often substituted for experiences which may produce real character change. The difficulties we are confronted with here are partly born of the fact that processes like "identification" and "modeling" are hardly understood. Also, the influence patterns for affectively growing children are varied and complex, involving parents, peers, and the internal conceptual system. The potential for change is in the configuration of the pupil's total life space, a most difficult system to bring into alignment. School mental health must address itself to this.

FEELINGS, VALUES, AND CURRICULA. As terminology is clarified so that a school can get down to actual planning, we face the second major problem: Is there really agreement on the goals for affective efforts? The developmental process for noncognitive capacities is much less clearly understood than those for the

cognitive ones. In a multiple value society, any direct effort to
deal with feelings and attitudes stirs up divergence, and what
school desires more than a reluctant quota of dissension? Yet it
is quite clear that most people subscribe to certain affective
states as desirable. The enhancement of personal self-esteem is
seen as a valid function for schools. Parents want happy children, self-directed children, and involved children. But the possibility of any change in school practice to enhance such goals
produces a great deal of fear on the part of many people. There
are those who see concern about attitudes as an invasion (rather
than a supplement and support) of the family and church. Because of the lack of understanding of how children and youth
develop values, books are banned lest they contaminate, flags
are waved, hair is cut, and youngsters are excluded, all in the
name of helping them or protecting their gullible peers.[37]

Perhaps the basic reason we are in such a quandary in the affective area is that we have not developed techniques for discussion, exchange of opinions, and the settling process which
gives reasonable consent to a working set of propositions. To
begin with, it is necessary to find techniques to use in dealing
with value divergence and even conflict. True, the school is but
one of the educative forces in the affective domain, but it is the
one broad universal social institution, a community agency with
responsibility. Schools cannot move ahead in this area without
parent involvement.

AFFECTIVE TEACHING IMPROVES COGNITIVE LEARNING. A third
problem is the degree of support for a major school mental health
effort. The test of seriousness for any school contemplating a
mental health program has first to do with the time it is willing
to commit to this aspect of school. It is safe to say that at least
half the school's energy and resources will need to be invested
in thoughtful, positive participation in the affective area. Most
schools are reluctant to become involved except when there is a
major outcropping of social failure, a child, adolescent, or whole
group whose behavior cannot be ignored; yet haphazard, ill-
designed, unintentional participation in affective life takes place
all the time in schools. Pupils succeed or fail, they are involved
or bored, they exercise choice or are forced, they torment or sup-

port each other, they trust or they fear. Every day, in classrooms all over the country, there is affective learning. It can be shocking to bring it to light. This emphasizes the fourth problem, in the school itself (let alone the country): To mount an effective mental health program means the reexamination of the total school program with the possibility of many changes and the involvement of many persons.

MENTAL HEALTH: NOT ONLY A PROFESSIONAL CONCERN. This leads us to the fifth problem. Mental health has been the exclusive domain of the specialized professionals, the psychiatric, social work, and psychological trinity. One has to recognize that this area of professional work, like all others today, is undergoing the shock of reexamination. As Hersch [18] has pointed out, the certainty has gone. While formerly a clear image of therapy existed, now there is no agreement on who is the patient, individuals or society. Who helps, professionals or recovered victims? How is help provided, through psychotherapy or primal scream? We are not even certain about improvement. The advantage of this open system is not without its difficulties for school mental health. Schools have long sought to broaden the school mental health complex and free it from the overattachment to the clinical aspects. The danger is that we forget the spectrum of mental health work—from enhancement of the normal child to work with the autistic child. The procedures along this spectrum differ. It is not clinical or quasi-professional. The schools cannot rest with classical therapeutic concepts alone. Those mental health professionals who have become immersed in the schools and applied their expertise to the problems of the school milieu as co-workers will provide the help needed. It is a far cry from the old clinical view, however. We will return to this in a subsequent section.

Classroom teachers and school mental health personnel alike have sensed that we can never win if we continue as at present. We must be concerned. But the activation of concern is not simple, not only because of the lack of appropriate skills by school personnel, but because of the difficulty of resolving value problems as previously indicated. There are also instances of efforts which abort because of poor preparation or the esoteric nature

of the procedure chosen. But, fortunately, more and more serious efforts toward an approach in depth to affective concerns in
school are being made.

SCHOOLS AS THE RESOLUTION POINT OF MANY PRESSURES: CHIL-
DREN'S RIGHTS THROUGH MANY EYES. As we examine the role of
mental health influence in public schools, we immediately become involved in the new complications of this particular social
agency in our changing times. Here we have to deal with the
school as an advocate for children, and also child advocates
pressuring schools. Since the school is a public agency, it is the
meeting point of many sets of rights and obligations. We think
first of pupils and their rights, but it must not be forgotten that
this is only one set; teachers have rights too, as do parents and
the community. Unionization in one form or another is designed
to protect the rights of teachers. Parents have learned how to
assert themselves, sometimes to the point of the right to control.
The community at large tries to use political muscle through
control by boards of education. Of course, everyone claims to be
speaking for the welfare and rights of children as seen through
their eyes. And where are the opportunities, obligations, and
responsibilities which are the other face of rights? As we focus
on the rights of children and youth in the educational enterprise,
we should not forget that the school, as a societal agency, is the
fusing point of a whole complex of forces. It can never be responsive to only one of the groups, whether it be the students,
teachers, parents, or a special interest faction. There is no stability, but an ebb and flow as various changes take place in
society.

Parenthetically, it is well to remember that the school is vexed
not only with a confluence of rights and obligations and a variance of values; there is an even more severe problem. The science of psychology has not been convincing either in revealing
the nature of human nature or in the process of guiding the
learning-maturing evolution of that nature.[10] There are those
who hold that children are intrinsically antimoral and become
"humanized" only by punishment and force, and there are those
who see only a positive nature always pushing through with inevitable higher mental codes. The view of man and his development which underlies the direction taken in this chapter has

been stated in distilled form by Valett.[44] Part credo and part substantiated by psychological data, it avoids both the negative and the romantic polarization:

A few of the principles are as follows:

Psychological wholeness (or "happiness") is essentially a self-transcendent state of rational altruism.

The process of becoming individuated or self-actualized requires meaningful involvement, personal commitment, and work.

Self-actualization can only be achieved when basic needs, such as food and love, are gratified.

The life instincts or drives for actualization, creativity, etc., can best be furthered under organizational and political systems of social democracy.

Self-determination, ego control and instinctual sublimation are essential for psychosocial integration and must be learned by the individual.

The above principles can and have become guidelines for instructional purposes within a few schools and community educational organizations. They can serve as the basis for program development whereby psychologists and other specialists design total systems so the child will learn to grow and develop toward psychological wholeness.

Beyond such generalizations are the myriad of psychological studies which focus on affective and value matters. Piaget,[35] Kohlberg,[26] and Berkowitz[1] have given serious consideration to research on moral development. Skinner[43] takes on the whole social order. Harlow[17] does a masterful job on learning to love, describing five phases of the affectional system as well as fear and anger and the social process. While the psychological pundits do not speak with a single voice, what they discuss is not at all academic. What a teacher believes about human nature and the learning process becomes the guideline for designing the school. Or, to reverse the order, the way we react to growing children reveals our assumptions about human nature. A free school cannot provide a comfortable format for those who question the innate goodness of human nature.

THE SCHOOL AS A HUMANIZING FORCE IN CHILDREN'S LIVES. The new concept of school mental health has added ecological or community mental health to the clinical heritage which for a long time dominated the orientation. As we shall see, the school has the need of classical mental health work. Its major invest-ment must be in the type of a total school milieu which will con-tain the essence of mental health. It is not far off the mark to say that mental health provisions are everywhere, in relationships, tasks, evaluation, and morale factors, for example. School mental health is not something added to education; it is in the form of the total educational experience. This brings us to a considera-tion of the school as a humanizing force for children and youth.

CAN OUR SCHOOLS CHANGE? Schools have, in fact, been decried as evil, dehumanizing agencies. There is no doubt that some schools are dehumanizing and certain conditions in many schools operate to such an unfortunate end. However, the major prob-lem is that what some citizens and teachers consider humaniza-tion is indeed not at all so to others. Both goals and means differ. Public compliance is evidence for some that matters are going well, while student rebellion satisfies others. Contrary to certain assumptions now popular, schools do make an impact. As some have demonstrated, schools can and do make a difference in the affective sphere. For example, the "progressive" school en-hanced inner directedness. When it comes to making changes, one of the major obstacles is the ever-present willingness cf edu-cators to put form above substance, to create a new slogan each year without engaging in the very hard work required for the creative evolution of really innovative processes. Modules, free schools, open classrooms, family groupings, accountability, con-tract learning, local control—the list is endless. It is easier to write up new verbal statements than to alter a complex social structure like the schools. Most of the new concepts are enablers for change under given conditions. But often these same en-ablers become empty vessels when borrowed by others who have not undergone the original insight generated by the social proc-ess underlying the development. The career critics of education, flagellating obeisant educators, have exploited this condition while true advocates, working in the midst of the actual con-fusion, have been chewed up by those who only write and do not have to put their effort where their mouth is.

TEACHER AS MODEL. Kozol [27] covers this as only those few can who face their own development. He asks for some direct attacks on slogans such as, "The real teacher is the one who best succeeds at the pretense he knows nothing." Kozol sees a teacher's greatest impact through what he is, and even what he wishes to do. The candor of this position exemplifies the issue. Children need to have interaction with adults who can help them find their way. The subtle quality of the necessary interaction between the child and the adult has been presented by Dennison, [15] who exposes the whole authority problem for the charade it is. The useful adult embodies functional maturity rather than role authority. For the vast majority of children, this creates the bridge of trust. Only by self-awareness as a balancer can the adult be protected from the seductive illusion of the power of authority or the abdication of the adult as role model.

Student's bill of rights

A Bill of Rights for school pupils can serve to elucidate propositions which will orient the curriculum, the administrative practices, and the social design of educational processes.

THE PROCESS, NOT THE FORM, COUNTS. *The first right of the child is to a school which is process conscious.* The *way* things are done is equal in importance to *what* is done. Few would question that there are things children and adolescents need to learn, which require limits to their freedom to act on the impulse of the moment. While there are those who advocate ultimate sexual and political discretion to junior high youngsters, such a position is obviously not an acceptable guideline for our country. The solution is not to be found via *Lord of the Flies.* There is always a constituted authority and always an ebb and flow of contention against it by children and youth as they grow up. Cottle [14] puts it clearly when he indicates that abdication of adult authority is not a solution. The solution lies in a new mode of working with pupils, especially adolescent pupils. To meet mental health expectations, the new school requires a process to replace old style arbitrary authoritarianism which robbed the growing child of both the need and the right to be self-responsible. We cannot make decisions for pupils, but we must participate with them in the decision-making procedure. There is no longer the question of youngsters being exposed to divergent values. Mass media present every possible variant as acceptable.

The problem with pupils today is twofold: first, to consciously recognize the overt and covert values which are being portrayed; second, to study the significance and implications. Thus, the school will need to relate beliefs to relevant philosophical and psychological guidelines. This is the connecting phase in relating what children are experiencing to basic concepts. Next is the phase that involves sorting out which of these divergent views best fit the tenets of the individual in a society striving to be democratic. The time of a controlled monolithic society is past. Variance will exist, but variance will be within the parameter of the basic tenets of a democratic society. While there are always those times when the risk to a student by impulsive behavior is so great that a pupil's freedom may be curtailed, these should not constitute the substance of school life, especially if we are willing to forgo adult-established deadlines for certain performances. There will need to be a wide variety of ways to help children if the right to a process-oriented approach is met.

STUDENT AS PARTICIPANT. *Pupils have a right to a school which cultivates their sense of identity, their worth, and their independence by taking their needs, attitudes, and ideas seriously.* What they think, feel, and wish is legitimate material for interchange with adults. When there are significant decision points regarding behavior, the pupils' perception of the situation is of primary importance. Perspective, possible implication of given options, alternatives not envisioned, the implication of given behavior on others—these are part of the contribution of adults in schooling. The adults in the environment must be knowledgeable about children and how they grow, must have teaching skills suited to these new areas, and methods to humanize the school, and they must, above all, be skilled mentors in the process of effective and satisfying living. Essentially, the teachers constitute models for identification. This modeling cannot be of a pseudo-adolescent mod style (as a teacher who advertises himself as a two-cycle freak!) or of a superficial life-style. The essence of the modeling is of the human mode, the embodiment of hope, living self-satisfying lives, demonstrating the substance which helps them to cope openly with minor and major confrontations of the times. Are they viable models? If they are not happy, zestful, and purposeful, how can they expect to be images for the human qualities needed in the next generation? At the same time, their realization of the state of constant flux and change keeps open a freedom gap, so that youngsters can mold variant patterns around the essential credo. The power of the adult lies not in verbal talk, but living exposition of values which produce a useful and satisfying existence. The demonstrations of modeling take place in the myriad of daily transactions between adults and pupils in the school milieu.

A developmental teaching-learning model. Developmental psychology provides guidelines to help prevent over- or under-loading the youngster's capacity for understanding, reasoning, and decision-making. Otherwise, on the one extreme, we ask sixth-graders to decide now what job they want to prepare for or what college they choose or, on the other extreme, we deny them the freedom to state their current goals and work through changes step by step. Youngsters must have the right to be responsible for their lives. This balance between asking neither too much nor too little is indeed the vortex of professional skill of child upbringers, whether it be parents or teachers.

Growth occurs with decision-making. The "rights" process of decision-making includes the participation of those who will be influenced by the outcome of the decision. In little things, in larger things, and in big things, students participate. Humaneness means listening, trusting, asking questions, and knowing how pupils feel and what they think. The great "cop-out" of mental health personnel, that is, school counselors, psychologists, and social workers, is to exploit immaturity under the guise of giving assistance. Here the matter is a diagnostic one of deep significance. We must distinguish between those children who, at a given time, because of personal limitations—biological and cultural—need significant protection and those who must not be protected from a graduated exposure to the reality of responsibility for their lives. It is interesting how even preadolescents have sometimes asked mental health workers not for protection from what appears to the adult to be a devastating life situation, but for support to cope with the situation.

We tutor pupils with diagnostic learning handicaps in a specialized way because their problems require the additional sophisticated assistance coming from a recognition of their limiting conditions. On the other hand, if we tutorially force-feed young-sters who have capability but an attitudinal malaise and never get to why, they will only go through the pretense of "learning" when confronted by a tutor; we are likely to stand in the way of their real growth. Old-style diagnosis of the status condition and surmises about the personal history which generated the con-dition are inadequate for school mental health. What is required now from diagnostic specialists is guidance in designing the sup-portive program in such a way as to maximize the child's poten-tials. For an autistic preschooler, the useful reality will be quite a different design than for an omnipotent, elective mute child. The adolescent with identification deficit will not learn what is needed from the same pieces of reality as the oversocialized, in-hibited youngster. School mental health programs will always be vexed in finding the necessary elements to build restorative en-vironments for the more complicated aberrations. The elements come not only from classical approaches or from consultations, but by designing the whole school milieu, school rules, and class-room operation to meet certain criteria. Decisions may not al-ways be palatable or acceptable to everyone, but they are arrived at by a deep sounding of all involved. A responsive en-vironment, concerned with attitudes, values, and feelings, recognizes that the cutting edge of growth is at the point of decision-making. This is the right to responsibility for self-gov-ernance in keeping with the pupil's individual level of develop-ment.

LEARNING, COMPETENCE, AND SELF-ESTEEM. *The student has the right to a school experience which serves to enhance one's self-esteem.* Self-concept is the nature of the person, the content of the self. Self-esteem is the result of an evaluative process, the judgment of the worth or value of the substance of the self. The nurturing of self-esteem is elusive, yet it lies at the core of the individual's mental health. Sometimes, it becomes a clinical mat-ter to discover the manner in which a pupil finds self-suste-nance. One pupil may feel enhanced by overcoming the same level of adversity which overwhelms the next. We know that more than a minimum percentage of failure will not be helpful to the self-esteem of most students. In fact, students soon reject that which diminishes their esteem if they possibly can. Pupils, therefore, must feel they are progressing and that their achievements are valued by both peers and adults. So much of the educational process takes its cue from the way the pupils develop their esteem. Some children will need little external reinforcement, feeling strong when they, in their own view, have done well. Others require considerable external support for their accomplishments before feeling good about themselves. Since the erosion of self-regard is such a catastrophic phenomenon, bringing on depression and excessive defensiveness, youngsters will seek out reinforcing subsystems which enable them to feel good about themselves. As Coleman [11] has shown, adolescents quickly band together with those who will induce their own good self-feelings. The peer group may be establishment or delinquent. What makes a particular school task relevant is not its arbitrary up-to-date characteristics. Relevance is a psychological phenomenon, feeding back high self-esteem.

The school's obligation is to bring a reflective self-awareness as the student goes through the grades. It is not enough to have self-esteem, for it must be that which is understood by the youngster and is related to his world. The products of the person, be they completed arithmetic problems, a drawing, a broad jump, or a bit of social service, must be recognized by the child's VIP's, adults and peers in the school environment, if self-esteem is to be enhanced.

SENSITIVE TEACHERS: AN EDUCATIONAL MUST. *The right to interact and relate to sensitive, trained adults, teachers who have gone this way before, is essential for children.* Each one of us must find anew on our own, in our own way, much about the accomplishments of mankind. Yet, through symbolic representation, much time can be saved.

Knowledge, apart from the significance to the knower, is not sufficient. The mysteries of life are exciting to youngsters if they are part of living with adults who care, who lead, who point out ways but give the child the leeway to move at his or her own pace. Teachers who know developmental psychology and the nature of individual differences can be facilitators. *The humanization of knowledge is the addition of meaning and feelings to the facts.* Those who have the role of assisters are sympathetic and knowledgeable concerning the riddle of growth and its

cycles as well as the human quest for understanding. They become adept at arranging the conditions which bring the younger
person in touch with the broadening experience. Their profound
respect for living things and mankind's struggles becomes the
touchstone. The pupil has the right to persons who are experts,
both in child upbringing and the world around them in their
curriculum areas. While many of those who teach will continue
to be professionals, there will be many others from the community who take various roles. Since the basic right is for a synthesis
of life in a meaningful way, the interaction of school and family
becomes essential rather than adjunct.

The child and youth assisters have a most difficult complex to
master. In an oversimplification, three positions can be stereo-
typed for making the point: (1) We are beset with human
nature worshippers—Rousseauites who trust blindly and who
expect the child spontaneously to master life. (2) On the other
extreme are the somewhat paranoid, who are freedom misers
and psychological fascists and trust only their capacity to force
and condition children into their way of behaving and perhaps
thinking. (3) The third system evolves from developmental
psychology and emphasizes individuality of children and understanding of growth process without being blind to the consequence of particular experiences in the progressive building of a
life-style. As Piaget,[35] Bruner,[8] Cottle,[14] and Rogers[39] have
pointed out, the social being is a consequence of interacting with
"teachers" as well as with things. It is a subtle process which few
of us manage well. The interesting thing is that the evolution of
the self, where the internal workings are responded to gently and
sympathetically by adults who are confident in themselves, helps
to develop a new young self far stronger and more able to cope
with problems of living and learning. The invention of the "generation gap" relieves adults of their responsibility. The interac-
tive process of the young and the old always has had and will
have elements of friction and dissonance as well as elements of
nurture and assistance. We keep looking for a way to pretend
away the required socialization. For adults to say the young
won't listen is a convenient "cop-out." It is a more difficult relationship, to be sure, because living is itself more difficult.

THE COMPETENCE IN LIVING AS STUDENT AND ADULT. *Children*

have the right to cognitive-skill experiences which will enable them to cope with life's demands. Without the tool skills for reading, computation, and social interaction, one is doomed to be a hanger-on in a compacted, symbol-ridden culture. With the complexities of society, knowledge about the physical, social, and internal universe of man becomes the precursor for choices and decision-making. Life is not simply concepts to know or skills to be learned, but processes to be used to function in the society. The sense of aloneness of modern man can only be counteracted by a personal perspective which produces an internal locus of control, a sense of self-direction, and the feeling of some power over one's destiny. Humanization of knowledge produces a commitment to be involved.

The individual side of this cannot be ignored. Pupils' talents must be brought out, engaged, and enhanced for their present and future, with the expectation of time for living in addition to earning a living. The arts and recreational activities, whether for professional performance or personal satisfaction, are looming as more and more vital to the quality of life. A school presents opportunities for individuals to find themselves in these realms as well.

SCHOOLS FREE OF FEAR. *Children have the right to work, play, and learn in a school milieu which is free from fear and, more than that, which is organized to provide for maximum social growth.* In a manner of speaking, there are many schools which are unworkable under the typical concepts of school design. On the face of it, adults are a minority group who can operate with arbitrary control only when their role authority is accepted by youngsters and community at large. This used to be the case. Now, power resides not in role authority, but in the viability and veracity of what the adult can communicate. The shock waves of the populist participatory movement are even now being felt by the teaching profession. It is changing lives. The symptom one hears in meetings with teachers is, "No one respects me any more." The solution to this lies in the style of interpersonal relationship between the adult and child, which has already been discussed.

There is a tendency to forget that there is never an absence of authority. Authority is just expressed through new dimensions.

Thus, it is not that there is no authority left, but rather that increased authority resides in the peer culture instead of in adults. Bronfenbrenner's [5] contrast of Russian and American peer culture emphasized how much power peers exert in American schools and how this is basically antagonistic to, rather than supportive of, adult mores. We have long recognzied this at adolescence and the college age, but it is equally potent in the preadolescent as well. Thus, there is no freedom for the youngster unless the peer culture operates to support integrative problem solving.

School problems as learning experiences. What then assures the right to a safe school milieu? For one thing, it is the protection a child needs from the very few sadistic and driven-to-the-wall educators. Schools must have codified procedures for dealing with problems without resorting to physical or psychological harassment. Rules must be open and openly arrived at with humane procedures and built-in safeguards for pupils and parents. The focus is on resolving the issue and meeting the problem in a way which constitutes a learning experience. Punishment, discipline, winners and losers, supporting the staff, the rights of children, all are beside the point. The point is, every problem situation, crisis or no, becomes the place where the parties attempt to create a learning environment to help children and youth learn how to cope with reasonable expectations.

The way some disciplinary situations are handled, one could hardly say the event was a short course or even a cram course in adjustment. If these events are to be used for "teaching," especially with disturbed youngsters, the utmost care must be taken in diagnosis and planning. It is the last place for only amateurism in ihe decision-making process. There are still mental health workers who want to be the "good guys" and not contaminate themselves with such problems. Regular school personnel, suspicious of mental health workers, often covet the discipline function under their control to "keep the school from falling apart." The new school mental health reinterprets "disciplinary situations." Discipline situations are breakdowns in social learning; therefore, special planning must be employed to facilitate the proper design to foster the child's maximal social learning.

Much parent and child concern about the school environment

revolves around the right to travel in safe halls, which is just as real an issue as safe streets. To the right to humane treatment by adults is added a safe peer culture. In the most primitive sense, we are speaking of body safety, for there are schools where extortion and overt harm are threatened. There are children who are afraid to go to school. Adolescents do not use the bathrooms out of fear of the hassling that takes place. A school must have an announced code and enforce it. A pupil has the right to a school which gives protection to both his person and possessions.

SOCIAL DEVELOPMENT: AN EDUCATIONAL OBJECTIVE. *Children and adolescents have a right to more than an absence of the primitive-level threat; they should be able to mingle, cooperate, argue, organize, and relate to many of their age as well as cross-ages.* They should learn to make friends, organize in groups, work for common goals, and find their individual roles and unique capacities substantiated by their fellows. As social beings, they need a laboratory for social development. The right to sustaining group life includes the right to feel, think, and act with independence. In fact, the group code and its power often overwhelm the individual with threats of rejection. The current pseudo-solution of "doing your own thing," regardless of others, is of course no answer. Many of the present singers of the freedom song for the individual are willing to do so even at the expense of others. As a result, they have encouraged the cult of narcissism. The essential dual responsibility to self and to others involves rights and obligations which can be studied, experienced, and absorbed in school group life. The differences between individualistic matters which violate no other's rights and those which deny the most fundamental rights of others is an endless discussion of social values. But the image of a freer society with increased individual choice is around and about us, ranging from style of dress to social contract and refusal to go to war. The introduction and exploration of this dilemma is every youth's right and obligation.

There is still another aspect to adult responsibility needed to bring about a hygienic school environment. Teachers, as up-bringers, must learn to work with and through groups, since groups are so vital to youngsters. Thus, teachers must be able to help children and youth understand group codes and group roles. How group life develops, the negative and coercive aspects as well as the positive resources of groups, must be understood by the members. In fact, how to be free in a group-organized world becomes a major learning sphere and one major key in the search for independence.

SOCIETAL PROBLEMS: OBJECTS FOR STUDY AND LEARNING. *Children must be guaranteed the right to systematic opportunities to study the quality of life and personal growth.* "Courses kill learning" is an adage of many, young and old. Somehow, excitement and relevance die as textbooks and assignments get into the picture. And yet, we can no longer be amateurs or depend upon happenstance and still live insightfully. The challenge is to incorporate systematic attention to the quality of personal growth without generating negative learning conditions. Most teachers who work continually in a group setting have had little help in learning how to utilize the group process for learning. Group dynamics, methods of working with groups and effecting change and learning in individuals through groups, are all needed learning experiences in the teacher's repertoire.

Many persons, Ojemann [34] among the first, have seen that the school is in the intellectual business and have developed curricula which deal directly with these matters. Glasser's *Schools Without Failure* [16] is another approach, incorporating group discussions of important matters in the classroom. Attention to the broader context of how people learn and how classrooms should be designed is presented by Rogers.[39] These, in one way or another, depend upon the idea that schools can use their major channel, consciously planned experiences, to foster mental health goals. Particular mental health programs are dependent upon the specialists who may come and go with change in personnel. All day long, children and youth are involved in the curriculum. This is a far more natural and enduring channel for schools to utilize in enhancing mental health. If we can build part of the mental health program into the substance of the school, it may gradually be incorporated. This is at once promising and difficult. In the subsequent section, we will discuss these issues. Here, the point is that the pupil has a right to a school which directs curricular attention to mental health processes. To ignore such processes is to deny students' rights.

THE STUDENTS' ADVOCATE: A MENTAL HEALTH RESOURCE. *The*

right to rescue. Regardless of ideals and hopes, any social institution with the population magnitude of the school is bound to put some participants in a bind now and again and others very often. Therapeutic and social agencies can never accommodate to the variety of individual needs at any one time for the possible clientele in need. There must be a mental health rescue operation in the school. An always accessible resource must be available at times of stress and conflict. This is the advocate or ombudsman function and more. When there is a crisis, human resource must be available to pupils for immediate assistance. This does not mean that the pupils' position or interpretation will become the law of the school or that their wishes will eventually be seen as necessarily correct. But they will be listened to and the matter at hand will be explored for possible resolutions. The provision of a nonmoralizing, clinically aware crisis service in depth becomes more necessary with the increase both in population and in expectation from schools. As the study of a crisis progresses, it may be the system which is at fault or it may be the individual pupils who need to think through their behavior and ways of adapting in school. Again, the pupil-adult interaction process is crucial to demonstrate how difficulties of life can be met rather than resorting to arbitrary dicta by adults. Some communities have walk-in clinics, and schools need their counterpart.

This right of rescue includes the right to compensatory and restorative efforts and not just diagnosis. While the school cannot be expected to do all things for all students, it must embody resources far more intense than the mental health "band-aid." Immediate crisis handling is an important and integrative learning experience. Continued troubles require the skilled efforts of the school mental health professionals to help unravel the confusions which underlie the problem behavior. When necessary, community services should be utilized. The continuum ranges from the teacher's effort to specialized clinical attention.

TRAINING FOR CITIZENSHIP IN A DEMOCRACY IN THE SCHOOL. *The student has the right to an explicit code of social expectations.* So much of schools' expectation for pupils remains in the hands of the authority. It may be arbitrary and even at times generated on the spot around an incident. What is required is the development, redevelopment, and constant interpretation of the code of how we live together in schools. It is a constantly evolving social process. This school microcosm of society at large offers many possibilities. Often the legislative, executive, and judicial powers are held by one person. Whenever possible, the rules of life should become codified by consent of all parties. All should at least participate. The code must always be open to analysis and alteration. The underlying principle of governance is again process, due process.

The matter is not simply a code regarding peripheral aspects, such as length of skirts and hair, but embodying the most important concepts about how people live together, maximizing individual freedom without violating others' rights. This never-ending quest and how one gets commitment to given codes become the laboratory of learning about social organization. In fact, this right could be stated in reverse, as the right to have a never-ending laboratory of social organization permeated with the democratic ethic. There is, in fact, a whole new vista opening up in this context, with the "mini-school" such as the New York elementary program where the school is transformed into a subculture wherein problems and solutions for social living can be learned in a "safe" environment. This takes the concept of simulation as far as one can. From the mental health point of view, it represents the ultimate in taking values and attitudes out of the book and into the lives of children.

ASSESSMENT AS INFORMATION FOR CHANGE. *Evaluation research —individual and systems assessment—must also be considered a right of children since it involves continuing responsiveness of schools to students' needs.* Most schools know the achievement level and ability potential of their students. In fact, some whole states conduct massive testing programs on a periodic basis. But where is the concern for the affective growth of these same students? What is the quality of their school and total lives? What are the values they are developing, the attitudes they hold, and the feelings they have about themselves, their peers, and the school at large? What are the hopes of the youngsters, their self-concept level, and self-esteem? Old-style mental health screening concentrated on finding those with problems. The current view is concern for all children. Both formal and informal soundings can be taken. The results are not sacred; they are findings for students, parents, and staff to discuss. Adolescents and pre-adolescents can design questions and process certain information themselves.

We are concerned as well with how the total system is functioning. Administrators, teachers, pupils, and parents have perceptions of the system which need periodic reassessment in order to incorporate information on the mental health quotient. The Bank Street group (Minuchin et al.) [31] has begun the long and arduous task of changing goals to relate to processes with actual efforts to assess and evaluate the design.

Strategies and procedures for integrating mental health in schools

We turn next to conceptualizing school mental health practice to integrate the propositions discussed into an overall design. What are the resources of the school in its concern with positive values of life, especially the affective components? Three elements can be brought into focus—the child-adult relationships, peer relationships, and tasks or substantive work. School mental health is dependent upon the proper functioning of these elements. Adults serve as models and transmission vehicles for effective behavior. The authenticity and willingness to be open, especially with adolescents, is crucial. Rogers [39] goes into detail concerning the practice of education on an existentialist basis. His model is again one of process, gradually evolving from the current status to one with more humaneness. The fundamental concern for the pupil-teacher relationship has been discussed at length in prior sections. The second resource, peer relationships, has also been discussed. The need for each pupil to develop acceptable roles and be nurtured by peers is essential. And third, the substantive experiences must have personal relevance and commitment to enhancement of competence. "Lock-step education" gives way to concern with individual style and rate in learning. Filling in of learning gaps through out-of-school learning and synthesizing of experience takes precedence over "filling the empty vessel." Further, there are new ways to blend the affective with the cognitive, of which more will be said later.

From the mental health point of view, the school loses its

walls. Sometimes working out a useful educational experience will involve the home in a joint effort with the school. Rather than expecting everything to be brought to school coded in symbols, presented in books, or as images on a screen, the setting for learning moves to the locale of the actual event whenever possible. The basics of life still are concerned with acquiring food, clothing, and housing. For example, when some otherwise knowledgeable youngsters were asked how their parents obtained the roof over their heads, the responses indicated a sad lack of awareness of the financial complexities upon which housing is dependent. They had no real understanding of rents, mortgages, taxes, and the like. They did not know what happens when people lack the resources to pay for housing. Government is not in a civics text but in the daily transactions and decisions which affect people. Employment is not the result of a vocational aptitude test but a vast array of experiences which impinge on a vulnerable self. Relevance ceases to be a surface interest popularity contest in school. Relevance becomes a reflection of the realities of one's life, now and in the future.

The matter of relevance opens a myriad of avenues to new learning endeavors. Is the glorious history of the country an appropriate sequence for school study if one lives in poverty in a rundown block, amid crime? When the school begins to deal with the conditions surrounding the growing child or youth, it often comes into conflict with certain community interests. This has been evident even in the recent emphasis on ecology. The radical educational critics have said that the real curriculum should deal with how one obtains food, clothing, shelter, and health. If one can read, but what one reads does not apply to solving one's problems, is learning to read relevant? Piaget's concept of discovery taken seriously would mean confrontations with life problems, leading to competence. There are students who graduate without learning the tool skills: Would they not be more ready to learn if skills were seen as the key to solving a problem? Other students graduate with the skills but are incompetent. Their illiteracy is in the application of their skills. Even the able manipulation of symbols which are devoid of personal significance does not represent competency. Youngsters in a

New York school who set up a mini-economy within the school learned their math for "economic" survival. Government evolved as the students struggled to live together equitably. Another innovative public school had a civics class which met in the committee chambers of the city council. Youth unemployment stimulated another student group to survey the community for possibilities and examine legal statutes for employment of minors in their struggle to find jobs. Again, one high school finds its courses in "psychology" (understanding the self) oversubscribed, while many traditional subjects are kept going only because of state requirements for graduation. Why? Because the psychology course speaks to problems of real concern and is so recognized by that age group.

School "hot lines" should be more than a telephone service; they are one source of organizing the study of the community culture. Competence for living is dependent upon participation, though it need not always be self-serving as in those just described. One school sees student team service projects in the community as the source of much learning and an activated citizenship. Will schools embrace the actual living rather than being content to play intellectual games?

The curriculum of the humanized school is about human beings. As the children mature and their horizons expand from their own inner and outer life through the family to the community and thence to the world, the school places them in strategic situations for increasing their functional understanding. They grow through using their skills in confrontation with real life situations. That this can be done is amply demonstrated; it is well known that many urban children are sophisticated in the life of the streets, which have become their real school.

The school evolves to become a center for educational planning for the child and family rather than the single source of only formal learning. Some have even seen the educational complex as the viable setting in which to generate the new child development multi-services center, in contrast to a whole new agency superstructure. Health and other services would be incorporated around the elementary and secondary school.[22] Starting with family planning, well-baby clinics, preschool and on through continuing programs even in adulthood, the developmental center would be responsible for protective services as well as the life enhancement experiences.

Three specific levels of school mental health programming

Before turning to the specifics of a tri-level design for school mental health, it must be emphasized that no mental health program can substitute for meeting the primary needs of children and youth. The hungry child, whether due to chronic malnutrition or the sporadic empty refrigerator, is not going to be available for even the most exciting school experience until he is fed. The Black Panthers have understood this well. There are schools which provide breakfasts as well as lunches. Further, educators can serve as advocates for destitute children. In such matters, it is not only providing for the physical needs of children and youth but providing without the degradation of welfare stigma. The humiliation of poverty in a country of affluence cuts the heart out of the child's sense of self-worth. One school, rather than giving a pair of shoes to a child in need, had a clothing store, where the youngster chose from a selection. Older pupils were provided with opportunities to earn their purchases to give them independence.

Children also need a safe place to sleep as well as freedom from fear going to and from school. The right of children to have their physical needs met is a precursor to formal learning, whether in a ghetto or rural setting. But we want them nourished not simply so that they will have the energy to learn to read when they should. It is their birthright. Many of these matters can become the stimulus for relevant school studies dealing with real problems. The curriculum of a poverty-ridden school must speak to these issues.

We turn now to the task of analyzing how affective components which make up mental health can be infused into the life of the school. The range of expectation is on three levels: (1) primary prevention; (2) compensatory efforts to fill in for deficient life experiences; and (3) educational programming for those who come with serious difficulties. The strange thing is, we are better versed in the second and third than in the first.

PRIMARY PREVENTION. When it comes to primary prevention, we are discussing the strengthening of the lives of children, positive growth or building of "strens" as Hollister [20] called them. There can be no separate course in ego strength or goodness of life. The affective and cognitive synthesis is where it must begin, as Sanford [40] has shown. When Bruner [8] developed his course of study on man, Jones [23] added the basic synthesis of cognitive feeling, which is required to strengthen the affective life. Others have emphasized humanizing curricular experiences.[3,6,29]

The start of affective education lies in the recognition and discussion of feelings when they arise in the normal course of school experiences. Jones presents specific examples of the way emotional aspects of happenings are ignored or even repressed, even when they are clearly present in the normal course of school experiences.[23] For example, emotions of fear, love, death, and aggression are all about us, as well as generated by history, literature, and other curricular content. Each human being lives with his or her personal wishes, hopes, cares, and angers. The oft decried boredom of students is itself an affective state all too common in some schools.

The point is, whenever there is an emotional component in an experience, it is the function of education to consider this along with the cognitive material. Jones describes how, dealing with Bruner's story of man, the pupils were aroused affectively by many features of Eskimo life, such as their killing seals, prizing only one sex in their offspring, and dealing with old age, to say nothing of their favorite foods and the strange dangers of their lives in general. These are typically ignored in the "lesson."

The school does not need to create special emotional components—it is a matter of responding to those which are a natural counterpoint to the cognitive experiences. Typically any such arousal is dampened or repressed. When children are angry with a peer, they may well be told to stop being angry, that it is bad to have such feelings. This denial of a part of normal, valid expression of an individual is like a surgical incision; part of our very being is cut off. Thus, when in the natural course of events, there are feeling components, these must be recognized, discussed, evaluated, and digested. This blending of cognition and feeling is the way we learn to deal with affective aspects.

It is interesting that many of the modern sensitivity training situations invent affective displays. We have been so distant in dealing with feelings, that some would enshrine them in contrast to cognitive processes. This merely reverses the present error of cognitive emphasis to one of emphasis on the affective. The key is not one or the other, but both. The precursors for dealing with values and attitudes are found in the blending of feeling and thinking. Obviously, teachers and mental health workers are not at home with this combination. In fact, except for polite and noble affective states described in historical heroes, schools tend to deny the whole matter of feelings. Those who work with youngsters will always be confronted with this component of growing up. It cannot be left to chance alone, sporadic attention, or peer-culture teaching. It requires conscious, purposeful adult-child interaction.

Real feelings clarify real present problems. The goal is not permissiveness nor undue and indiscriminate emphasis of feelings but responding to feelings openly and thoughtfully. Teachers will have to become comfortable and knowledgeable about their own personal feelings before they can help children synthesize many of the feelings which affect their lives. Here is the first-level mental health component for pre-service and in-service teacher training. As many psychologists have made clear, adults need to learn how to build upon their own persons, to grow in maturity if they are going to be teachers of affect. Maslow [30] presents many issues which are relevant here. However, teacher education related to primary prevention cannot rest on sensitivity training or encounter groups alone. It must be backed up by a study of the affective processes in such work as that of Kohlberg,[26] Piaget,[35] and Kay [24] on character development, which has been noted previously, Berkovitz [1] on the nature of altruistic experience, Branden,[4] Coopersmith,[13] and Sears [41] on the self-concept and how attitudes can be changed. Even the concept of trust is more stated than understood. Cognition is the warp and affective states are the woof; together they create the fabric of the educational experience.

Curricular approaches. If we are to have equal time for affective components with those of reading, there are many things which can be added to fortify the normal youngster attempting to master the affective domain. Since the schools are curricular in orientation, many new approaches of this nature are developing. Here we bring together the emphasis referred to previously. The curricular orientation is exemplified by such workers as Ojemann [34] and Mosher [33] (at Harvard, in his course for high school adolescents). Weinstein and Fantini,[45] as well as Raths,[36] have taken this track. Weinstein and Fantini found that the major concerns are about self-image, relationship with others (the disconnectedness of life), and control over one's life. These pervasive concerns serve to direct the design of their curriculum of affect, and they include specific content suggestions and methodology. Lyons,[29] Borton,[3] and Brown [6] have all given directions for affective curricula. Bruck and Vogelsong [7] have a series of teachers' guides and workbook activities which change the direction of guidance to affective education. What can be said is that the curricular approach is now a most active concern in the educational field and there is no dearth of stimulating material for classroom use.

In the curricular realm, there is also a place for the inclusion of material which has affective significance in daily living for learners. Part of this is the linkage of phenomena which create impact in the news and daily life events and the child's feelings through the model of the teacher who can demonstrate and generate empathic feelings. One can also see the use of vivid and meaningful books and movies to include literature and exposition which is directly related to the life experience of children at given ages. The world of the adolescent has been taken over by the popular press, leaving the schools holding on to that which they cannot make meaningful. It need not be so; for the welfare of adolescents, it must not be so.

Figures for identification. At the deepest level, primary prevention in the positive sense of building strength rests upon identification. The adults in the environment must be models. Their style of life can offer examples of involved and meaningful living to young people. Can youngsters expect to solidify values from adults who are not joyous, vibrant, purposeful, and, to a degree, sound? It is through identification that we transmit the values of society. Not only must we look to the adults, but to important peer figures who are being highlighted. Must these be only in athletics and cheerleading? All of the capable students, whether in the arts, sciences, and/or social skills can, by featured example, help mold the life-style of all youngsters.

The vital role of school administrators. It is interesting how many educational experiments owe their vitality to charismatic leadership. The tone of the building, the style of its operation, the morale of the staff, the sense of teamwork—so much is a consequence of the top leadership. If the directions indicated are to be followed, the principal will have to be concerned and effective. Staff training, generating new ideas, reducing the anxiety about change are among the many functions dependent upon the leader.[32] Downtown, the central office sends out memos and visiting dignitaries, but it is the on-the-line local agent who does or doesn't respond. The vast differences in schools, even neighboring schools with similar situations, verify the critical role played by the principal. With the emphasis on decentralization, the school unit becomes the operating system for the generation of goals, assessment of process, allocation of resources, and accountability.

COMPENSATORY MENTAL HEALTH PROGRAMMING FOR CHILDREN AT RISK. Compensatory programs are particularly important in schools where social conditions are such that the school can predict a high incidence of failure and dropouts. The inner-city schools must meet the many needs of children not answered in the community at large.

Many ghetto schools are in the midst of the "ill-housed" or "ill-fed" areas; they cannot be viable without engaging in these matters. Some see the school as the core compensatory agency for all of the special needs of deprived children, physical, social, and educational. It is the one agency with the available contacts.

Beyond sustaining and enhancing the affective life of the normal child are the intensification and individualization of efforts needed for the 10 to 12 percent * whose problems place them in high risk. Their current life patterns are not satisfying to themselves and/or to others. There may be failure, frustration, or a lack of hope. While many are sad and depressed within their own shell, most high-risk students behave in such a

---

* Identified by the Government Commission on Mental Health of Children.

way as to result in their schoolmates suffering as well. Others, while apparently satisfied within themselves, have incorporated values which seriously violate societal norms and curtail freedoms of others. They have not yet acquired humaneness, so to speak. Some of these children are reacting to temporary stress while others have suffered from stress for many years, resulting in chronic difficulties.

It is well known that particular times, such as the first grade, third grade, the start of junior high and the adolescent period, will be periods of high emotional fallout. Resources must be expanded for high-risk youngsters, especially at critical times. The resources range from care for their physical and health needs to mental health crisis intervention and remedial education, with school and community mental health agencies working conjointly. While classical therapeutic interventions will continue, group programs and cross-age activities of peers such as Big Brothers-Big Sisters present a potential resource to supply identification opportunities.

Therapeutic educational assistance implies response not only to the learning problems, but to the person with those problems, since attitudes and feelings enter into the picture. The isolation of learning disabilities as if there were no emotional components involved is the latest example of faulty separation. This means that more clinically trained teachers, whatever their designation, are needed to man special school services. Need exists for smaller size classes and special interest groupings with outstanding teachers.

Mental health workers in the schools, guidance, social work, and psychology are only starting the role change necessary to provide individual and group counseling opportunities, particularly around aggression, sex, and drugs for preteens and adolescent youngsters. Since discipline is the counterface of socialization, those responsible for this phase of the school's work are "up to their exclusions" in affective education. They do not usually see it in the modern light. New styles of intervention emphasizing crisis handling, life space interviewing, and reality confrontation have to be utilized.

Teachers need an omnipresent responsible resource when they find it impossible to help a pupil in the classroom setting.

Referral to the crisis person without rancor or stigma is the "right to rescue" which works to both the student's and the teacher's advantage.

Developing resources. Given the scarcity of resources, it will be necessary to retain present personnel and readjust services rather than expect to add all new personnel or add new services. Some schools have counted up their resources, assessed the work which their milieu demanded, and designed a cooperative effort with all disciplines. For example, early morning mini-clinics on problem situations, conducted by trained personnel, met a real need of teachers in handling disturbed children. By reassignment of personnel, it took no longer than two weeks from a teacher's request to the first state of action planning. Usually, specially trained personnel visited the class setting and made on-the-spot assessment for the planning.

Parents need to be brought in early in the work with a pupil, not to be lectured but to help plan, *with the child actually participating*. Then more comprehensive strategies can be evolved. Humaneness means not doing things *to* people but *with* people, toward mutually recognized goals. Schools are advocates for child welfare but they are not the parent or even surrogate parents, although at times this does happen. Most schools have all they can do within their resources to develop a school climate for effective learning and living without expecting to take over for the parent or other agencies. Working with parents means collaborative efforts to suggest goals or counseling and exploring means toward mutual goals. Court suits are forcing schools to be responsible for all children. At the same time, the pupils' total lives are not their responsibility alone.

It is interesting how the parent voucher proposal has axed into the power of decision, chips flying in every direction. In itself, the voucher plan, by giving parents power, could as well encourage repressive educational practice as innovation. Some parents are demanding basic education—the three R's and nothing else—while others are demanding open schools with no structure and no emphasis on skills. Behind it we see parents as co-participators with the schools which are major upbringing institutions complementing the family. It is not easy as a teacher to be working for 30 parents, or a whole parent constituency.

The answer lies not in an advisory relationship but in a shared responsibility by parents, pupils, and teachers. In one such process, the potential teachers in a public school were interviewed, ranked, and hired by just such a joint committee of parents, pupils, and teachers. The role of parents should rest not only in decision-making but should include giving service as volunteers. In one urban school, a class of young children visits all the homes of the members and talks with parents. As the school moves down to preschool-age level, some teachers work half time in the homes as well as regular teaching. After all, the real teachers are the parents, especially the mothers of young children. The concept of school from age 0 to 25 will mean significant new designs.

RESOURCES FOR THE SERIOUSLY HANDICAPPED. The third level follows naturally after the primary and secondary mental health prevention models described above. Figures show that up to three percent of the school population remain in dire straits from the mental health point of view. The quality of their life is indeed meager and their future desperate. This is not to imply that schools can solve everything for all children, though with mandatory education, the implication is that there will be expectations. It does mean that most of this three percent will have schooling of some type for more waking hours than anything else. With the extended day programs, the seriously disturbed sometimes spend more hours in a school than the normal youngster.

We know this much: These pupils will require a very high investment and a high quota of skill on the part of their upbringers, teachers and parents. While the specific patterns will differ from place to place, the essentials which are needed in order to rehabilitate these very disturbed pupils are vividly clear. The first is maintenance of all possible regular relationships to enhance the child's normality. Pupils should be removed from the mainstream of the school only when necessary for helping them and not as an administrative convenience, and then only when required additional assistance is actually provided. Rather than coming back to the regular class "on probation," they are "on loan" to special services and belong with the regulars. The crisis teacher, resource room, helping teacher, counselor, and Hewett's

resource center [19] are examples of specialized input with minimal specialized stigma. In addition to the crisis provision and
the work of the mental health team discussed before, there is
the need for refuge and security rooms where pupils can find
assistance over a period of time. When they can return, they do.
It is important that their feelings, as well as their academics, are
responded to. One significant provision is the individually
planned day where the best match in subject matter and teacher
is worked out to fit each child's particular needs. As the elementary school becomes more fluid in its grouping patterns, and
as the high schools work on modules, new scheduling, and new
school designs, it will be possible to make more precise fits for
special cases.

In the very few extreme cases, it may be a long-time loan of
the pupil to special services. And there will be those, even with
a broad and variant total school complex, who will be best protected by considerable long-term separation, during which they
should be building toward a normal school experience.

There will be special classes; the cry that they are dehumanizing ipso facto has been shown to be in error. Yet we know that
when the pupil, especially at adolescence, is forced into a class
with a punitive tone as a last stand by frustrated adults, such a
class will be no haven of refuge. The child's feelings about the
style of help often are more critical than the substance of the
resource itself. Programs for delinquents are notorious for personal insult, and yet there are examples of milieu programs and
clinical services which do work, such as the education program
under Dr. Besoville of the University of Montreal. On the other
hand, some pupils have, on their own, recognized their need for
a sustained protected environment. The question is how a helping service fits with the goals and plans of the pupils and their
families. How well is it conducted? Are their needs being met?
Are all possible contacts with mainstream youngsters being
maintained? Special education must examine both the prescrip-
tive aspects and quality of programs. It is the psychological
nature of programs, rather than the administrative format, which
must be evaluated.

For those whose handicaps cannot be remediated, the program must look ahead to what can be done to find a suitable

long-term life pattern. It is clear that, for many young children and more adolescents, the way to develop a quality life pattern is not through education as it now exists in any but a few rare places. This is the further step of attention to the life stream rather than mainstream. The assistance will have to be thought of in terms of the life stream, the eventual participation in the society outside of school as adulthood approaches. Work therapy differs from co-op programs because in work therapy, work is a means to help youngsters find themselves as well as jobs. The disturbed pupil will have troubles and will falter. In fact, for some seriously disturbed students a sheltered workshop will be necessary in youth and even for life. In effect, their problems in school are but a screen for their eventual real problem: How are they to live most independently and with the greatest sense of self-adequacy? Until the educative enterprise incorporates real work, it will have missed a crucial channel.

Many experiences which offer both developmental growth and therapeutic potential for the normal child are often denied the ten percent and the three percent we have just discussed. Art, music, dance, creative crafts, and drama are the birthright of all children and youth, though they may have a special mental health function here. Yet many specialized programs do the least with these media. One of the most profound opportunities for restorative social feelings is often denied the disturbed child. The role reversal when problem youngsters tutor or help younger peers is dramatic and provides a more realistic pattern of enactment of a "good and giving life" than any moralizing.

It should be emphasized that referral for outside help and various aid will still be needed for some children. No one expects all children to be helped solely by the school.

Touch and go

School mental health has changed. We have seen the welling up of the humaneness revolution, sometimes in caricature, to be sure. But, beneath it all is the quest for an affective life with quality. A better life is the activation of the mental health concepts. Nothing is inevitable about the future; we may lose to reaction rather than find the new, which is ready to emerge.

Above all, teachers need assistance in articulating these

broader goals of education and especially in techniques to bring about the needed action components. It will be slow going but the direction for school mental health is neither as confused, nor as dark, as some have thought.

REFERENCES

1. BERKOWITZ, L. *The Development of Motives and Values in the Child*. New York: Basic Books, 1964.
2. BIBER, B. Schooling as an influence in developing healthy personality. In R. Kotinsky and H. Witmer (Eds.), *Community Programs for Mental Health*. Cambridge: Harvard University Press, 1955.
3. BORTON, T. *Reach, Touch and Teach*. New York: McGraw-Hill, 1970.
4. BRANDEN, N. *The Psychology of Self-Esteem*. Los Angeles: Nash, 1969.
5. BRONFENBRENNER, U. *Two Worlds of Childhood*. New York: Russell Sage Foundation, 1970.
6. BROWN, G. I. *Human Teaching for Human Learning*. New York: The Viking Press, 1971.
7. BRUCK, C. M., & VOGELSONG, M. O. *Build—Teacher's Guide*. New York: Bruce Publishing Co., 1969.
8. BRUNER, J. *Toward a Theory of Instruction*. Cambridge: Harvard University Press, 1966.
9. CAMPBELL, A. Measuring the quality of life. Unpublished paper. The Institute of Social Research, The University of Michigan, October, 1971.
10. CHEIN, I. *The Science of Behavior and the Image of Man*. New York: Basic Books, 1972.
11. COLEMAN, J. S. *The Adolescent Society*. New York: Free Press of Glencoe, 1961.
12. COLEMAN, J. S. The children have outgrown the schools. *Psychology Today*, 1972, 5:9, 72–75.
13. COOPERSMITH, S. *The Antecedents of Self-Esteem*. San Francisco: W. H. Freeman, 1967.
14. COTTLE, T. J. Parent and child—the hazards of equality. *Saturday Review*, February 1, 1969, 16–19; 46–48.
15. DENNISON, G. *The Lives of Children*. New York: Random House, 1969.
16. GLASSER, W. *Schools without Failure*. New York: Harper & Row, 1969.
17. HARLOW, H. F. *Learning to Love*. San Francisco: Albion Co., 1971.
18. HERSCH, C. This discontent explosion in mental health. *American Psychologist*, 1968, 23, 497–506.

19. HEWETT, F., TAYLOR, F. D., QUAY, H. C., SOLOWAY, M. M., & ARTUSO, A. *The Santa Monica Madison School Plan: A Functional Model for Merging Special and Regular Class Programs in the Public School.* Santa Monica: Santa Monica Unified School District, 1970.

20. HOLLISTER, W. G. Concept of strens in education: A challenge to curriculum development. In E. M. Bower and W. G. Hollister (Eds.), *Behavioral Science Frontiers in Education.* New York: Wiley, 1967.

21. JERSILD, A. T. *In Search of Self.* New York: Teachers College, Columbia University, 1952.

22. *Joint special education study group regarding the report of the Joint Commission on the Mental Health of Children and Youth.* Nutley, New Jersey: Treatment Rehabilitation, Education for Children, Inc., July, 1970.

23. JONES, R. M. *Fantasy and Feeling in Education.* New York: New York University Press, 1968.

24. KAY, W. *Moral Development.* (Rev. ed.) Bristol, England: George Allen and Unwin, 1970.

25. KIRSNER, D. A. Instrumentation of Bloom and Krathwohl's taxonomies for the writing of educational objectives. *Psychology in the Schools,* 1969, *6,* 227–231.

26. KOHLBERG, L. Development of moral character and moral ideology. In M. L. Hoffman and L. W. Hoffman (Eds.), *Review of Child Development Research.* Vol. 1. New York: Russell Sage Foundation, 1964.

27. KOZOL, J. *Free Schools.* Boston: Houghton Mifflin, 1972.

28. KRATHWOHL, D. R., BLOOM, B. S., & MASIA, B. B. *Taxonomy of Educational Objectives.* Handbook II. *Affective Domain.* New York: David McKay, 1964.

29. LYONS, H. C. *Learning to Feel—Feeling to Learn.* Columbus, Ohio: Charles E. Merrill, 1971.

30. MASLOW, A. H. *The Farther Reaches of Human Nature.* New York: Viking Press, 1971.

31. MINUCHIN, P., BIBER, B., SHAPIRO, E., & ZIMILES, H. *The Psychological Impact of School Experience.* New York: Basic Books, 1969.

32. MORSE, W. C. *Classroom Disturbance: The Principal's Dilemma.* Arlington, Virginia: Council for Exceptional Children, 1971.

33. MOSHER, R., SPINTHALL, L. B., & NORMAN, A. Psychological education in secondary schools—A program to promote individual and human development. *American Psychologist,* 1970, *25,* 911–924.

34. OJEMANN, R. H., & SNIDER, B. C. F. The effect of a teaching program in behavioral science on changes in causal behavior scores. *Journal of Educational Research,* 1964, *57,* 255–260.

35. PIAGET, J. *The Moral Judgment of the Child.* New York: Macmillan, 1955.

36. RATHS, L. E., HARMIN, M., & SIMON, S. B. *Values and Teaching.* Columbus, Ohio: Charles E. Merrill, 1966.

37. REGAL, J., ELLIOTT, R., GROSSMAN, H., & MORSE, W. C. *The Exclusion of Children from School: The Unknown, Unidentified, and Untreated.* Council for Children with Behavioral Disorders, Washington, D.C., 1972.

38. RHODES, W. C. Psycho-social learning. In E. Bower and W. G. Hollister (Eds.), *Behavioral Science Frontiers in Education.* New York: John Wiley, 1967.

39. ROGERS, C. R. *Freedom to Learn.* Columbus, Ohio: Charles E. Merrill, 1969.

40. SANFORD, N. The development of cognitive-affective process through education. In E. Bower and W. G. Hollister (Eds.), *Behavioral Science Frontiers in Education.* New York: Wiley, 1967.

41. SEARS, P. S., & SHERMAN, V. S. *In Pursuit of Self-Esteem.* Belmont, California: Wadsworth, 1964.

42. SILBERMAN, C. E. *Crisis in the Classroom.* New York: Random House, 1970.

43. SKINNER, B. F. *Beyond Freedom and Dignity.* New York: Alfred A. Knopf, 1971.

44. VALETT, R. E. The existing psychoeducational revolution. Address presented at colloquium of the Alfred Bennet Center, Muskegon, Michigan, August, 1970.

45. WEINSTEIN, G., & FANTINI, M. D. *Toward Humanistic Education.* New York: Praeger, 1971.

The teacher . . . if he be indeed wise, does not
bid you enter the house of his wisdom, but rather
leads you to the threshold of your own mind.

KAHLIL GIBRAN

13

The School Mental Health
Consultant as
Community Child Advocate

IRVING N. BERLIN, M.D.

Mental health consultants trained in most school settings are
taught to help their colleagues in education to work more effectively with their students. Enhancement of the learning process
through the educator follows an understanding of the underlying
factors in students' behavioral and learning problems. The consultant involves the educator in mutual problem solving, based
on data about the student which are provided by the educator.
Options evolve from the educator's knowledge of the process of
teaching and learning, and the consultant's understanding of behavior and motivation.[3,4,5,6]

Mental health consultants in the schools are usually not at all
concerned with community needs and priorities. Most remediation of student problems ignores the community's priorities and
its frustrations with a nonresponsive school district. Relevant
interventions which involve the community, students, parents,
and educators as collaborators are rare.

The Woodlawn Mental Health Center was given a goal by the
community to help the first graders "make it" in school, where
traditionally most of them had failed. This was the basic condition for the mental health center to come to the Woodlawn
community.[9,13,14]

In a few other instances a community's priorities have been made conditions for a mental health center's existence. In these situations school consultants are forced to act on these mandates. In contrast, consultants hired by the school behave like other school personnel. They are usually not attuned to, or even aware of, the community's concerns, especially if it is a poor or minority community.

Professional training and community responsiveness

Professional training and background also influence the responsiveness of the mental health consultant to community needs. The psychiatrist and psychologist, trained in individual psychotherapy, research techniques, and testing, know how to interact with middle-class patients who are like themselves and who respond to the methods they have learned. Social workers, historically concerned with community needs, especially with poor and economically powerless persons, have become the emulators in practice of the well-paid, high-status psychiatrists. Recently, through their community organization curricula and field work in welfare and the ghettos, some have become increasingly concerned with the needs of their clients and have begun to espouse the clients' positions in their welfare councils. Only recently the National Assembly of NASW has endorsed national health insurance, taking positions of advocacy for mal-treated clients and the shift of defense funds to health and welfare. Most social workers, like most psychiatrists and psychologists, are still too firmly entrenched in secure, financially remunerative, establishment positions to venture forth on behalf of the needs and priorities of their communities. Perhaps the most involved mental health professionals are those nurses in public health and community mental health centers who, through their ongoing service to the poor and minorities in their homes and in community well-child and mental health clinics, come closest to knowing the needs and respecting the acumen and the potential of their patients. Some of them have helped enunciate and clarify the needs of the communities to the organizations with which they collaborate. Most, however, see their service as an end in itself. Community involvement is still infrequent.

Strikingly, few if any mental health workers consider the students themselves or the young people in the streets, who enunciate their needs and priorities forcibly, as representing an important part of the community. This is despite the grudging acknowledgment from all professionals in close contact with students and young people that their complaints are valid and that many of their suggestions for change are very relevant to solving urgent school and community problems.

Thus, in one Black community, only the persistence of the community council in response to continued pressure of parents of school children and adolescents in and out of school forced mental health workers to help the community representatives find methods of clearly documenting the failure of the agencies that were supposed to serve them. Thus data were gathered by the parents on the ineffective job of teaching which took place in primary grades. Similarly, parents documented both how welfare and public health agencies failed to provide needed services and their basic disrespect for their constituents. A study revealed the police precincts' neglect in protecting civil and property rights of the Black community while harassing their youth.[2]

The data were presented to the school board, city council, welfare department, public health department, and police authorities by the community council whose presence was reinforced by the involved mental health professionals and representatives from their professional organizations. Changes soon began to be noted. At first these were token changes; however, when the organized community and its professional workers persisted in their data collecting and would not be appeased by token changes, real and continued change began in response to continued community pressure and vigilant documentation of agency performance. A corollary of these activities was greater community awareness of their political clout and a more unified, effective selection of representatives to elected office.

Obstacles to professional involvement

Why are professionals reluctant to involve themselves with relevant elements of the community in their role as school mental health consultants? It is clear from some of our studies that professionals are turned off by lack of actual prior experience in working with community members and students who have their own ideas about what is important. Since their only experience is with patients who ask for help or the usual school consultees whose troubled existence makes any offer of help welcome, they know no other role. Thus community participants, students, and adults may want help, but for their specified goals and in their own fashion. Mental health consultants may require consultative help in tuning in to community needs and learning how to work with members of the community. They need to learn to hear, behind the anger and the rhetoric, the issues that require their expertise in evaluating and documenting the data the community can use most effectively. Traditional mental health professionals employed by the schools are in competition with each other and seek power by serving the educational establishment. Thus they cannot think in terms of community needs.[12]

Psychologists' sophistication about learning theory and the use of behavior modification as a tool to help teachers to work with students who have learning or behavior problems are rarely used to effect a meaningful collaboration between student and teacher to realize the student's particular goals. Child psychiatrists, as consultants, are often well trained in normal and abnormal physical and emotional development as well as in the stages of cognitive and affective development which, if correctly interpreted and understood by educators, could be helpful to them. However, it is striking how often the need to be omnipotent and omniscient interferes with a problem-solving, scientific approach to a child's dysfunctional behavior that might involve the educator, the administrator, the child, and the parents in a collaborative effort. Since most social workers have had little training either in child development or learning theory and behavior modification, their most frequent tool is to try to understand the student's problems in light of past behavior and intrafamilial conflicts. Often, working in this way, they are helpful to student and parents, but as consultants they have not been trained to help educators do a more effective job. They therefore are seen as persons to whom administrators can give the problem for solution rather than as enhancing the capacities of educators to do a more effective job with students and their families. Certainly none of these "mental health" professionals are by training concerned with the preventive aspects of their work.

Prevention: A new role

Prevention requires an analysis of the precursors to disease and disorder, and intervention to reduce or eliminate the problem. Thus the data that malnutrition in prospective mothers and their newborn children leads to mental defect, learning difficulties, and apathy, depending on the variables of degree and time of onset of the malnutrition, point clearly to dietary intervention in *high-risk populations*. Data on how the impact of poverty leads to maternal depression, with its effect on babies and children of all ages, led to studies which revealed maternal depression in other socioeconomic classes. Research has shown that educating mothers to play with and stimulate their children reduces maternal isolation and depression and infant-stimulus deprivation. Thus, prevention may well require widespread early help to mothers to stimulate their babies as well as quality day care programs for young children, with mothers and fathers as potential trainees and employees. It also means awareness of how poverty on the one hand and a poorly responsive environment and educational system on the other hand produce dropouts, delinquents, and drug users throughout society. Adults who make it in school are usually not trained to compete in our technological society for jobs in industry, health, welfare, education, or the vast service and repair networks so essential to our communities.

Mental health professionals and educators find themselves alienated from a community they don't know or understand, or which they fear. Community priorities in education, jobs, or health care are difficult for middle-class professionals to respond to and facilitate since these professionals usually conceptualize problem solving from their own middle-class framework. They have no way of understanding the feelings of impotence with regard to altering any part of the system and the mistrust they evoke as representatives of the system when they seek to be helpful. Students and other adolescents in the community are seen by professionals as strident and difficult patients rather than as participants in a process of mutual learning. Especially difficult for mental health professionals is to reconsider their role as one of using their expertise on behalf of the community, placing their skills at the disposal of the community, of parents, adults, and children to accomplish those tasks most vital to them.

Comfort in usual professional role

The usual professional role, the one most comforting, is to use one's knowledge in a traditional way. That is, the professionals know what is best for their patients or the community and provide those services as they see fit. For example, in public health care there can be little question that wiping out disease in every contagious form is a professional's job. However, when it comes to ridding the same population of dangerously contaminated drinking water, pollution which comes from the effluent of a nearby industry, unsanitary housing conditions, or serious overcrowding injurious to health, mental health, and child development, then the public health physicians must have the vigorous, informed, sustained backing of the population they serve. Without it, their knowledge and authority are not sufficient to offset the wealth, propaganda, promises, and rhetoric of a well-financed company or non-responsive city, state, or national government. Thus, in the instance of environmental pollution, health professionals put themselves in the position of lending their expertise as educators, with important information, to the community and its leaders so that they may use it for the community's benefit. The real leadership in the fight against environmental pollution and environmental hazards must come from the concerned and articulate citizens and communities who utilize the data provided by the health professions. Citizens have begun to learn to do this effectively on the local and national political scenes.[8,10]

In a number of instances, mental health professionals and educators, primarily concerned with working within their established system, have developed methods to help their problem students. Thus team teaching, therapeutic groups for adolescents, or even more advanced encounter groups for faculty, although helpful in themselves, do not take cognizance of the core issues of concern to the community. Therefore the general sterility and irrelevance of curricula and the nonhuman treatment of children, which produce failure and alienation from learning, are not altered. The Plowden Report altered elementary education in England by parent involvement and experimenting with methods to help children to be creative, to explore their environment, and to learn by participating in projects relevant to their lives which makes for more involved and exciting learning. Despite publicity and praise for this report, its relevance for our schools is rarely utilized or examined by our educators.[10]

New roles for student, teacher, and consultant

It is clear that helping children learn early how to gather facts, assess their validity, and come to relevant conclusions makes for involved and relevant learning. This problem-solving approach, learned early, becomes a way of life.

The educator and mental health consultant need to collaborate to overcome the many obstacles within any institution to introducing new methods of teaching and learning. The mental health consultant knows from other experiences that any system changes are upsetting to many within the hierarchy. Such efforts also mean that the community members, through their children, learn how to utilize fact finding and data analysis to attack their community problems. Usually students' desires for meaningful education and a community's concern that their children get an education that will have some payoff in meaningful employment and betterment of their lives are strongly resisted by all the establishment. Teachers and administrators who have to learn new styles of education and of relating to students and parents resist change. The school system, with its rigid curriculum, is fearful of innovation which it cannot control.

Those mental health workers who have helped pioneering educators to venture forth and demonstrate how they can effectively relate to community and student needs find concerted and powerful opposition. Political forces are very much concerned that an informed citizenry will alter political patterns and power. In the few instances where such efforts have approached success, the community has had to withstand pressure from city, state, and other vested interests who seek to discredit and sabotage accurate fact finding, but especially concerted and politically effective action.

The role of the consultant clearly becomes one of helping concerned community participants and pioneering school personnel anticipate resistance and mobilize to minimize it. Mental health consultants need to be in constant touch with key people in the schools and the community who will be subject to the greatest pressure, the most anxiety, and in some instances even threats so that they can be supported through this onslaught and be helped to maintain their position despite pressures to revert to the status quo. Often the mental health consultant's greatest allies are students who, once they experience problem solving and real participation in meaningful learning, are not going to settle for anything else. Their determination and clarity of vision and purpose have been sustaining to adults under pressure because it is clear there are no other alternatives.[10,16]

Mental health workers learn to their benefit that once the integrative potentials in human beings, especially children, are mobilized and used, they cannot easily be turned off. They also learn that such a process reduces mental health problems. Those persons whose capacities for meaningful and productive human interactions are enhanced and whose capacities to influence the institutions which determine their lives are increased serve as models to other students and to teachers, community leaders, and mental health professionals. In such a role the mental health worker is an advocate for the community and its children in school.

REFERENCES

1. BECKER, A., WYLAN, L., & McCOURT, W. Primary prevention—whose responsibility? *American Journal of Psychiatry*, 1971, *128*, 412–416.
2. BERLIN, I. N. Professionals' participation in community activities: Is it part of the job? *American Journal of Orthopsychiatry*, 1971, *41*, 494–500.
3. BERLIN, I. N. Preventive aspects of mental health consultation to schools. *Mental Hygiene*, 1967, *51*, 34–40.
4. BERLIN, I. N. Mental health consultation for school social workers: A conceptual model. *Community Mental Health Journal*, 1969, *5:4*, 280–288.

5. CAPLAN, G. *Theory and Practice of Mental Health Consultation.* New York: Basic Books, 1970.
6. CAPLAN, G. Types of mental health consultation. *American Journal of Orthopsychiatry,* 1963, *33,* 470–481.
7. ELSON, A., & ELSON, M. Educating teachers and children in law: An approach to reduced alienation in inner-city schools. *American Journal of Orthopsychiatry,* 1970, *40,* 870–878.
8. GEIGER, H. J. Hidden professional roles: The physician as reactionary, reformer, revolutionary. *Social Policy,* 1971, *1:*6, 24–33.
9. KELLAM, S. G., & SCHIFF, S. K. An urban community mental health center. In L. Duhl and R. Leopold (Eds.), *Mental Health and Urban Social Policy: A Casebook of Community Actions.* San Francisco: Jossey-Bass, 1968. Pp. 113–138.
10. LEININGER, M. Some anthropological issues related to community mental health programs in the United States. *Community Mental Health Journal,* 1971, *7:*1, 24–28.
11. OJEMANN, R. H. Self-guidance as an educational goal. *Elementary School Journal,* 1972, *72:*5, 247–257.
12. SARASON, S., et al. *Psychology in Community Settings.* New York: Wiley, 1966.
13. SCHIFF, S. K., & KELLAM, S. G. Historical parallels between public education and community mental health: Implications for planning. Presented at the 44th Annual Meeting of the American Orthopsychiatric Association, Washington, D.C., March 22, 1967.
14. SCHIFF, S. K. Community accountability and mental health services. *Mental Hygiene,* 1970, *54:*2, 205–214.
15. SCHONFELD, W. A. Comprehensive community programs for the investigation and treatment of adolescents. In J. Howells (Ed.), *Modern Perspectives in Adolescent Psychiatry.* New York: Brunner/Mazel, 1971. Pp. 483–511.
16. SHELDON, A. On consulting to new, changing, or innovative organizations. *Community Mental Health Journal,* 1971, *7:*1, 62–71.
17. THARP, R. G., CUTTS, R. I., & BURKHOLDER, R. The community mental health center and the schools: A model for collaboration through demonstration. *Community Mental Health Journal,* 1970, *6:*2, 126–135.

For it is patently true that respect for medicine
stems from faith in curative medicine. Prevention
may be better than cure, but that is little consolation
to a sick person.

N.R.E. FENDALL

Thus . . . medicine is the science of agencies
helpful and harmful, the helpful being alike
those which conserve existing health and those
which restore it when deranged; while the
harmful are the opposite of these.

GALEN in *DeSectis* (2nd Century)

—————————————————— **14**

Physical Illness or Injury:
The Hospital as a Source
of Emotional Disturbances
in Child and Family

DANE G. PRUGH, M.D.
KENT JORDAN, M.D.

Editor's note

*In this volume we do not discuss in a separate chapter the
usual mental illness treatment services—these are incorporated
in chapters 15, 16, and 17. Because prevention of, early intervention in, and treatment of mental illness in children are our
major concerns they are placed in the context of the community
needs and services. New kinds of services are developing and
new kinds of early interventions make it appropriate to discuss
mental health services in a community context. These problems
and issues are discussed throughout the volume as a recurring
theme.*

This chapter focuses on harmful mental health practices affect-
ing physically ill children. In this setting the means to remedy
these services are within the power of the physicians, nurses, and
especially the administrators of the hospital. It is certainly within
the power of knowledgeable parents to create a demand for
different treatment of their children.

Hardly any informed pediatrician has not read the Robertsons'
essay, "A Two-Year-Old Goes to the Hospital," or other relevant
papers in pediatrics. Yet antediluvian methods persist. Why?

In a few hospitals parents spend time freely with their children,
and are encouraged to help care for them, etc. Parents are there
especially when children are seriously ill or during critical mo-
ments before surgery and while they are recovering from
anesthesia, to provide reassurance at times of critical emotional
need.

One might also ask why hospitals continue to be built like
factories, why they continue to be run as impersonal, nonhuman
institutions.

Let me indicate only one of the many reasons. It is theoretically
more efficient and less burdensome for nonhuman oriented ad-
ministrators, planners, and some professionals to work in such a
system. The reality is that a humane hospital saves both valuable
professional time, human suffering, and lives. Since this is the
hospital's actual mission it means real increased efficiency.

Mechanization and efficiency always mean depersonalization.
However, the separation of parents from sick children is not a
new procedure and stems from the germ theory of disease. Hos-
pitals must be antiseptic. It was only when pediatricians like Holt
and others recognized that infants were dying for lack of nurtur-
ance that nurses were encouraged to ignore sterile techniques
and to pick children up.

The fight for human treatment of children as patients goes on
despite the knowledge available, because, as I have heard time
and time again, it is more convenient not to have parents under-
foot while treating their children.

As in all such efforts, Dr. Prugh, a pioneer in the reversal of
this process, not only documents its evils but also reveals the
kinds of pressures required from parents, public, and newly-
trained physicians to reverse such a harmful effect on our

*children. He also emphasizes that "hospital-bound" professionals
and insurance companies find it easier to talk about beds rather
than the now clearly necessary greatly enlarged outpatient services.*

*We feature this paper because the necessary changes in hos-
pital policies do not require new legislation or money. Primarily
education and new attitudes and policies are required. We urge
our colleagues in pediatrics to join us in this advocacy for child
mental health in the hospital. We urge them to join those of us
who more frequently recognize parents as our therapeutic allies
and their potential capacity in caring for their children in an
overcrowded hospital. We welcome the physicians' use of parents
to reduce the emotional impact of painful and frightening procedures done in strange places by strangers. Together we can
humanize hospitals for both children and adults.*

Introduction

In this chapter, an often neglected topic will be dealt with in
a straight-forward and candid fashion, in the interests of the
welfare of children. Hospitalization for illness or injury is an experience which affects millions of children and adolescents each
year. However, the harmful emotional impact of this experience
upon young people and their families is consistently disregarded
by our society, which calls itself "child centered." How this can
happen and what can readily and gradually be done to change
this shameful situation are the focal questions of this chapter.

For the past 23 years, one of the authors (D. G. P.) has attempted, as have many other workers, to deal with this problem
from a reasonably dispassionate "scientific" approach. He, like
others, has carried out controlled investigations which show the
importance of specific preventive measures in minimizing the
emotional impact of hospitalization upon children and families.[23,38,41,72,100,102,103] These findings have been repeatedly
published and presented at meetings where pediatricians,
nurses, and hospital administrators could learn about these advances. Yet, at the present time, there has been *very little*
change in most hospital programs in this country. Thus, in his
middle age, he welcomes this opportunity, with the help of his

young and energetic co-author (who has also done work in this area), to join with James Robertson in England, likewise a scientific investigator, in bringing the shocking facts to the public, especially *the parents* in this nation.

Only parents and the public can bring pressure upon hospital administrators, pediatricians, nurses, and other professional people to change this destructive state of affairs in the direction of the interests of children and youth. In fact, not in rhetoric, our children are our most important resource and, indeed, *our only hope* in this world of technological excellence and disordered human values.

Both of the authors know that it is not evil or organized opposition to the welfare of children which has allowed the present situation in our hospitals for children to continue. Pediatricians, pediatric nurses, and other people involved in such programs are by nature kind and compassionate people. They love children and make great sacrifices to obtain the long and arduous training necessary to learn how to treat their illnesses or injuries. However, *inertia and the difficulties in changing the "system,"* once it is set up by human beings, are the human problems involved. The authors believe these problems can be mastered, but only if parents, health and mental health professionals, and an aroused public *demand* that such changes be brought about for the welfare of their children. Some physicians, nurses, and hospital administrators may feel, if they should read this "angry" chapter, that it is not completely fair to the few very good hospital programs for children in this country. It is not, but they will feel as anguished as we do for young people who are hospitalized in poor programs.

Let us briefly note the number of children affected and the nature of the problems before we elaborate and document them.

THE PROBLEM. Most hospitalization has a serious and often long-lasting "bad" psychological effect on the child and family.

SIZE OF THE PROBLEM. The number of children involved is enormous. About one-fourth of our population of 200 million is under 14 years of age, about one half under 25 years. Three-and-a-half to 4 million children under 15 years are hospitalized each year.[99] Aside from the number of children with chronic illnesses hospitalized over and over again, at least one-third of all young people will have been hospitalized once by the time they become adults.

The most serious causes of emotional problems due to hospitalization

1. Hospitals on the whole have not considered the developmental needs of children in planning for hospitalization. Most hospitals treat children from infancy on as if they were little adults. Therefore, the need for infants and children to be nurtured and sustained by their families during hospitalization is rarely recognized or understood as a critical aspect of care, and even more rarely implemented.

2. Rarely are there "living-in" facilities for parents with hospitalized children of from six months to six years, the developmentally most vulnerable period. Many hospitals still do not even permit daily visiting.

3. Active free play for children physically able to be up and about is rarely provided. Restriction of movement increases children's tensions resulting from hospitalization and impairs their sense of physical mastery, essential to a sense of competence in the hospital.

4. Children and parents are rarely talked to clearly and simply before, during, or after hospitalization. Often they don't understand the need to be hospitalized or what procedures will be carried out. The parents frequently are not asked to help and support their children during this difficult period away from home and family in a strange and threatening environment. Bedside discussions by staff do not take into account the children's limited understanding or their tendency to become seriously upset by what they hear. Progress reports are all too rarely given to parents and children and, when given, are often couched in professional language which is difficult to understand.

5. Most hospitals lack educational facilities to engage children in continued learning, in classrooms where possible or at the bedside. Such a program not only helps children keep in touch with learning but, more importantly, imparts a greater feeling of competence to children in a situation where they have little opportunity to feel mastery of the environment and where they feel at the mercy of the institution and its staff.

6. The child's concept of time is limited. Temporary separations and brief moments of pain feel like forever to a child. The small child's tendency to misinterpret these events as punishment, desertion, or mutilation is rarely considered. Most hospital personnel are not trained to understand children, to talk reassuringly, and help them over tough spots.

7. Small children and children from deprived social and economic backgrounds are most vulnerable to separation from home and family. The signs of anxiety, withdrawal, and fear are rarely recognized and dealt with. Instead, children are often told to "behave" and stop crying or being a "nuisance." Usually they are blamed for being troublesome.

8. Many procedures which can be done on an overnight or outpatient basis are done in the hospital, with unnecessarily prolonged hospitalization. Inactivity after surgery, already proven harmful to the recovery process in adults, is the rule with children, who need especially to be up and active within the limits of their abilities.

What kinds of emotional problems result from such hospital procedures?

1. Psychological disturbances in young children result from regression or "slipping backward" in response to stress. These involve the loss of capacities for washing and dressing or bowel and bladder control, the return to baby talk or loss of speech, and demanding, dependent, "baby-like" behavior.

2. Anxiety reactions and intensified fears result from separation from parents and from pain or restrictions in the hospital. Clinging to mother, nightmares, fears of the dark or death, and sleep disturbances are often seen. Sudden withdrawn behavior often represents self-protective behavior in children who fear separation from the family and have difficulty in trusting them to prevent such pain and fear again.

3. Angry, hostile, and aggressive behavior may occur, associated with destructiveness and temper tantrums. Such children clearly blame parents and family for the hurts they have suffered, and are "getting back" at them. "Testing out" of parents by misbehavior to see if they still love them is seen in some children.

4. Self-gratifying behavior may appear when young children seek the nurturance and security they lack by sucking their thumbs or blankets, masturbating, rocking back and forth, or occasionally chewing or eating inedible objects like paper, hair, or dirt.

5. Other reactive disorders appear in early school-age children. Reading, writing, and other learning difficulties are common as a result of anxiety, regression, and loss of self-confidence arising from hurt and threat to the self in the hospital.

All of the above problems can disappear gradually, but they may become fixed and thus continuingly harmful to children's personality development, particularly their ability to learn and to socialize. Prolonged separation and "maternal deprivation" in an impersonal hospital environment may produce, in infants under two years, lasting inability to socialize, to develop a conscience, or to explore and learn (with an appearance resembling gross mental retardation).

WHAT CAN BE DONE? Major preventive measures are available. Parents, especially mothers, can help care for their children in the hospital. Pediatricians and nurses can be educated to recognize the vulnerabilities of children and to nurture, protect, and stimulate them according to their needs. Preparation of child and family for hospitalization and for post-hospital reactions can be offered, together with prompt follow-up by doctors and nurses after hospitalization, with help for child and family. One experimental program, involving the use of "foster grandparents" to provide the arms and laps for children whose parents can't be with them, will be mentioned. Other important measures will be detailed in the section on "What can be done to alleviate hospitalization problems of children."

Changes in patterns of hospitalization

Over the last 30 to 40 years there have been striking changes in the reasons for which children are hospitalized, as well as in the number of children admitted.[2,99] These changes have come about, in large part, as a result of the many advances made in biological medicine over the last several decades. Public health measures, such as immunizations, the provision of vitamins, improved sanitation, and particularly the advent of antibiotics, among other developments, have prevented or controlled many illnesses that previously required hospitalization. Pediatric wards are no longer filled with children with serious cases of acute infectious disease or nutritional deficiencies. (Both these conditions still do occur, however, with tragic frequency in children from urban and rural poverty areas, who receive inadequate prophylactic care, or none at all.) Now, hospital beds are more and more occupied by children with chronic illnesses or handicaps, such as congenital defects and diseases of genetic origin or chronic complications of accidents. Children who would have died at birth or in early childhood 40 years ago are now living into their teens or adulthood. These include many very small premature babies, children with chronic diseases of vital organs, birth defects and inherited diseases, and even cancer, especially blood diseases.

Children with chronic illnesses or handicaps often require highly specialized surgical and medical therapy currently available only in inpatient settings. In addition, the "technological revolution" in medicine has produced many new, complex, and important laboratory tests. Because of convenience, necessity, or the problems of insurance coverage, these specialized diagnostic tests today frequently involve hospitalization. These new tests have made it possible to diagnose many diseases which would have gone unrecognized some years ago. Such tests also are often used to "rule out" physical disorders in emotionally upset children, who often have physical complaints but turn out to have no physical diseases. Children with emotional problems frequently are first taken to a doctor because of "failure to thrive" in infancy, that is, failure to gain weight and grow normally, or abdominal pains, headaches, or fainting in later childhood and adolescence. Such children are often hospitalized for extensive (and expensive) laboratory tests to rule out diseases such as a kidney problem or a brain tumor.

CHANGE IN HOSPITAL CARE FROM ACUTE TO CHRONIC ILLNESS. Thus, important advances in medicine have changed the types of illness for which children are hospitalized. Children with

chronic physical and/or emotional disorders have largely replaced those with acute physical illnesses in many hospital
wards, especially in university hospitals. These changes also have
increased the total percentage of children who are hospitalized
(as for diagnostic tests) and have increased the percentage who
require repeated hospitalizations for recurrent or chronic physical problems.

Another cause of change in patterns of hospital admissions in
recent years has been the increased number of poor and mi-
nority-group children who are getting better medical care. With
the development of Head Start Programs and Neighborhood
Health Centers, many more children have recently received
medical attention. Previously unsuspected physical and emotional problems have been detected in a quarter to one-half of
these children and adolescents. Some of them have required
hospitalization. Medicaid has made it possible for some of these
poor and minority group youngsters to be admitted to hospitals
previously "reserved" for white, middle-class populations.

FAMILY MOBILITY—NO FAMILY DOCTOR—NO CONTINUOUS CARE.
Finally, the percentage of children being hospitalized has undoubtedly increased because doctors today often only see sick
children in families whom they do not know. Around the turn of
the century, children usually were cared for by family physicians
who had known the children and their families for many years.
With the trend toward specialization, family physicians virtually
disappeared, although very recently they are being resurrected.
Increased family mobility (changes in jobs, neighborhoods, and
cities), with one of five families moving each year, has also decreased continuity of care. Thus, a sick child is often taken to a
doctor who knows little or nothing about the child's past history
or present circumstances. If the parents are upset about the
child's illness, they may not be able to recall important details.
If the doctor has any significant doubt about the degree of seriousness or the nature of the illness, a child may be hospitalized
with a relatively minor illness "to be on the safe side."

The increased number and different types of illnesses for
which children are currently being hospitalized have presented
many new problems and challenges. The number of hospital

beds for children and adolescents has been considerably increased, some through private funding, but mainly from city, state, and federal funds. There still is a shortage of hospital beds and of adequate inpatient facilities in some areas, especially large inner cities and some remote rural areas. The primary focus of this chapter, however, is on what happens to children once they are admitted to a technically adequate, "scientifically modern" hospital unit. Such units need to be prepared to handle children from various racial and socioeconomic backgrounds, some with acute illnesses but most with chronic physical and/or emotional problems. These days they have to be prepared to cope with children and adolescents who are not acutely or seriously ill, who can and should be ambulatory (up and around), and are able to lead a fairly normal life even though they are hospitalized.

Continuity of care, concern for ill persons rather than diseased organs, and the prevention of chronicity and disability from illness or handicap are issues which need higher priorities in both outpatient and hospital medicine. The acute "episodic" or "crisis" medical model of traditional hospital care needs to be supplemented by a more comprehensive model of care. This applies to the emotional as well as the physical aspects of the problems of children in all age groups. Traditional and valid medical concerns to decrease illness and to save lives need to be coupled more effectively with equally valid (and equally traditional) medical efforts to improve the "value of life," to decrease the incidence of illness, and to adhere to the Hippocratic principle of *primum non nocere* (first do no harm). Hospitals do save children's lives, but it is the authors' belief that most hospitals, as they are now operated, often without awareness, make life miserable for children and parents. They promote or fail to prevent emotional problems. They isolate children from families. Advances in biological and technological aspects of medicine have not been matched by advancements in the psychological and humanistic areas of medical care.

SIZE OF THE PROBLEM. The problem of children's hospitalization is of monumental proportions, as pointed out earlier. The U. S. population is now over 200,000,000; half of that population is under 25 years of age. If one-third of these latter are hospitalized at least once, this is a staggering figure—over 30,000,-000 young people. Thus, if the experience of hospitalization were only occasionally harmful, it still would affect a huge number of children and youth. The authors contend that the majority of hospitalizations have a "bad" effect on children and their families. The nation's youngsters do not need any more problems added to the ones they have already. They have enough difficulty coping with poverty and racism (one-fourth to one-third of children) as well as in dealing with the contemporary instability of family life. Divorce occurs in one-fourth to one-third of families in addition to the frequent moves mentioned earlier. There is little contact with extended family members, such as grandparents, uncles and aunts, or cousins. It is no wonder that raising children today seems to involve bigger problems than was the case 50 years ago. It is a tribute to the resilience and resourcefulness of children, not to our society, that as many as do reach maturity without serious emotional problems.

Why are today's hospitals often harmful to children?

THE ADULT MODEL USED FOR CHILDREN. What is it about hospitals that often makes them undesirable places for children? The main reason is that children's facilities traditionally have been built and run with the implicit (and sometimes explicit) assumption that children are simply miniature adults. The special needs and problems of children in general and of sick children in particular usually have been ignored by well-meaning people who unfortunately know little about children's age-appropriate needs or feelings. Traditions and policies established for adult wards usually have been largely or completely transferred to children's services. There has been some recent progress toward change in a few, *but not the majority,* of hospitals. The greatest change has occurred in children's hospitals and in special children's units on one floor of a general hospital. Even in some of these, there is much room for improvement. Little or no change is even possible when children are admitted to general hospitals without adequate pediatric facilities. The latter, unfortunately, is still the situation for the overwhelming majority of hospitalized children across the country.[75]

The "adultomorphic" approach to the care of children is obvious in the traditional policy, in most hospitals, of limiting parents' visits. The assumption seems to have been in the past (and still is in the majority of hospitals) that children do not need their parents around any more than adults need their families. Very little knowledge of child development is necessary to understand that parent visits are important for children under 12 and are especially critical for those under the age of six years.[14,22,40,73,79] Nonetheless, many hospitals continue to limit parents' visits to several times a week, while most limit visits to a short period a day. Very few hospitals have *"live-in" facilities* for mothers to stay overnight with their infants and preschool children.[75] As shown in a recent survey,[101] only 28 out of over 5,000 general hospitals (and only a little over half of the children's hospitals [75]) have such facilities, and most of these are makeshift arrangements. Not all mothers can or wish to stay with their children, but the opportunity should be available. As James Robertson in England has emphasized,[79] and Clare Fagin in this country has documented in a controlled study,[22] such an approach is the only really effective way to prevent psychological distress for very young children.

PHYSICAL ACTIVITY IMPORTANT TO CHILDREN. Many other hospital policies and programs show a lack of concern and a lack of understanding of children's special needs at different ages. Toddlers who can move about are not provided with play pens. Many children up to four or five years of age or older are put in cribs (for fear they might fall to hard floors from beds of adult height). If an older preschool child becomes disturbed at being confined "like a baby" and tries to climb out of the crib, a net is often placed over the crib, or the child may be tied down while receiving an I.V. Preschool and young school-age children are rarely provided recreational areas for active free play. During these ages, especially in a strange and often frightening setting, children need opportunities to run around, ride tricycles, and engage in other "large muscle" activities in order to work off tensions through motor activity. These younger children also are rarely provided facilities to engage quietly in creative play, by themselves or with other children or an adult. Young children need opportunities to paint, to play with clay, to play "house," or "doctor," or "nurse" in order to help them master their worries through creative fantasy. Even children confined to bed need play materials to help work off tensions as well as to enjoy themselves.

LEARNING AND SCHOOL IMPORTANT FOR SIX- TO EIGHTEEN-YEAR-OLDS. In addition to such inadequate facilities for play, the "business" of the young child, most hospitals lack educational facilities for school-age children and adolescents. If children are hospitalized for more than a few days and there is no one to help them continue with their studies, or at least with their interest in learning, they may be seriously penalized on their return to school. If they are hospitalized for several weeks, neglect of their education may prove disastrous, especially if they are from a ghetto background. In many ways there is a parallel in the policies and programs of most hospitals and many public elementary schools. Both types of institutions try to confine children to small areas and expect them to be quiet and cooperative, as if they were small adults. They are expected to have adult-like self-control and interests as well as to conform obediently to many rigid rules, which are often inadvertently designed more for the convenience of the adults in charge than for the benefit of the children themselves. Learning is involved in children's mastery of their environment and feelings of effectiveness. This is especially important in a situation of fear, with children feeling at the mercy of the hospital rules and personnel and feeling they have no way to cope with their anxieties.

CHILDREN ARE BLAMED FOR SHOWING ANXIETY. It is not simply that most hospital programs deprive children of the attention and support of their parents, as well as the facilities and opportunities to play and learn in an age-appropriate manner. Most hospital personnel also expect children not to be particularly upset by these deprivations. Furthermore, they usually expect children who are feeling unwell to accept living in an unfamiliar hospital environment, where frightening or painful procedures are performed on them, much as an adult would. Most mature adults can, when required, adjust to the realities of hospitals and of being mildly to moderately sick. However, children are not "little men"; they do not automatically and readily adjust to the realities of hospital and illness; even most adults do not, under certain particularly stressful circumstances, as a recent article in the *New Yorker* magazine indicates. In fact, the tragic truth is that busy and sometimes harassed hospital personnel not only rarely provide active help, but often actively make adjustment more difficult by being critical of children who "unrealistically" get upset. Out of lack of knowledge or understanding, they frequently become irritated, ridiculing, and even scolding toward children who have "silly" or "unreasonable" fears and fantasies, or who "resist" accepting the "necessary" rules and procedures of the hospital.

AWARENESS OF REALITY DIFFERENT FOR CHILDREN. Youngsters, especially under the age of six or seven, lack the capacity to assess realities as adults can. They tend easily to misinterpret events and to view relatively benign situations as serious threats or potential "attacks" upon them. They may be upset by what they overhear of the conversations of medical personnel on ward rounds. (Things are often said, within children's hearing, which it is assumed they will not understand, without the awareness that children understand a great deal, particularly tones of voice. Children often are disturbed also by what they do not understand.) Young children still lack a good understanding of *time relationships* and may view a relatively brief discomfort as intolerably long. Temporary separations from parents may be misinterpreted as desertions. Finger pricks or venipunctures may be viewed as possible mutilations or *punishments*. Children often need repeated explanations and reassurances, as well as opportunities to talk about their fears and worries with sympathetic adults. Younger children, particularly, need the help of warm, friendly (and preferably familiar) adults to master their unrealistic fears and fantasies before they can begin to make a realistic adjustment to being sick and to living in a hospital.

NEED FOR PARENT SUBSTITUTES TO HELP CHILDREN. When the parents are not with the child, then hospital personnel need to assume this role. Unfortunately, the majority of nurses and doctors who take care of hospitalized children are not intellectually or emotionally prepared to give such help. This professional deficiency is especially prevalent when medical personnel have little or no training in child development and pediatrics. Relatively few hospitals have personnel who have or will make the time to explain procedures or to reassure children repeatedly, in words and ways they can understand and appreciate.

ANTIQUATED HOSPITAL TRADITIONS. Besides the mistaken expectation that children have needs and reactions which are no more or no less than those of adults, most hospitals have other irrational practices which contribute to their young patients' maladjustments. These mainly fall into the category of outmoded hospital traditions which once were thought to be necessary and helpful. These traditions are perpetuated in the majority of hospitals for a variety of reasons, despite their having been repeatedly and unequivocally shown to be useless, at the very least, and, at the most, positively harmful. Possibly the main reason is that many hospitals have become tightly-knit, hierarchical, regimented institutions, run by administrators who often exhibit little concern for people.[41,65,96]

Whatever the reasons, many hospital practices are determined more by "blind" adherence to tradition than by rational concerns for the needs of children. One example of this traditional expediency is the common policy of limiting parental contacts with a child. Besides being an "adultomorphic" policy, limitations on parent-child contacts have been rationalized for many years as "good for the child" and necessary for its hospital treatment. As the result of several controlled studies, few hospitals today are more than mildly afraid of cross-infection from the visits of parents.[73,106]

Children often get upset after the parent leaves, especially when the parents only see their child a short period in the day or a few days a week. Also, parents "get in the way" of rigid hospital programs. Parents and child often want to stay with each other; they sometimes resist the child going off for diagnostic or therapeutic procedures (again especially true if parent-child contact is limited). It is true that many parents get upset being around their sick child in the hospital. It is also true that a few of these upset parents may, in their agitation, upset their children more than they soothe them. Finally, it is true that a few parents make unreasonable demands of and are critical of hospital staff. This usually results from their irrational fears or mental anguish at seeing their child suffering. Nurses often complain that these "demanding" parents take up too much time for explanations and reassurance. They also may impede nurses and doctors carrying out their hospital duties.

Why not exclude, or at least limit, the visitations of difficult and "disruptive" parents? One reason is that temporary "parentectomy" (removing parent from child) is rarely effective (in achieving an unkind goal) and it ignores the fact that the child belongs to and wants to belong to the parents, rather than to the hospital staff. A more basic reason is that partial or total "parentectomy" is usually undesirable for both child and parents and is harmful to both.[22,45,73,103] Even though talking with and giving emotional support to parents are time-consuming, sometimes difficult, and emotionally exhausting for the hospital staff and even disruptive of tight hospital schedules, it usually *"pays off" for parent and child, who after all, are the consumers who are paying for hospital care.*

Other irrational hospital "traditions" for children include prolonged hospitalization following surgery. The length of hospitalization for surgery has been shown to be very arbitrary and to vary greatly among hospitals. Although long abandoned for adults, long post-surgical hospitalization is frequent for children.[99] Enforced bed rest is still used too freely;[33] this in spite of the fact that several controlled studies have shown that even serious illnesses, such as rheumatic fever [47] or acute nephritis,[57] do not show more later complications in children when they are allowed moderate activity (the child's natural state). Children, even those with chronic heart disease,[47] adjust their activity intuitively to their physical limitations.[25,43] Confinement to a bed, as is the routine in most bed-oriented hospital units, ignores the fact that most children are not acutely ill today and tends to promote a regressed sick role which children both resist and are tempted by and which can complicate convalescence. Rigid diets, which children instinctively (and wisely) resist, and which have been proven unnecessary for most children and adolescents with diabetes, obesity, and other disorders, are still prescribed too frequently. Excessive use of restraints and sedatives are still prevalent, supposedly to keep kids quiet but serving only to confuse and agitate them more. Physical isolation of children to prevent cross-infections is still used too widely, in spite of the fact that it is only occasionally necessary [2] and has been shown to be often ineffective. When it is indicated, isolation is often prolonged unnecessarily with little or no attention to the need for parental visiting [2] in spite of the child's lonely, frightened feelings.

What kind of problems do hospitals cause children and families?

The commonest kinds of problems are temporary (though sometimes prolonged or permanent) psychological disturbances. These represent reactions by children to traditional, "adult-oriented" hospitalization. Children between the ages of six months and six years have been shown to be the most vulnerable.[23,40,73,79,84,104] Traditional hospital programs without "live-in" facilities for mothers are the least successful in meeting the developmental needs of this age group. Such very young children are most hurt by separations from their parents under strange circumstances.[12,34,82] Not all separations are traumatic for young children; they need some "practice" in separating from their parents (and the parents need some time by themselves). Such separation should take place under the right circumstances, however, with a familiar person as a parent substitute. This age level also is most prone to regress psychologically or to "slip back" to more immature behavior under stress. Finally, because of their active imaginations, children three to six years of age are most likely to misinterpret and to distort reality; they often have frightening fantasies and unrealistic fears. After as little as one week in a traditional hospital, a high percentage of younger children develop emotional disturbances lasting weeks and even months after discharge.

REGRESSION. One of the commonest emotional problems that occurs is *regression,* with loss of recent developmental age-appropriate skills and increased dependent behavior. This may include loss of bladder or bowel control, the return of baby talk, or of decreased vocabulary (and even loss of speech in toddlers). There is increased whining and crying, as well as loss of self-help skills like feeding and dressing one's self. Such children often demand that the things which they could do for themselves before hospitalization be done by the parents.

ANXIETY. A second type of problem involves *anxiety reactions.*

Clinging behavior (following mother around at home) and fears of needles and doctors occur; great anxiety when briefly separated from parents (e.g., when left with a babysitter) is seen. Other younger children show *detached* (or sullen) and withdrawn behavior when they get back home, especially after being hospitalized for over a week with very little contact with parents. Such children behave as if they have temporarily emotionally detached themselves from their parents. They seem (nonverbally) to say to their parents, "You deserted me, so I gave up on you."

ANGER AT FAMILY. A third type of emotional reaction to hospitalization is the appearance of *anger*, with hostile and aggressive behavior. These youngsters may become destructive of their own or other people's property. They may be "mean" to younger siblings, taking out their feelings on them, or may develop temper tantrums which include screaming, spitting, biting, hitting, or throwing things at parents and siblings who frustrate them. Such children seem to be saying to their parents, "I blame you for putting me in that awful place and now I'm going to get back at you." Their "getting back" anger may, however, be totally or partially diverted and turned in upon themselves, with resulting guilt or depression, rather than being directly expressed toward the parents or objects the parents value.

MISBEHAVIOR. Another common reaction is "testing" of the parent's concern and love by misbehaving. While this paradoxical behavior obviously includes a certain amount of anger at the parents, the primary motive seems to be to misbehave in order to test the reactions of the parents. Will the parents show they feel sorry for what they did in hospitalizing the child and "make it up" to the child? Do the parents still want the child around or (as the preschool child may fear) will they get rid of the child if he or she misbehaves or isn't "good" all the time? These or other questions the children may be asking through their misbehavior, questions they cannot, or dare not, put into words. The misbehavior can also be a way in which children tell their parents (nonverbally), "Look here, I got upset in that horrible place you put me and now I need some special concern and attention from you."

SELF-PLEASURING BEHAVIOR AND OTHER PROBLEMS. A fifth type of behavior reaction shown by many younger children involves the appearance of *self-gratifying* (*or self-pleasure-giving*) *behavior*. These children may regressively (or for the first time) begin to suck their thumbs, may become attached to a security blanket (which they rub against their face or put up their nose), may rock back and forth for long periods (especially at bed time), may show increased masturbation, or may chew on or even eat inedible objects (paper, hair, dirt, wood, or cloth).

These five types of emotional and behavior disturbances resulting from hospitalization are not the only ones children may show. They are simply examples of some of the most frequently seen acute reactions, or reactive disorders, which include also depression, anxiety, sleeping or eating disturbances, hyperactivity, and certain psychosomatic reactions involving diarrhea or vomiting. It should also be noted that two or more types of reactions often are found in the same child. These are problems which even emotionally healthy children often "pick up and carry home with them," when hospitalized for as little as one or two weeks. They usually disappear within weeks to several months, if the child was previously emotionally healthy and if the parents are able to handle the emotional disturbance appropriately after hospitalization, letting the child be more dependent and "baby-like" for a few days and then "weaning" it gradually back to its previous level of adjustment. These acute emotional disturbances, or reactive disorders, are not specific or unique to hospitalization. They are commonly seen in children under the age of six or so, in the face of a wide variety of stresses. Similar reactive disorders appear in young children after the loss of a parent through divorce or death, the loss of a limb, eye, or other body part, prolonged neglect or physical abuse, or most frequently (as when a sibling is born) when children feel that they are being ignored by parents.

REACTIVE DISORDERS. Reactive disorders are most common in preschool children but are not uncommon in early school-age youngsters (six to nine years old). They also occur in emotionally healthy, older school-age children and adolescents, if the stress is severe enough.[45,72,83] However, most children over the age of seven or eight years can "weather" up to several weeks of adult-oriented, traditional hospitalization without developing a reactive disorder (though they should not have to do so). The major exception is when a child over six stays longer than one or two weeks in a hospital without a recreational or, in particular, an educational program. This often leads to transient difficulties in returning to or functioning in school, especially if there has been a history of a previous school adjustment or learning problem. Early school-age children are especially prone to develop "school phobias" (absenteeism due to reluctance to leave home and go to school) following hospitalization. Finally, temporary learning and school discipline problems often occur in children who fall significantly behind their schoolmates. Youngsters with chronic illnesses, requiring repeated hospitalization, may have repeated reactive disorders which result in chronic psychological disability, if not anticipated and worked with.

Children of six or seven years of age may show reading or writing difficulties on return to school. These may result from regression or the temporary "losing" of skills. They also arise from any diseases involving the brain, even if complete recovery occurs, or sometimes from an illness involving a high fever.[60,72] Children are especially prone to develop a delirium with high fever, and may show perceptual-motor difficulties (problems in coordination among the eye, the brain, and the hand) which can persist for at least several weeks before disappearing. Such children should not be pushed hard to return immediately to their previous level of academic functioning, but should be permitted to take it easy for a week or two, gradually being weaned back to full performance. This can prevent a child from feeling pressured and becoming resistant, or from experiencing a feeling of inadequacy, thus developing a negative attitude toward learning which may last for years.

It must be emphasized that hospital reactions are temporary only if the child, family, home, and school situation were previously healthy and adaptable. But these are big "ifs." If the child had preexisting, significant emotional difficulties or school problems (present in at least 10 to 20 percent of children), then hospitalization may be "the straw that breaks the camel's back." A disturbed but functioning child may become permanently nonfunctional after one or two weeks in a "depriving" hospital setting. Even children who did not have preexisting problems may develop long-lasting or possibly permanent disturbances after hospitalization.

Parents may overreact to their child's post-hospitalization behavior because of emotional problems in themselves, because of temporary family trouble, or simply out of ignorance. When parents become angry and punitive with a child who withdraws or misbehaves after hospitalization (which is easy to do when there seems to be no reason for the behavior), the child may become even more withdrawn, hostile, or testingly provocative. On the other hand, when parents try "to make it up" to the child by being markedly overindulgent and overprotective, post-hospital regression is likely to greatly increase. Vicious cycles or "struggles for control" may develop, with parent and child each intensifying and perpetuating the other's disturbed behavior and maladaptive reactions. Sometimes a brother or sister may become upset because of the increased attention given to the hospitalized child, or the parents may get into battles over serious differences in methods of handling the child's altered behavior, blaming themselves, each other, or the hospital for something which is no one's fault, but that of the system.

Even with infants under five or six months old, who do not yet show conscious stranger or separation anxiety, the infant's global reaction [84] of fussiness or crying to different methods of feeding or bathing, perhaps overcome in the hospital, may reappear on return home. The mother then may herself feel a stranger to her own infant, who now reacts with fussiness to her care, having gotten used to different methods of handling in the hospital. Not knowing that this is simply the baby's temporary response to any change in conditions of handling, the mother, by urging feedings or in other ways, may try to prove herself a good mother, with resulting feeding resistance or other problems.[101]

The return of children to certain rigid elementary schools may be stressful. These schools are unable to individualize their handling of students. Therefore, what might be temporary school readjustment or learning problems may become serious, prolonged, or even permanent school maladjustments or learning disabilities.

Recently, evidence has accumulated to indicate that many children who experience stresses, such as losing a parent, may seem to get over it. However, they may have increased risk for later emotional problems in adulthood. This is especially likely if they have not been able to mourn or cry openly,[1,12,42] or if they have not been able to develop other close, warm relationships. No long-range study has been done on children with apparently temporary hospital reactions to see if they have more than normal problems as adults. However, it is reasonable to speculate, on the basis of some evidence, that a significant number of apparently "temporary" hospital disturbances may never completely heal.[48,66] Some of the more severe hospitalization reactions may just superficially seal over. A latent problem may persist, predisposing to later emotional illness if the right (or the wrong) precipitating experience occurs in adult life (such as being deserted by a person one depended on, or having to be hospitalized for a serious illness).

MATERNAL DEPRIVATION. An important type of reactive psychological disturbance, which hospitalization may produce, is so-called maternal deprivation in infants under the age of one or two years. This problem fortunately is not common today, although it was only a few years ago. It arises only if an infant is kept in a hospital for many weeks or months without receiving adequate substitute mothering. Maternal deprivation can result when an infant (especially under one year old) remains in an emotionally (as well as bacteriologically) sterile hospital setting for a number of weeks, during which time it is rarely picked up, cuddled, or otherwise nurtured and pleasurably stimulated by anybody. It can also arise if a child under the age of two or even three years is kept in a hospital for a number of months without receiving consistent "mothering" from parents or parent substitutes. Though rare today, these deprivations of mothering care can produce profound and long-lasting disturbances in a child's total development. Among other repercussions, such children may develop major defects in conscience formation, intellectual abilities, and their capacity to relate to other people, as well as chronic depression and failure to thrive.[12,71,94]

UNNECESSARY HOSPITALIZATION. Another problem that arises not uncommonly today is that of unnecessary hospitalization mentioned earlier. Some physicians hospitalize young children with minor illness because mothers (or fathers) seem overly anxious about their child's illness. The rationale for hospitalization is to reassure the parents that the child will be all right and to alleviate the parents' anxiety. The long-range result, however, may be just the opposite. The next time the child gets sick, the parents tend to be even more overconcerned and anxious than before. In the parents' eyes, a child is hospitalized only if it is very sick and can't be adequately cared for at home. Similar problems arise in older children with emotionally caused physical complaints who are hospitalized for extensive diagnostic evaluations. The fact that the child is hospitalized and elaborate physical tests performed tends to implant the idea that he or she is physically ill, no matter what the tests show. Both the child and the parents may come to believe that there is an underlying physical disease which doctors can identify, if only they look hard enough.

REPEATED HOSPITALIZATION. A final group of problems may arise when a child with a chronic illness or handicap is repeatedly hospitalized (which should occur only if it is absolutely necessary to save its life). Children with chronic physical disabilities need to lead as normal lives as possible. The more such children are hospitalized, the more they may begin to look at themselves as more seriously ill and disabled than is true. They may tend unnecessarily to assume a helpless, sick role in life outside as well as inside the hospital. More problems are produced if the hospital program is a rigid or traditional one and if parents are excluded from much contact with their children. After multiple and prolonged hospitalizations, these children may begin to view hospital personnel as their main parent figures. Their difficulties in reliance on parents who are never around are very frightening. They need to rely on someone. They may begin to feel doctors and nurses know how to raise them better than their parents do. The professionals may replace the parents as the children's principle authority figures and sources of comfort and support. If the parents' child-rearing opportunities and practices are undercut in this way, parent-child conflicts tend to arise at home, and the children's adjustment to their illness tends to become more and more difficult.

What can be done to alleviate hospitalization problems of children?

There are a number of steps that could be taken *now* which would greatly decrease, if not eliminate, most of the problems created by hospitalization. First, however, hospital administrators, physicians, nurses, and especially parents need to become more aware of the seriousness of the problems and the staggering number of children who are adversely affected by hospitals. It is understandable that the general population is not aware of the amount of harm hospitalization can cause children. They have not been adequately informed. It is harder to understand why hospital administrators and most health professionals do not seem aware of, or have done very little about, the many problems which arise from hospitalization. The literature in pediatrics, child psychiatry, and nursing over the last 30 or more years has been full of articles which have more than adequately documented the problems and their solutions. Most bureaucracies only change, not as a result of knowledge, but as a result of pressure.

Indeed, as a glance at the selected references at the end of this chapter will indicate, the pioneering articles of Beverly,[8] Richards and Wolff,[76] Pearson,[66] Jackson,[37] and Bakwin[4] were published in American journals at least 30 years ago, with others not long after.[9,17,39,44,45,48,65,74,83,105,108] Even earlier, the work of Chapin[15] in this country and that of certain German physicians in the early 1900's had already supported the observations of Charles Dickens and the Bronte sisters in England regarding the seriously detrimental effects upon infants and children in long-term hospitals or orphanages. To bring this knowledge to bear, parents and parent groups, and the health and mental health organizations need to contact administrators and professionals and to let them know forcefully that *the public does care what hospitals do to children.* In England, James Robertson, an eminent research worker in this field and his wife, Joyce, also an investigator, have stimulated the formation of a parents' organization to work for changes in children's hospital programs; they have used books,[79] articles,[81] parents' reports,[80] and films [111,112,113,114,115] to educate the public. Such changes have been slow in coming about in Great Britain also, despite the fact that the work of Robertson, Bowlby, and others resulted in an official government statement, the Platt Report.[14] It recommended building facilities for "living-in" in all new hospitals along with other changes supported by other reports.[30,64]

PRE- AND POST-HOSPITALIZATION COUNSELING. Of the steps available, first would be *improved pre- and post-hospitalization counseling* by physicians, nurses, or the new "nontraditional health professionals," such as nurse practitioners or child health associates. Children could be better prepared for hospitalization by being given simple explanations and reassurance and also by talking or "playing out" their anticipatory fears and worries in structured doll play or other situations.[21,54,58] This is feasible for elective admissions as for certain surgical procedures, and could occur in one or two 15- or 20-minute interviews a few days before being hospitalized. At the UCLA Medical Center, all children are brought for a visit to the pediatric play program before elective admission, and they and the parents are routinely prepared. Even in emergency admissions, children can be briefly prepared by a reassuring discussion about what is going to be done, if they are conscious. In addition, parents should be counseled about how to prepare their child. Usually, they are confused and uncertain about what will happen. Booklets for parents to read themselves or for them to read to children are helpful, and are available,[28] including one in Spanish.[19] These, however, are no substitute for an interview with a warm supportive person which gives opportunities for questions. Parents also should be told of possible post-hospital reactions they might expect in their child before the child is discharged, along with anticipatory guidance in how to handle these reactions.[72]

REGULAR POST-HOSPITAL COUNSELING. Skillful and routine preparation of all children undoubtedly would decrease the number, severity, and duration of adverse reactions to hospitalization and surgery, as one controlled study in England shows.[102] Special preparation for anesthesia prior to surgery has been demonstrated by Jackson[38] in a controlled study, to cut down on vomiting and other post-operative reactions,[107] with less anesthetic required. In addition to less tension and fear, this means a greater margin of safety for children with chronic heart and respiratory disease. However, a major limitation of this approach is the difficulty in preparing those children who are the most vulnerable, those under five years of age. Young children have a limited capacity to comprehend and communicate about future, unknown situations. They also have a strong tendency to deny, or block out from awareness, unpleasant realities they are afraid of and would rather not think about (as may older children and adults, to a lesser extent).

Hospitalization reactions, when they occur, can best be dealt with soon after the child is discharged. If child and parents were seen within one week after hospitalization, problems could be detected and counseling provided which would shorten reactive disorders and prevent chronic problems. A one week post-hospitalization visit should be a *regular* procedure for physicians who care for and about children.

Parents should be encouraged to call earlier if puzzled or troubled by their child's behavior, using such a "telephonic lifeline" for support or arranging an earlier visit if necessary. Although not the most crucial change, better pre- and post-hospital care may be the most feasible and practical change which could occur soon. This change is at least something individual parents and physicians have control over by simply asking the doctor or nurse. The remaining recommendations involve changes in the ways large numbers of professionals function together in established systems, with long traditions less immediately susceptible to change, though change *must* come.

CHILD AND FAMILY ORIENTED HOSPITAL PROGRAMS. A second, more direct and effective means of decreasing the negative influences of hospitalization would be a change from adult oriented to *child and family oriented hospital programs*. This requires major alterations in established hospital systems. The most obvious alteration needed in hospital care is the elimination of the widespread practice of putting children in general hospital wards for all ages. Such wards mainly contain adults, especially elderly people, and cannot help but be adult oriented. Children need their own wards, either completely separate pediatric sections in general hospitals or exclusively children's hospitals. They need relations with other children and understanding adults. Frequent contact with family continues previously established relationships and home contacts. In addition, there should be further subdivisions of services according to age groups within pediatric facilities.

The type of age grouping in the pediatric services under the direction of Dr. C. Henry Kempe of the University of Colorado Medical Center has proven very practical and beneficial since its initiation in 1965. Besides a newborn service with "rooming-in facilities" offered by Obstetrics, and an Intensive Treatment ward, there are separate areas for infants and toddlers (up to age three years), preschool children, school-age children, and adolescents (12 to 19 years). Adolescents have their own *recreation area* where they can listen to records, dance, etc. There is a *game room* where adolescents and school-age children can play quiet games, a large sun-deck area and a large recreation area, with swings and other equipment for active play. In addition, there is a separate *play area* for preschool children, equipped with painting material and toys appropriate for the creative play of this age group. The recreational and play activities of children (especially preschoolers) are supervised by a full-time *Child Activity Coordinator* (or "playlady" as she often is called) with volunteer assistants, working closely with teachers and members of the medical and nursing staff. These play and recreational areas are separate rooms or outdoor areas off the wards, "down the hall" from treatment and sleeping areas. This arrangement allows kids to get away from reminders that they are ill and to forget temporarily that they are in a hospital. The Child Activity Coordinator also makes appropriate play materials available to children who are truly bedridden and includes them in a group activity whenever possible. Other recreational programs in other settings involve similar or related features.[6,16,67,68,98]

UNRESTRICTED PARENT VISITING. An even more important change needed in children's hospital care is *complete elimination of restrictions on parental visiting rights*. This should apply from the moment of admission, which should be a positive experience from the start, with emotional support for parent and child. For parents and children from Spanish-speaking or other minority backgrounds, an interpreter should be available if needed. Even those who speak English well may need help when anxious or frightened. There should not only be unlimited parent visitation; parent (and sibling) contact and involvement with the hospitalized child should be actively promoted and facilitated. Parent contacts with their child should be viewed as much more than just casual "visits"; really, they are a vital part of the child's therapy.[11,23,40,73] Parents should be encouraged to feel and to be important, active participants in their child's hospital care. As Moncrieff, an English pediatrician, has said, "The emotional needs of the sick child need as much consideration as his food or drug therapy." [62]

A *therapeutic alliance* needs to be established between parents and hospital personnel; each have their own separate but interrelated roles in providing care for hospitalized children.[73,74,92,108] The parents' role is primarily one of providing a connecting link between home and hospital nontechnical care and child-rearing practices, as well as giving most of the emotional support and comfort. On the other hand, the hospital staff should not expect, or allow, the parents to assume responsibility for specific, technical aspects of medical care, such as giving shots or other medication, making or recording biological observations and measurements (e.g., temperature, urine output), or restraining an anxious child during especially painful procedures. Similarly, if parents can be available, nurses and doctors should not assume nontechnical, general care of a child, such as feeding, bathing, diapering, soothing pain or minor emotional upsets. Parents should be allowed and encouraged to accompany their children while they undergo painful or emotionally traumatic procedures. When a sedative is given in preparation for an operation, the parents should be able to be present in order to hold the child's hand and give comfort and emotional support *if* the parent is emotionally able and willing to do this. This type of care should be the parents' responsibilities, without competition from nurses.[10,18,27,35,59,97] It is also helpful for parents to accompany infants and young children to x-ray or other new strange experiences on or off the ward.

It should be emphasized that hospitals need actively to facilitate parents' involvement. Thus, there should be *living-in* facilities for the parents of all infants and preschool children.[55,63, 69,70,79,93] This term is used to distinguish such facilities from rooming-in units [37,61] for newborn infants, which should be available in every obstetrical service (but are not available in most) for mothers who wish to use this method of getting to know their babies early and intimately. It is very important, and must be encouraged, for at least one parent to sleep next to the child or to stay 24 hours somewhere on the ward, in order to be available for a child under six years old. New hospitals should be planned to include folding, Pullman-type beds or other arrangements. Older hospital units can provide cots, convertible couch beds, or at least a sleeping chair in a small room, *all at no extra cost to the parent*. Parents should also be close at hand to nurture a frightened and seriously ill child. In the type of living-in unit developed by Dermond MacCarthy [53] in England, a lounge for parents is provided, as well as a cooking area for preparation of the child's routine diet or favorite foods.

Sibling visits also should be encouraged. Children in hospitals need contacts and interactions with their *entire* family. Siblings over the age of two or three usually should be allowed to visit in an area just off but adjacent to the ward to prevent the possibility of cross-infection from mumps, measles, or other contagious diseases. Siblings three to six could be included, at times, in preschool hospital play programs. Such programs should be available to permit parents long hospital visits, free of anxiety about their preschool children.

Other hospital changes that are necessary to underwrite child and family oriented hospital facilities include the setting up of *educational programs*.[52,56,72,101] There must be school teachers available to give daily tutorial help (as much as can be tolerated) to every school-age and adolescent child on the ward. Ideally, there should be a *classroom* adjacent to the pediatric ward, so that children can leave the ward and "go to school."

WARDS WITH HOME-LIKE ATMOSPHERE. Children's wards should have a *home-like atmosphere* insofar as possible. The sleeping rooms should be small (e.g., two to four children per room) except in Intensive Therapy and newborn nursery wards.[2,101] There is need for only a few single rooms. Comfortable chairs and couches should be in each room. Ideally, nurses wear street clothes, not uniforms, a change that is already beginning to take place. Rocking chairs must be available for mothers to hold and rock infants. Infants and young toddlers need *play pens* and other protected areas to crawl and walk in. *Family style group eating* areas ought to be available, as well as a separate lounge for parents and private interviewing rooms for talks with doctors, nurses, etc. Children should wear their *own clothes* from home and not wear depersonalized hospital "johnnies" and garments. *Early and complete ambulation* must be strongly encouraged whenever possible. It permits more effective play, social, and educational experiences and avoids emphasizing the sick role for children and adolescents.

An important service for all children who are under six, or for older children who are seriously ill or regressed, is a *substitute mother* program. This is crucial when the real mother cannot or does not wish to assume the mothering role on the ward. The University of Colorado Medical Center has a foster grandmother O.E.O. program set up by Dr. C. Henry Kempe, Chairman of the Department of Pediatrics. This consists of older women who are paid to "mother" (hold, rock, comfort, sing to, play with, or feed) younger or regressed children who do not have their natural mothers available to them. The "grandmothers" themselves derive dignity and a feeling of worth from their contributions to sick children's welfare. They can be of great help to emotionally deprived infants and young children who may benefit from the positive use of pediatric hospitalization [95] for severe feeding problems, diarrhea, failure to thrive, or other psychosomatic disorders; these may respond amazingly to such replacement mothering therapy.[51] Other "mother bank" programs have drawn on volunteers. *Social services* should also be available, with social workers who can help parents who are having parent-child relationship problems. Consulting child psychiatrists and psychologists must also be on tap. Unfortunately, they are not available at present to most general hospital programs.

Finally, there should be a pediatric clinical coordinator or clinical director for each ward, whose full-time job would be supervising total ward care and activities. This physician would coordinate technical, medical, and psychosocial aspects of ward activities and have an interest in research on methods of delivery of inpatient care. He or she would also chair a weekly or twice-weekly "ward management conference"; this helps the members of the different disciplines on the staff to exchange observations and ideas and to implement the 5 C's—*communication, collaboration, coordination, consultation,* and *consistency* —which are vital principles in any such complex undertaking.[72]

ALTERNATIVES TO HOSPITALIZATION. Even more fundamental than improving hospital programs is to do away with unnecessary hospitalizations. One way to accomplish this is through the widespread establishment of new alternatives to hospitalization. These new facilities could be attached to existing hospitals and could serve as a type of "partial hospitalization" for many children who currently receive, but do not require, full inpatient services.

One major innovative program would be small, informal *overnight emergency facilities for children and their parents,* attached to hospital emergency rooms or acute care clinics.[101] Many children with acute illnesses could be kept overnight, with a parent staying with the younger patients, while being observed or treated. In this way, 24-hour formal hospitalization of many young children could be avoided. The child would not have to be separated from the mother; the mother also could be supported and better helped to care for her sick child (increasing instead of decreasing her confidence and competence in her caretaking role). The relatively small, highly selected, and homogeneous patient population of such a facility could be managed by one or two nurses with a minimum of routine procedures. The child would not have to adjust in so short a time to a big ward.

Another new type of partial hospitalization program that would be very helpful is a *motel-like family facility* attached to ambulatory, acute care, and diagnostic clinics. One parent and the child patient, or even the entire family, could move into such a facility and the cost would still be only half or less than that of current hospitalization. It now costs realistically at least $50 to $60 for one person to just stay overnight in a hospital; every diagnostic or therapeutic procedure significantly increases the bill. Much of family functioning could proceed without disruption, especially if day-school facilities were available for the families' children. Many children who currently experience several days or even weeks of hospitalization could be handled in these hospital motel units. Formal hospitalization for purely diagnostic reasons could be virtually eliminated. Likewise, the majority of chronic illnesses or handicaps of children could be managed in this type of facility. Several nurses and doctors could be available to make two or three "motel-rounds" a day, as well as for emergency care. Dr. Morris Green of the University of Indiana originally developed such an approach,[31] and the Children's Hospital in Boston also has such a motel unit. With such programs, formal hospitalization usually would only be necessary for children requiring very close nursing observation and immediately available therapy on a 24-hour basis. The majority of children's hospital beds could eventually be closed, excepting those offering intensive treatment, surgical treatment, and newborn illness care. The empty space could be remodeled into motel-type or other facilities. These and the other foregoing considerations underwrite the importance for the future of innovative planning in hospital design.[13,14,29,61,64,91,101]

An important kind of *partial hospitalization* should be available for children with complicated chronic illnesses needing prolonged, hospital-like care. Large institutional-type convalescent homes fortunately have disappeared today. However, a certain number of children still need long-term, 24-hour care, for periods of months to several years, outside their own home. These children have physical illnesses, often combined with emotional problems, which are beyond their families' capacities to manage. The demand for hospital beds and the cost of hospitalization are too great for long-term inpatient care. Furthermore, hospitals which provide pediatric care are not now, and probably never should be, prepared to "raise" children for one or more years. When children are kept in hospitals for many months or years, serious emotional problems are almost inevitable consequences. Currently, most of these chronically disabled children, often with multiple handicaps requiring a great deal of care, must either return to their families or be placed with untrained foster parents if they come from broken homes. In either instance, they receive grossly inadequate care, often ending up as totally and permanently disabled adults, some on welfare. Most of this misery and burden could be prevented by a sufficient number of *medical foster homes,* where small groups of these children could be cared for by trained, semi-professional foster parents, with adequate nursing services and medical or surgical consultation.

Probably the best way to avoid problems of hospitalization is to handle many more children by *ambulatory care*. Though the highest in priority, this probably will be the most difficult to accomplish. It involves the greatest change in traditional and established systems of delivery of patient care. One simple, but apparently not so simple, change that would go a long way to avoid the need to hospitalize is *modifying medical insurance policies*. Most insurance companies do not adequately cover outpatient treatment and will not pay for many of the more expensive diagnostic tests unless the patient is hospitalized. *Almost all of these tests could just as well be done on an outpatient basis.* Thousands and possibly tens of thousands of children are unnecessarily hospitalized each year because of these clearly irrational insurance programs. The insurance companies (and/or hospital administrators they deal with) undoubtedly have good reason to believe these policies are in their own best interests. Whatever benefits accrue to insurance companies (and/or hospitals), however, there is no doubt that such policies are not in the best interests of children (or families who have to pay inflated insurance premiums to cover large numbers of unnecessary, expensive hospitalization bills).

Next, physicians need to become more comfortable and competent in ambulatory pediatrics, or improved outpatient care. A current and firmly entrenched tradition exists in medical education which emphasizes training in inpatient settings and still largely neglects ambulatory training; there is only one recent textbook specifically devoted to this subject.[32] Medical students still spend most of their time on inpatient services; outpatient training is often optional or brief and without continuity of care to children and families. Interns and residents still have the bulk of their training focused on hospitalized patients. They often learn a great deal about rare and unusual diseases; they typically learn very little about diagnosing or managing the common and chronic illnesses or the emotional and developmental problems of children. Most of the clinical faculty of medical schools still focus their interests and attention on hospitalized patients and specialty clinics, such as a clinic for children with blood diseases. Few really effective educational programs are offered in the medical center's general pediatric clinics, and family practice training programs are just beginning. It is not surprising that physicians often unnecessarily hospitalize children who present any difficult diagnostic or therapeutic problem. Physicians have been firmly conditioned to do this by the "system" and have not learned how to treat many children as outpatients.

Unnecessary hospitalization of children often occurs in relation to surgery. A number of pediatric authorities believe that far too many tonsillectomies are performed which in no way benefit children.[26] Tonsillectomy is one of the commonest operations during childhood, and usually is performed on a preschool child. There also is evidence that a large percentage of surgery on children, traditionally done in hospitals, could be performed on an outpatient basis [46] (e.g., tonsillectomies, hernia repairs) or with overnight stay by mother and child in a facility close to the Emergency Room.

A major decrease in the number of children requiring hospitalization would result from *improved "reach out" services*. These should include more and better homemaker services to help mothers when a child is significantly sick at home. Too many children are hospitalized primarily because mothers are too overwhelmed with home and child-rearing duties to take care of a moderately ill child (who could otherwise stay at home). Also, there need to be increased *visiting nurse services* available to assist with home care of sick children. It was shown originally by Sir James Spence [92] in England, and since confirmed by others, also in England,[5,86] that improved home care programs can handle many children once thought to require hospitalization on an ambulatory basis. It has also been proven that children's adverse emotional reactions are markedly decreased in time and intensity if their illnesses are treated in the home.[86] In urban areas in the United States, doctors have difficulty in making home visits. However, nurse-practitioners and child health associates—two new disciplines "invented" by Dr. Henry Silver at the University of Colorado Medical Center—are beginning to work in neighborhood clinics and in the private offices of pediatricians, and are able to make home visits as well as offer other important contributions to pediatric care.[88,89,90]

Conclusions

In summary, hospitalization of children, especially under the age of six years, has been and still is causing children and their families a great deal of unnecessary grief and misery. A large number of temporary, and many prolonged or permanent, psychological problems are precipitated by hospitalization. The reasons hospitals cause children so many problems are found in the many archaic and irrational features of hospital care programs. Hospitals usually treat children as though they were merely small adults. But their physical and psychological development is not complete and their needs are very different from those of adults. Hospitals still do not seem to recognize, and certainly do not meet, children's special psychological and developmental needs.

In general, the younger the child and the longer the hospitalization—the more the child is deprived of its emotional supports, the parents—the more the child is harmed. There are many things that could and should be done to diminish or eliminate harmful hospitalizations. At the very least, children and parents could be given *better preparation* before elective (non-emergency) hospitalization, as well as regular *post-hospitalization follow-up* by physicians and other professionals. More effective would be changes in hospital programs so they become *child, instead of adult, oriented.* Even better still would be *innovative alternatives to formal hospitalization,* such as motel-type family live-in units attached to hospitals; the child then would not have to be deprived of family support and care. Best of all would be *improved ambulatory or outpatient care* in doctors' offices, outpatient clinics, and home-care programs. Ideal ambulatory care could eliminate the need for any kind of hospital care in the majority of children's illnesses. But these urgently needed changes will not occur until *parents unite and demand* the psychologically best care for their children.

REFERENCES

1. AINSWORTH, M. D. The effects of maternal deprivation: A review of findings and controversy in the context of research strategy. In *World Health Organization Public Health Papers*, No. 14. Geneva, Switzerland: World Health Organization, 1962. Pp. 97–165.
2. American Academy of Pediatrics. *Care of Children in Hospitals.* Evanston, Illinois: American Academy of Pediatrics, 1960.
3. BAKWIN, H. The hospital care of infants and children. *Journal of Pediatrics*, 1951, 39, 383–390.
4. BAKWIN, R. M. Loneliness in infants. *American Journal of Diseases of Children*, 1942, 63, 30–40.
5. BERGMAN, A. B., SHRAND, H., & OPPE, T. E. A pediatric home care program in London—Ten years' experience. *Pediatrics*, 1965, 36, 314–321.
6. BERGMAN, T. *Children in the Hospital.* New York: International Universities Press, 1965.
7. BERGMAN, T. Observation of children's reactions to motor restraint. *Nervous Child*, 1946, 4, 318–328.
8. BEVERLY, B. I. Effect of illness on emotional development. *Journal of Pediatrics*, 1936, 8, 533–543.
9. BIBRING, G. L. The child first. In *Long-Term Care of Children.* Washington, D.C.: U.S. Department of Health, Education and Welfare, Children's Bureau, 1949.
10. BLAKE, F. *The Child, His Parents and the Nurse.* Philadelphia: J. B. Lippincott, 1954.
11. BLOM, G. E. The reactions of hospitalized children to illness. *Pediatrics*, 1958, 22, 590–600.
12. BOWLBY, J. Maternal care and mental health, (2nd ed.) Geneva, Switzerland: *World Health Organization Monograph*, No. 2, 1952.
13. BUTLER, C., & ERDMAN, A. *Hospital Planning.* New York: Dodge, 1946.
14. Great Britain Play Committee. *The Welfare of Children in Hospital.* London: Her Majesty's Stationery Office, 1959. (The Platt Report).
15. CHAPIN, H. D. A plan for dealing with atrophic infants and children. *Archives of Pediatrics*, 1908, 24, 491–496.
16. COYLE, G. L., & FISHER, R. Helping hospitalized children through social group work. *The Child*, 1952, 16, 114.
17. DAVIDSON, E. R. Play for the hospitalized child. *American Journal of Nursing*, 1949, 49, 138–141.
18. DIMOCK, G. H. *The Child in the Hospital: A Study of his Emotional and Social Well-Being.* Philadelphia: F. A. Davis, 1960.
19. *En el Hospital.* El Hospital Neuva York—El Centro Midico de

Cornell. El Departamento de Pediatria. New York: The Society of the New York Hospital, 1970.

20. ERIKSON, E. H. *Childhood and Society.* (Revised and enlarged) New York: W. W. Norton, 1963.

21. ERIKSON, F. Play interviews for four-year-old hospitalized children. *Monograph of the Society for Research in Child Development,* 1958, 23, 1–77.

22. FAGIN, C. M. *The Effects of Maternal Attendance during Hospitalization on the Post-Hospital Behavior of Young Children: A Comparative Study.* Philadelphia: F. A. Davis, 1966.

23. FAUST, O. A., JACKSON, K., CERMAK, E. G., BURTT, M. M., & WINKLEY, R. *Reducing Emotional Trauma in Hospitalized Children.* Albany, New York: Albany Research Project, Albany Medical School, 1952.

24. FREUD, A. Film Review: A two-year-old goes to the hospital. *International Journal of Psychoanalysis,* 1953, 34, 284–287.

25. FREUD, A. The role of bodily illness in the mental life of children. In R. Eissler, et al. (Eds.), *The Psychoanalytic Study of the Child.* Vol. 7. New York: International Universities Press, 1952. Pp. 69–81.

26. GARROW, D. H. The tonsil and adenoid problem. *British Journal of Clinical Practice,* 1957, 11, 218–220.

27. GEIST, H. *A Child Goes to the Hospital: The Psychological Aspects of a Child Going to the Hospital.* Springfield, Ill.: Charles C Thomas, 1965.

28. *Going to the hospital.* Oakland, California: Child Development Center, Children's Hospital of the East Bay, 1951.

29. GOOD, L. R., SIEGEL, S. M., & BAY, A. P. *Therapy by Design.* Springfield, Ill.: Charles C Thomas, 1965.

30. Great Britain Ministry of Health. *Hospital Building Note No. 23, Children's Ward.* London: Her Majesty's Stationery Office, 1964.

31. GREEN, M. Integration of ambulatory services in a children's hospital: A unifying design. *American Journal of Diseases of Children,* 1965, 110, 178–184.

32. GREEN, M., & HAGGERTY, R. (Eds.) *Ambulatory Pediatrics.* Philadelphia: W. B. Saunders, 1968.

33. HARRISON, T. R. Abuse of rest as a therapeutic measure for patients with cardio-vascular disease. *Journal of the American Medical Association,* 1944, 125, 1075–1077.

34. HEINECKE, C. M. Some effects of separating two-year-old children from their parents: A comparative study. *Human Relations,* 1956, 9, 105–176.

35. HUNT, A. D., & TRUSSELL, R. E. They let parents help in children's care. *Modern Hospital,* 1955, 85, 89–91, 154.

36. JACKSON, E. B., OLMSTEAD, R. W., FOORD, A., et al. A hospital rooming-in unit for four newborn infants and their mothers:

Descriptive account of background, development, and procedures with a few preliminary observations. *Pediatrics*, 1948, *1*, 28–43.

37. JACKSON, E. Treatment of the young child in the hospital. *American Journal of Orthopsychiatry*, 1942, *12*, 56–63.

38. JACKSON, K. Psychological preparation as a method of reducing emotional trauma of anesthesia in children. *Anesthesiology*, 1951, *12*, 293–300.

39. JENSEN, R. A., & COMLY, H. H. Child-parent problems and the hospital. *Nervous Child*, 1948, 7, 200–203.

40. JESSNER, L., BLOM, G. E., & WALDFOGEL, S. Emotional implications of tonsillectomy and adenoidectomy on children. In R. Eissler, et al. (Eds.), *The Psychoanalytic Study of the Child*. Vol. 7. New York: International Universities Press, 1952. Pp. 126–269.

41. KLAUS, M., & KENNELL, J. Mothers separated from their newborn infants. *Pediatric Clinics of North America*, 1970, *17*, 1015–1037.

42. KLEIN, D. C., & LINDEMANN, E. Preventive intervention in individual and family crisis situations. In C. Caplan (Ed.), *Prevention of Mental Disorders in Children*. New York: Basic Books, 1961. Pp. 283–322.

43. KORSCH, B. The pediatrician and the sick child. In S. Z. Levine (Ed.), *Advances in Pediatrics*. Chicago: Yearbook Publication, 1958.

44. LANGDON, G. A study of the uses of toys in a hospital. *Child Development*, 1948, *19*, 197–212.

45. LANGFORD, W. S. Physical illness and convalescence: Their meaning to the child. *Journal of Pediatrics*, 1948, *33*, 242–250.

46. LAWRIE, R. Operating on children as day cases. *Lancet*, 1964, *2*, 1289–1291.

47. LENDRUM, B. L., SIMON, A. J., & MACK, I. Relation of duration of bed rest in acute rheumatic fever to heart disease present two to fourteen years later. *Pediatrics*, 1959, *24*, 389–394.

48. LEVY, D. M. Psychic trauma of operations in children and a note on combat neurosis. *American Journal of Diseases of Children*, 1945, *69*, 7–25.

49. LIGHTWOOD, R., et al. Home care for sick children. *Lancet*, 1957, *1*, 313–317.

50. LOOMIS, E. A. The child's emotions and surgery. In W. B. Kiesewetter (Ed.), *Pre- and Post-Operative Care in the Pediatric Surgical Patient*. Chicago: Yearbook Publications, 1956.

51. LOURIE, R. S. Experience with therapy of psychosomatic problems in infants. In P. H. Hoch and J. Zubin (Eds.), *Psychopathology of Childhood*. New York: Grune & Stratton, 1955. Pp. 254–266.

52. LUCAS, W. P. Education for hospitalized children. *Medical Women's Journal*, 1949, *56*, 22–29.

53. MACCARTHY, D., LINDSAY, M., & MORRIS, I. Children in hospital with mothers. *Lancet*, 1962, *1*, 603–608.

54. MACKEITH, R. Children in the hospital: Preparation for operation. *Lancet*, 1955, *2*, 843–845.

55. MANN, P. When he's in the hospital: Why can't you stay with your child? *Parade* (Newspaper magazine supplement), January 23, 1966, 6–9.

56. MASON, E. The hospitalized child——His emotional needs. *New England Journal of Medicine*, 1965, *272*, 406–414.

57. MCCRORY, W. W., FLEISHER, D. S., & SOHN, W. B. Effects of early ambulation on the course of nephritis in children. *Pediatrics*, 1959, *24*, 395–399.

58. MELLISH, R. W. P. Preparation of a child for hospitalization and surgery. *Pediatric Clinics of North America*, 1969, *16*, 543–553.

59. MENZIES, E. P. Nurses under stress. *Nursing Times*, 1961, *57*, 141–142, 173–174, 206–208.

60. MEYER, E. Psychological considerations in a group of children with poliomyelitis. *Journal of Pediatrics*, 1947, *31*, 34–48.

61. MOLONEY, J. C., MONTGOMERY, J., & TRAINHAM, G. The newborn, his family, and the modern hospital. *Modern Hospital*, 1946, *67*, 43–46.

62. MONCRIEFF, A. La Pediatrie sociale. *Courrier du Centre Internat. de L'Enfance*, 1951, *1*:3, 11–20.

63. MORGAN, M. L., & LLOYD, B. J. Parents invited: A. The mother's view. B. The nurse's view. *Nursing Outlook*, 1955, *3*, 256–259.

64. Nuffield Foundation. *Children in Hospital: Studies in Planning.* New York: Oxford University Press, 1963.

65. PARRY, L. A. The urgent need for reforms in hospitals. *Lancet*, 1947, *2*, 881–883.

66. PEARSON, G. H. J. Effect of operative procedures on the emotional life of the child. *American Journal of Diseases of Children*, 1941, *62*, 716–729.

67. PICKERILL, C. M. Plastic surgery clinic for babies: Where mothers reside with their infants. *Nursing Mirror*, 1947, *85*, 2210.

68. PICKERILL, C. M., & PICKERILL, H. P. Keeping mother and baby together. *British Medical Journal*, 1946, *2*, 337.

69. PLANK, E. N., CAUGHEY, P. A., & LIPSON, M. J. A general hospital program to counteract hospitalism. *American Journal of Orthopsychiatry*, 1959, *29*, 94–101.

70. PLANK, E. N. *Working with Children in Hospitals.* Cleveland, Ohio: Western Reserve Press, 1962.

71. POWERS, G. F. Humanizing hospital experiences. *American Journal of Diseases of Children*, 1948, *76*, 365–379.

72. PROVENCE, S., & COLEMAN, R. *Infants in Institutions.* New York: International Universities Press, 1962.

73. PRUGH, D. G. Children's reactions to illness, hospitalization, and surgery. In A. M. Freedman and H. I. Kaplan (Eds.), *Com-*

prehensive Textbook of Psychiatry. Baltimore: Williams & Wilkins, 1967. Pp. 1369–1376.

74. PRUGH, D. G., STAUB, E. M., SANDS, H. H., KIRSCHBAUM, R. M., & LENIHAN, E. A. A study of the emotional reactions of children and families to hospitalization and illness. *American Journal of Orthopsychiatry,* 1953, *23,* 70–106.

75. Report of Association for Child Care in Hospitals. (Mimeographed), 1965.

76. RICHARDS, S. S., & WOLFF, E. The organization and function of play activities in the setup of a pediatric department: A report of a three-year experiment. *Mental Hygiene,* 1940, *24,* 229–237.

77. RICHMOND, J. B. The pediatric patient in illness. In M. H. Hollender (Ed.), *The Psychology of Medical Practice.* Philadelphia: W. B. Saunders, 1958. Pp. 195–211.

78. RILEY, I. D., et al. Mother and child in hospital—Two years' experience. *British Medical Journal,* 1965, *2,* 990–992.

79. ROBERTSON, J. *Young Children in Hospital.* New York: Basic Books, 1959.

80. ROBERTSON, J. (Ed.) *Hospitals and Children: A Parents'-Eye View.* London: Victor Gollancz, 1962. (American Edition available).

81. ROBERTSON, J. A mother's observations on the tonsillectomy of her four-year-old daughter. In R. Eissler, et al. (Eds.), *The Psychoanalytic Study of the Child.* Vol. 2. New York: International Universities Press, 1956. Pp. 410–427.

82. ROUNDINESCO, J., DAVID, M., & NICHOLAS, J. Responses of young children to separation from their mothers. *Courrier du Centre Internat. de L'Enfance,* 1952, *2,* 66–78.

83. SENN, M. J. E. Emotional aspects of convalescence. *The Child,* 1945, *10,* 24–28.

84. SCHAFFER, H. R., & CALLENDER, W. M. Psychologic effects of hospitalization in infancy. *Pediatrics,* 1959, *24,* 528–539.

85. SHORE, M. F., GEISER, R. L., & WOLMAN, H. M. Constructive uses of a hospital experience. *Children,* 1965, *12,* 3–8.

86. SHRAND, H. Behavior change in sick children nursed at home. *Pediatrics,* 1965, *36,* 604–607.

87. SHRAND, H. Home care scheme for sick children. *Nursing Times,* 1964, *60,* 1113–1116.

88. SILVER, H. K., FORD, L. C., & DAY, L. R. The pediatric nurse practitioner program: Expanding the role of the nurse to provide increased health care for children. *Journal of the American Medical Association,* 1968, *204,* 298–302.

89. SILVER, H. K., & HECKER, J. A. The child health associate. *Hospitals* (J.A.H.A.), 1970, *44,* 47–49.

90. SILVER, H. K., & MCATEE, P. A. Health care practice: An expanded profession for men and women. *American Journal of Nursing,* 1972, *82,* 78.

91. SLOAN, R. P. *Hospital Color and Decoration.* Chicago: Physicians' Record Co., 1944.
92. SPENCE, J. C. Care of children in hospital. *British Medical Journal,* 1951, *1,* 125–130.
93. SPENCE, J. C. Mothers go to babies' hospital. *American Journal of Nursing,* 1954, *54,* 582–583.
94. SPITZ, R. A. Hospitalism: An inquiry into the genesis of psychiatric conditions in early childhood. In R. Eissler, et al. (Eds.), *The Psychoanalytic Study of the Child.* Vol. 1. New York: International Universities Press, 1946. Pp. 53–74.
95. SOLNIT, A. J. Hospitalization: Aid to physical and psychological health in childhood. *Journal of Diseases of Children,* 1960, *99,* 155–163.
96. STERN, R. A hospital is no place for people. *Resident and Staff Physician,* August, 1971.
97. STEVENS, M. Visitors are welcome on the pediatric ward. *American Journal of Nursing,* 1949, *49,* 233–235.
98. TISZA, V. B., & ANGOFF, K. A play program and its function in a pediatric hospital. *Pediatrics,* 1957, *19,* 293–302.
99. United Nations. Declaration of the rights of the child. *International Nursing Review,* 1960, *7,* 4.
100. U. S. Dept. of Health, Education, and Welfare, Children's Bureau. *Illness among children.* Data from the U.S. National Health Survey, by C. G. Schiffer and E. P. Hunt. Publication No. 405. Washington, D.C.: U.S. Dept. Health, Education and Welfare, 1963.
101. U.S. Dept. of Health, Education, and Welfare. *"Red is the color of hurting": Planning for children in the hospital.* M. F. Shore (Ed.), Public Health Service Publication No. 1583. Washington, D.C.: U.S. Dept. Health, Education and Welfare, 1965.
102. VAUGHN, G. F. Children in hospital. *Lancet,* 1957, *1,* 1117–1120.
103. VERNON, D. T. A., FOLEY, J. M., & SCHULMAN, J. L. Changes in children's behavior after hospitalization: Some dimensions of response and their correlates. *American Journal of Diseases of Children,* 1966, *111,* 581–593.
104. VERNON, D. T. A., FOLEY, J., SIPWICZ, R., & SCHULMAN, J. L. *The Psychological Responses of Children to Hospitalization and Illness.* Springfield, Ill.: Charles C Thomas, 1967.
105. WALLACE, M., & FEINAUER, V. Understanding a sick child's behavior. *American Journal of Nursing,* 1948, *48,* 517–522.
106. WATKINS, A. G., & LEWIS-FANING, E. Incidence of cross-infection in children's wards. *British Medical Journal,* 1949, *62,* 616–729.
107. WERRY, J. S., & DAVENPORT, R. T. Effect of surgery and anesthesia on post-hospitalization adjustment in children. *Scientific Proceedings of the American Psychiatric Association,* 1969. Pp. 208–209.

108. WESSEL, M. A. The pediatric nurse and human relations. *American Journal of Nursing*, 1947, *47*, 213–216.
109. WINNICOTT, D. W. Film review—Going to hospital with mother. *International Journal of Psychoanalysis*, 1959, *40*, 62–63.

FILMS

110. MASON, E. *Children's Reactions to Hospitalization.* New York: New York University Film Library, 1963. See also—Films on children's hospitalization and maternal deprivation: an annotated bibliography. *Commun. Ment. Health J.*, *3*, 240, 1967.
111. ROBERTSON, J. *A Two-Year-Old Goes to Hospital.* New York: New York University Film Library, 1952. (45 minutes, 16mm sound film, also abridged version, 30 minutes.)
112. ROBERTSON, J. *Guide to the Film: A Two-Year-Old Goes to Hospital.* London: Tavistock Publications, 1953.
113. ROBERTSON, J. *Going to Hospital with Mother.* New York: New York University Film Library, 1958. (40 minutes, 16mm sound film.)
114. ROBERTSON, J. *Guide to the Film: Going to Hospital with Mother.* London: Tavistock Publications, 1963.
115. ROBERTSON, J., & ROBERTSON, J. J. *An Infant in Hospital.* New York: New York University Film Library, 1969.

ORGANIZATIONS FOR IMPROVEMENT OF HOSPITAL PRACTICES

ASSOCIATION FOR THE CARE OF CHILD IN HOSPITALS, P.O. Box H, Union, W. Va., 24983. An interdisciplinary group, with an annual meeting and a newsletter, which welcomes members.
CHILDREN IN HOSPITALS, 31 Wilshire Park, Needham, Mass., 02192. A group of parents and professionals.

Man changes with the social milieu
which surrounds him.

EMILE DURKHEIM

_____ **15**

The Rights of the
Retarded Child
and His or Her Family

IRVING N. BERLIN, M.D.

A brief history of the rights of retarded children and adolescents

Prior to World War II, mentally retarded children and adolescents had no rights to any of the services in our society except custodial care. That care was for infants and very young, severely retarded children and for those retarded adolescents who had begun to cause problems for the community and therefore needed to be in a custodial setting. The advent of antibiotics extended the life of severely retarded children who otherwise died very young. As the number of custodial cases grew, it became clear that the custodial institutions for the retarded were no longer functional. However, society as a whole had little interest in retarded children and adolescents. In most of the United States, retarded and psychotic children were often placed in the same wards for custodial care. The basic purpose of "care" was to remove the child from home and community where the child might be a burden or troublesome. Little interest or concern existed on the part of either federal or state agencies to take advantage of the fact that retarded children now could live longer and potentially might be helped to become more competent persons. With training they could require less in the way of expensive custodial care and could contribute to their own care, and the less retarded could help those more retarded. Training and educational programs needed to be worked out.

Increased industrialization in our nation has eliminated jobs previously available to the mildly to moderately retarded in cities and small towns. Uncomplicated and routine jobs in the community, such as selling newspapers, cleaning the premises of small stores, helping with packaging and delivering groceries and other commodities have diminished and are disappearing. These jobs had provided viable employment opportunities for retarded adolescents as long as the community was protective of them. When these operations were small, personal interest in the retarded adolescents resulted in supervision of their work to help them function effectively. The adolescents not only did a good job and got satisfaction from it but also performed a necessary service within the community. It is still true, in some rural communities, that retarded children and adolescents are able to play a viable and important role within the family and the community. There are still a number of important chores both in housekeeping and in aspects of farming that retarded children and adolescents can learn to do very well. In such situations, they become an integral part of the community in which they exist, performing an important service for which they are paid. These youngsters receive respect important to their sense of accomplishment and worth.

As the family grocery store, dry goods store, hardware store, gas station, and other small establishments are replaced by supermarkets and large variety stores, and much of the work in industry, home, and farming has become automated, there is less and less place for the mildly retarded child and adolescent within the community. Urbanization, with all of its complex problems in living, has made it less likely that moderate to mildly retarded children can have opportunities to feel useful and wanted within the community.

RETARDATION AND TECHNOLOGY. Until the advent of President Kennedy and the concerns of the Kennedys with mental retardation, little national focus or funds were directed into the etiology of retardation or training of teachers to work effectively with the retarded.

A number of studies on mental retardation in the last 50 years, culminating with the Report of the President's Commission on Mental Retardation in 1968, have all indicated that the major causes of retardation are social and environmental factors, resulting in functional retardation. Thus, the large group of citizens on the lower end of the normal I.Q. spectrum in former days could learn to be independent, take care of themselves, earn a living and become viable members of the community. In our advanced technological society such persons of all ages have no place and no rights at all. Their retardation is compounded in a depersonalized, possession-oriented society, a society with little organized concern for human values and the worth of human life. Thus, the mild to moderately retarded children are increasingly treated in society as if they were severely retarded with no place for them within the community.

RESEARCH IN RETARDATION. Research in the social, cultural aspects of retardation has focused on the increased number of infants dying at birth and the increase in premature births, as well as a more accurate assessment of the impact of poverty on individuals in society. A number of very important findings began to emerge. First, the greater death rate at birth and the greater amount of prematurity in the poverty population had a great deal to do with poor medical care, both prenatally and at birth. Further, the overwhelming degree of malnutrition in mothers resulted in malnourished infants. Continued massive protein and vitamin malnourishment of infants and young children results in brain damage, fewer and smaller brain cells. Thus, poverty is closely related to the increased number of retarded among our child population. An essentially reversible process has, until now, been given very little attention. Despite the enormous amount of research data, there still continues to be very little effort to reduce the malnutrition of pregnant mothers and malnutrition of infants as well as of the entire poverty population. The issue of providing good prenatal, natal, and postnatal care has also received much publicity but very little action. We continue to multiply and increase the number of retarded children in our society with little attention to the aspects of prevention of retardation that are now possible. On the other hand, retardation based on biochemical-enzyme deficiencies and on a genetic basis has received a good deal of attention and research monies. These problems are of great interest to medical specialists and researchers, and a number of solutions have been identified. Methods of reversing brain damage due to phenylketonuria, maple sugar disease, and other genetic biochemical defects have been found; however, together they account for only about three-tenths of one percent of the retardation in our population.

RETARDED CHILDREN IN SCHOOL. The rapid movement of population away from rural areas in both north and south into industrial cities has also resulted in an enormous increase in the number of functionally retarded children in schools, which have few or no programs for them. One of the characteristics of the move from the rural setting and from the rural and urban south into northern and western cities is that these families find themselves not only displaced but unable to find jobs and therefore dependent on welfare and unable to find decent housing. They find themselves in an alien society without the support system of an extended family which has been important to them for generations. Many of these families come from a culture which is essentially nonverbal, and in which a variety of nonverbal signals are used. These signals are not at all understood in our verbal, urban society. School is difficult for these youngsters because the school's expectations are geared to those of the verbal urban children. Many children and adolescents thought to be retarded are actually youngsters of normal intelligence who function on a retarded level because the urban culture is in no way prepared to deal with them in terms of their own background and their own means of communication. Without the supports of extended family and community, they become increasingly withdrawn. The adult members of the family, because of their own anxieties about jobs, food, and housing, are often unable to be supportive of children who need their attention and concern. As a result, the total functioning of the family is in crisis.

RIGHT TO RELEVANT EDUCATION AND FAMILY SUPPORTS. Our society has given little attention to the rights of these youngsters

to have the requisite training and opportunities which capitalize on their nonverbal styles of communication. Society has not
recognized that many of these youngsters are bright and have a
variety of skills, especially manual ones, which could be built
upon and used as a transition to the development of verbal skills.
Such migrant families are part of the poverty population in the
ghetto, subject to the same threats of economic deprivation and
the same nutritional problems which have affected them as poor
people in both rural and urban areas. Their children, too, are
very likely to be born retarded with nutritional brain deficiencies. These data raise the disturbing question: Do these families
and youngsters have a right to the kind of employment opportunities, social economic supports, medical care, and nutrition
which will reverse this process?

THE MAJOR ROLE OF A.R.C. IN REFORM. The major concerns of
parents of retarded children are legislation and appropriation of
money for the education and training of all retarded children so
that their potential can be best realized. The purpose always is
that these children might therefore lead a life which makes them
a part of society rather than an isolated and sequestered segment of it.

The rights of retarded children and their families have been
of major concern to the Association for Retarded Children.
Middle-class parents of retarded children have done an enormous amount of work and have been effective in getting state
authorities to attend to the needs of retarded children and
youngsters. They have educated state legislators, congressmen,
and senators to understand the needs and write implementing
legislation in a few states making it a right for all retarded children to receive education and training commensurate with their
capacities.

Without the vigilant and aggressive efforts of these parents,
we would still be in the dark ages for the retarded child. Efforts
of these parents have increased the amount of space available in
schools and have resulted in special education programs and
sheltered workshops for adolescents and adults. Impact has
also been felt in initiation of professional training programs for
teachers, although these remain too few. More money has been
appropriated for specific research into etiology of mental re-

tardation and also research into methods of teaching and training the retarded to help them to become more effective and competent. Parent involvement has encouraged and supported research into congenital defects and birth defects which account for an important segment of the retarded. Recently, some state parent organizations are beginning to support the work in prematurity, which results in slow learning and often retardation. Another recent milestone, to which A.R.C. contributed, is the reduction of isolated and purely custodial wards for the retarded in state hospitals. These facilities are being brought closer to population centers. Continued pressure exists for these facilities to become geared to training and education programs. These programs are still infrequent and generally of poor quality. Perhaps the greatest impact of the A.R.C. has been in upgrading services for the retarded within the community. There are now, throughout the country, a number of preschools for retarded children, as well as elementary schools. A widespread movement occurs for the integration of retarded children into classes with normal children for at least a few hours a day. Thus, the usual segregation of the retarded can be reduced, resulting in fewer problems, as retarded youngsters learn to live with other youngsters in a community geared to understanding their needs and dealing with them as fellow human beings, rather than segregating and isolating them.

Rights of retarded children and families

THE RETURN TO COMMUNITIES. When we discuss the rights of retarded children and their families, we now talk about them within the context of the community. With the advent of community mental health centers some increased community services have been provided. Efforts have been increased to bring retarded children back from state hospital programs and into the community. While these efforts present opportunities for delineating new rights of children and their families, they also have some possible hazards which endanger the rights of retarded children and their families. For example, most states would like to reduce the number of state hospitals for retarded —because they are expensive—and return all retarded children into the community. While each state is prepared to underwrite to some extent the financial burden of returning retarded youngsters to the community, there is no real commitment to the support and development of quality programs. What has begun to happen is that in each community and each municipality, program quality depends upon the individual organizations and parents within the community and their ability to obtain local as well as increased state funds for their particular programs. No national, and very little state, commitment is made to quality programs for the retarded. Thus, in most states, the return to the community has meant decreased real services and care, especially for the severely retarded. The standards of care, education, and training have, in many states, steadily fallen.

Large cities, with their lack of resources, are unable to add these burdens to their other problems within the educational system. Neither state nor federal government has undertaken needed wide-ranging programs of training personnel to work with the retarded. Most teachers of retarded children are inadequately trained, or untrained and unskilled. Group homes for the retarded are rarely able to maintain quality programs because group-home parents and workers are not well trained or adequately paid. The programmatic development which is possible in a fairly large institution, by virtue of its size and capacity to employ a variety of specialists, is not as easily worked out in group homes. Small size also makes it easier to ignore the needs of retarded youngsters for effective education and training programs in community group homes. Usually the task is passed to the already overburdened schools. Thus, the burden of community care for the retarded has been shifted back to the family and community. Many families are ill-prepared to undertake these responsibilities. Most communities are unable to mount the kinds of programs which are required to give retarded children and adolescents a fair chance. The rights of both children and families are ignored when retarded children return to communities with no assessment of whether particular youngsters would do better in the large program with a wide variety of activities and, in some hospitals, a fuller social life. Assessment of capacity and supportive help are also necessary to work with those families that are unable to fully care for retarded children at home, because of other burdens which overwhelm them. In many cases, particularly in poverty families, health problems or other family and marital problems interfere with family stability.

RIGHTS FOR THE RETARDED INCLUDE FAMILY RIGHTS. The family and the retarded infant must have the right to early diagnostic assessment and accurate evaluation. Then, prognostic statements can be made about the degree of retardation and a plan can be made for a program to help the child and family. The family and the child have a right, after the diagnostic work-up, for a follow-through program which is continually concerned with the child and family and facilitates the family's becoming involved with the various community resources which might begin the education and training of their child. These agencies also should begin to help the parent to learn to live and to work with the retarded child. Such follow-through programs are very rare. Usually after the diagnosis of retardation is made, families are left to shift for themselves to find any community programs which might benefit them. They are often shuttled from one program to another. They have no help in assessing the quality or the particular aspects of a program which might be helpful to their child and to themselves. Most diagnostic and assessment programs are not concerned with the need for frequent and continued reassessment early in a child's life. Periodic reevaluation can help parents begin to recognize the particular requirements and assets of their special child and to plan with the resources in the community to meet these needs and develop the assets.

SOCIALIZATION: A RIGHT OF RETARDED CHILDREN. Perhaps the most critical right of parents of a retarded child, which is usually ignored, is the right to be helped to understand the necessary efforts required of them to help their child begin to learn and to socialize within the family setting. Families are usually not helped to recognize that the learning process, although it is much slower, still occurs in very much the same way as with normal children. They often do not realize that reinforcements to learning are necessary and vital and must be repetitive.

Agencies almost always fail to help parents recognize the critical and urgent role that discipline plays in the child's life. Early training in socialization and the use of gentle but persistent discipline to help the child learn the meaning of "no" are important. The child needs to recognize when parents and others are displeased, and to understand that certain behaviors are expected and certain behaviors cannot be tolerated within the home setting. Such slowly acquired understanding is critical for the child to be able to socialize and to live with others both in the home and in the school setting. All too often, these issues are not clarified early with parents. Therefore, because they feel some guilt at having a retarded child, they would like to make up to that child for his or her retardation. As a result, a tendency often exists not to insist on the kind of behavior which is important for that child's learning and socialization. Often parents expect other children in the family and the community as a whole to make allowances for temper tantrums, for aggressive and destructive behavior. They do not recognize that ignoring antisocial behavior begins a trend which reinforces such behavior and makes living in the home and socialized living in the school setting increasingly difficult for the child.

Most important is that, unless discipline is acquired, learning becomes extremely difficult for the child. For all children, learning is to some extent frustrating. For retarded children, if they are to learn, they need repeated practice until they acquire a skill. Frequent repetition is vital to their remembering and carrying out tasks. Unless these youngsters have begun to respond to discipline, to recognize the "no," and to react to encouragement by sustained effort, these youngsters tend to react with temper tantrums or withdrawal to the demands that are made upon them for recurrent and often trying efforts in learning. As they grow older, they respond to frustration with destructive and assaultive behavior or extreme isolation. Either makes both learning and socialization impossible. Since these patterns are established very early in life, it is indeed a right of both the parents and the children to have the process anticipated and spelled out for them. They then must have the necessary help to begin the socialization process of the children early so that the capacity for learning and for adaptive behavior in the community is enhanced early.

The ability of children to live in the home, to be part of the family, to begin to learn to do some of the chores within the family—which makes them a valued member of their family and helps them feel competent and wanted—depends upon their capacity to respond to family rules, to praise, and to encouragement and prohibitions. The capacity to look for praise and warmth and to react to prohibitions quickly spells the difference between a child who is unfairly treated and permitted to tyrannize the family because of his or her defect or one who lives as a member of the family. Thus, the family's role of enhancing the child's capacity for living and learning is a critical one. The right to be helped to such an enhancement on the part of the family is one that does not exist today.

THE RIGHT TO COMPETENT TEACHERS. Another right that both child and family should have, but often do not, is the right to skilled teachers educated to work effectively with retarded youngsters of various developmental levels. Few teacher training institutions help teachers learn to work effectively with the retarded. Most teachers of special classes for the retarded have had little, if any, education in teaching or training retarded youngsters. They know little, if anything, about child development and the learning process. They have not been taught to use the kinds of reinforcements and behavior modification techniques which would be effective for these youngsters.

Teachers' frustration in working with children who do not respond readily is usually noted in their giving up on the education and training of their students and becoming resigned to a babysitting job. Such an attitude is harmful to the mental health of the student, the teacher, and certainly the parents.

Differences between trained and untrained teachers. It has been of interest to me in working as a consultant in classrooms for retarded children to note the difference in the expectations between those teachers who have been trained to work with retarded children and those who have not. Trained teachers have clear ways of assessing the developmental stages of a child. They can evaluate individual capacities and begin to help each child take the next small steps in learning necessary for continued learning and development. The work is individualized and the teacher uses the reinforcement of both verbal praise and a variety of special tangible reinforcements, meaningful to each child, such as food, opportunities to play records, games, etc., as a means of motivating each of the children. In those classes where there are no trained teachers, the entire class of children is seen as having exactly the same kinds of problems, being at essentially the same level of development, with the same potentials. Untrained teachers teach reading in groups, knowing that some children cannot even recognize letters whereas others have already been helped at home to begin to read at an elementary level. All the children in that class are penalized because none of them are helped to advance at their own speed, beginning at their own level, toward the next stage of learning.

Another distinguishing characteristic of the trained vs. the nontrained teacher is the insistence upon discipline in the classroom. Trained teachers know very clearly that unless there is discipline in the classroom, no learning occurs and the socialization which is an important part of the class activities also deteriorates. Such teachers therefore use every means at hand, but especially the means of positive reinforcement, to help children to become disciplined students. They also take the requisite time with those children who may have difficulties until each child knows that the teacher really means it when he or she insists that the child carry out certain tasks and is expected to perform to capacity.

The third area of difference is that the trained teachers have clear expectations of collaborating with parents. In classes for the mentally retarded, possibly more than in any other educational effort, close collaboration between parents and teachers is essential to the successful learning of the child. Trained teachers know this is a critical factor in their students' learning and social adaptation. They work closely with parents so parents can continue and thus reinforce some aspects of the program developed in school. Such reinforcement makes the child a more viable member of the family and makes it clear to the youngster that what is learned in school is important to the family. Thus, parents and siblings talk about the achievements of the child and reinforce them within the family setting.

For example, in one instance, a girl of nine had begun to learn to set the table and to cook simple recipes. These achievements were not solidified until the parents and the older siblings were made aware of the youngster's new skills. They then encouraged the youngster to set the table at home and to cook the recipes she had learned for the family. They all enjoyed and praised her accomplishments. Her pleasure came from being able to do something for the family which was praiseworthy. These activities brought continued comments of pleasure from family members and greatly enhanced the youngster's position within the family. Her capacity for learning and moving on to the next step in learning in school was also clearly enhanced.

Thus, one of the important rights of mentally retarded children and their families is the right to skilled teachers, trained to work with child and family.

RIGHT TO EFFECTIVE SOCIAL SERVICES. Another right is the access to effective social services. One of the problems encountered by families with retarded children is the difficulty of moving among agencies that provide partial services for their youngsters. Thus, youngsters who require a variety of medical services as well as educational and recreational services should have the timing for the provision of services individualized to fit the needs of each child and family. Services not immediately available within a community must be obtained as close as possible to home. Preparation of children and family for medical services or for camp would reduce the trauma of separation and make the services more effective.

RIGHT TO VIABLE PLACEMENTS. Another right for the child and the family is that of being in a state-supported setting if the home and community placement cannot help a child. Such a state-supported setting can be within the community but must have state and federal support in order to be viable. Thus, there should be group homes with trained workers and a system in which a variety of specialists rotate through various group homes to provide their specialized services to the children. Ongoing training must be provided for the group-home parents and other personnel. Each group home must be part of a well-developed program within the community which includes school and recreational opportunities as well as effective socialization opportunities in the home itself. It is no longer tenable for children to be placed in a group home dependent upon personnel who are untrained and who have very little understanding of the retarded child.

RIGHT TO ASSESSMENT OF CHANGE. The family's right to alter

decisions is important. The circumstances of many families change throughout the lifetime of a retarded child. Thus, children who may be able to live within the family fairly well at younger ages may have difficulties when they get older as, for example, when there are new, smaller children within the family. At that time, they may find it very difficult to compete and to live in the family. Changes of employment for the family also may make it difficult to have the retarded child with the family in a new community which does not have the same kinds of facilities which the former community had available. Therefore, the child may be better off in a group home in which its needs are more fully met in education, training, and socialization.

Various family crises may make difficulties for a mentally retarded child or other children in the family. A physical or mental health problem within the family may make it necessary to reassess the capacities of the family to live with the retarded child. Family circumstances may make it difficult for children within the family setting to reach their potential. The critical question about where retarded children can have the greatest opportunities to develop their potential must be faced. That question needs continuous collaborative reassessment by both parents and professional workers involved with those children.

At certain milestones in children's lives, it may be advantageous for the children to participate in particular programs which would help them learn certain skills. For certain children, the opportunity for independent living makes it important for them as they reach adolescence to become part of an adolescent living group. Constant reassessment of the opportunities to help a child develop—become more independent and more effective— is a right of both the child and the family.

THE RIGHT TO INDIVIDUALIZED CARE WHEN NEEDED. One of the critical needs in the mental retardation field is the training of expert paraprofessional workers. It is clear that in this area, as in many others in the health, education, and welfare field, professional workers are all too few and unable to handle the volume of work required. Training programs for paraprofessionals become very important for mounting effective long-term programs. It has become clear that paraprofessionals can be very well trained, if chosen for their sensitivity, empathy, and understanding of children. The use of paraprofessionals permits greater individualized attention to children and results in enhancement of their individual capacities. It is certainly a right of the child to have individualized attention as needed or prescribed.

THE RIGHT TO WORK EXPERIENCES: AN INCENTIVE TO INDEPENDENCE. We have a lesson to learn from the retardation programs that have been mounted by the Russians. Several of our authorities on mental retardation were impressed in a recent visit by the high quality of the mental retardation programs in the Soviet Union. They were struck first with the fact that there was a much higher ratio of adults to children than exists in any program in the United States. In most institutions there was usually at least one adult for each child and sometimes a ratio of one-and-one-half trained personnel per student.

There was a wide variety of programs, designed to fit the gamut of needs and capacities of various children. Efforts were made to adapt some home industries to fit programs for the mentally retarded. The retarded children and adolescents were being paid for doing the kind of detailed but uncomplicated work which was necessary for many products. They were not just carrying out subassembly jobs. They were involved, for example, in the making of fine furniture, which entails a great deal of hand rubbing, waxing, and varnishing to finish the wood and build up a patina characteristic of fine furniture and cabinetry. The assembly of parts of the furniture was taught to children who were moderately retarded. They could learn to assemble these fairly large parts in a systematic way so that they could see the entire product when it was finished, to the great satisfaction of the youngsters. All sorts of baskets and containers for packaging food, fruits, and vegetables were being made in schools for the retarded. Youngsters were frequently taken to stores and markets to see how the products they made were being utilized. Thus, the wide adaptation of home industries to programs for the retarded, as well as paying retarded youngsters a standard wage for their labor, was an important part of the incentive program for the retarded in Russia. Our children deserve the same opportunities to work and to feel the dignity of meaningful contribution to community life.

Conclusion

The critical questions are: Do retarded children and their families have a right to the best of care from birth on? Do they have the right to the most effective use of our knowledge on behalf of children and their families? Do they have a right to the expenditure of federal and state monies to bring them the best of care and promote their mental health and the mental health of their families, as well as to help them become the most effective citizens possible?

Our answer to these questions through organized parent, community, and professional support must be a resounding "Yes"! That yes must now be translated into legislative action, financial support, and operational programs in every community. Retarded children and their families are citizens who do have inalienable rights to care which maximizes the child's potential for living and reduces the parents' concerns about their child's future.

REFERENCES

1. ALLEN, R. C. The retarded offender: Unrecognized in court and untreated in prison. *Federal Probation,* 1968, 32:3, 22–27.
2. BEGAB, M. The mentally retarded and the family. In I. Philips (Ed.), *Prevention and Treatment of Mental Retardation.* New York: Basic Books, 1966. Pp. 71–84.
3. BERLIN, I. N. Consultation and special education. In I. Philips (Ed.), *Prevention and Treatment of Mental Retardation.* New York: Basic Books, 1966. Pp. 279–293.
4. BRABNER, G., JR. The school years—Program design. In I. Philips (Ed.), *Prevention and Treatment of Mental Retardation.* New York: Basic Books, 1966. Pp. 262–278.
5. BURT, R. A. Legal restrictions on sexual and familial relations of mental retardates—old laws, new guises. In F. F. de la Cruz and G. D. LaVeck (Eds.), *Human Sexuality and the Mentally Retarded.* New York: Brunner/Mazel, 1973. Pp. 206–214.
6. CRANEFIELD, P. F. Historical perspectives. In I. Philips (Ed.), *Prevention and Treatment of Mental Retardation.* New York: Basic Books, 1966. Pp. 3–14.
7. DEAN, D. B. Psychiatry and the problem of mental retardation. In S. A. Szurek and I. N. Berlin (Eds.), *Psychosomatic Disorders and Mental Retardation in Children.* Palo Alto, Calif.: Science and Behavior Books, 1968. Pp. 156–166.

8. DE LA CRUZ, F. F., & LAVECK, G. D. (Eds.) *Human Sexuality and the Mentally Retarded.* New York: Brunner/Mazel, 1973.

9. DOLL, E. A. Recognition of mental retardation in the school-age child. In I. Philips (Ed.), *Prevention and Treatment of Mental Retardation.* New York: Basic Books, 1966. Pp. 59–68.

10. FRIEDMAN, P. *Mental Retardation and the Law: A Report on Status of Current Court Cases.* Washington, D.C.: Office of Mental Retardation Coordination, Department of Health, Education and Welfare, 1972.

11. GALAZAN, M. M. Vocational rehabilitation. In I. Philips (Ed.), *Prevention and Treatment of Mental Retardation.* New York: Basic Books, 1966. Pp. 294–307.

12. JOHNSON, W. R. Sex education of the mentally retarded. In F. F. de la Cruz and G. D. LaVeck (Eds.), *Human Sexuality and the Mentally Retarded.* New York: Brunner/Mazel, 1973. Pp. 57–66.

13. KATZ, E. The mentally retarded adult in the community. In I. Philips (Ed.), *Prevention and Treatment of Mental Retardation.* New York: Basic Books, 1966. Pp. 308–333.

14. MATTINSON, J. Marriage and mental handicap. In F. F. de la Cruz and G. D. LaVeck (Eds.), *Human Sexuality and the Mentally Retarded.* New York: Brunner/Mazel, 1973. Pp. 169–185.

15. NAROT, J. R. The moral and ethical implications of human sexuality as they relate to the retarded. In F. F. de la Cruz and G. D. LaVeck (Eds.), *Human Sexuality and the Mentally Retarded.* New York: Brunner/Mazel, 1973. Pp. 195–205.

16. PERRY, S. E. Notes for a sociology of mental retardation. In I. Philips (Ed.), *Prevention and Treatment of Mental Retardation.* New York: Basic Books, 1966. Pp. 145–176.

17. PHILIPS, I. Children, mental retardation, and emotional disorder. In I. Philips (Ed.), *Prevention and Treatment of Mental Retardation.* New York: Basic Books, 1966. Pp. 111–122.

18. PHILIPS, I. Common misconceptions concerning mental retardation. In S. A. Szurek and I. N. Berlin (Eds.), *Psychosomatic Disorders and Mental Retardation in Children.* Palo Alto, Calif.: Science and Behavior Books, 1968. Pp. 144–152.

19. PHILIPS, I. (Ed.) *Prevention and Treatment of Mental Retardation.* New York: Basic Books, 1966.

20. PHILIPS, I. Psychopathology and mental retardation. In S. A. Szurek and I. N. Berlin (Eds.), *Psychosomatic Disorders and Mental Retardation in Children.* Palo Alto, Calif.: Science and Behavior Books, 1968. Pp. 182–191.

21. RICHMOND, J. B., & GARRARD, S. D. Some current concepts of mental retardation: Implications for diagnosis. In I. Philips (Ed.), *Prevention and Treatment of Mental Retardation.* New York: Basic Books, 1966. Pp. 15–23.

22. ROBINSON, H. B., & ROBINSON, N. M. *The Mentally Retarded Child: A Psychological Approach.* New York: McGraw-Hill, 1965.

23. SCALLY, B. G. Marriage and mental handicap: Some observations in northern Ireland. In F. F. de la Cruz and G. D. LeVeck (Eds.), *Human Sexuality and the Mentally Retarded.* New York: Brunner/Mazel, 1973. Pp. 186–194.
24. STONE, N. D. Effecting interdisciplinary coordination in clinical services to the mentally retarded. *American Journal of Orthopsychiatry,* 1970, *40,* 835–840.
25. SUSSELMAN, S. Comments on the diagnosis of the mental retardate. In S. A. Szurek and I. N. Berlin (Eds.), *Psychosomatic Disorders and Mental Retardation in Children.* Palo Alto, Calif.: Science and Behavior Books, 1968. Pp. 153–155.
26. SZUREK, S. A., & BERLIN, I. N. (Eds.) *Psychosomatic Disorders and Mental Retardation in Children.* Palo Alto, Calif.: Science and Behavior Books, 1968.
27. SZUREK, S. A., & PHILIPS, I. Mental retardation and psychotherapy. In I. Philips (Ed.), *Prevention and Treatment of Mental Retardation.* New York: Basic Books, 1966. Pp. 221–246.

Child Advocacy is the participation in public decisions on behalf of children. True participation requires power to change thought, laws, attitude notes, services, behavior, and use of money. It also requires responsibilitiy for follow-through and for adverse effects of change.

Statement of THE AMERICAN PUBLIC HEALTH ASSOCIATION in *The Nation's Health*, October 1973.

_____ **16**

One Model of Operational Advocacy: A Neighborhood Program

IRVING N. BERLIN, M.D.

Definition

The definition of operational advocacy has been delineated by Norman Lourie in Chapter 7. Operational advocacy has as its aim the evolution of a system of providing services which deal effectively with the needs of the population of children and their parents in a defined geographic area. To be maximally effective, such a system must be able to provide continuous diagnostic assessment of the needs of a population. Thus, there must be methods to understand how and why these needs exist. Operational advocacy as we define it must also have the capability of introducing preventive and interventive measures for both individuals and the community.

Structure of program to fulfill objectives

In this chapter the term *neighborhood* is used to describe a circumscribed area usually served by an elementary school. The term *community* has two meanings: (1) a combination of sev-

ONE MODEL FOR ORGANIZATION OF
A COMMUNITY ADVOCACY PROGRAM

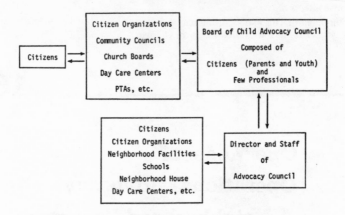

Figure 1a. INFORMATION FLOW CHART

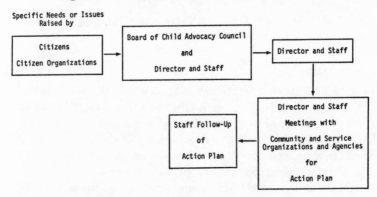

Figure 1b. ACTION FLOW CHART

eral neighborhoods adjacent to each other usually served by at
least a junior or senior high school; and (2) a rural area of several hundred families served by the same school and other
county governmental services, often comprised of one or more
towns or political subdivisions.

One of the basic objectives of the model operational advocacy

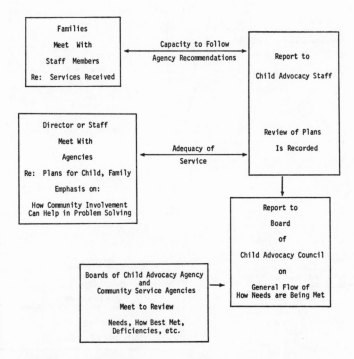

Figure 2. FOLLOW-UP SYSTEM FLOW CHART

program to be described here is finding the resources to provide the required services, not to provide the services themselves. Such a program has a major objective in discovering and developing models of viable neighborhood citizen organizations. Such organizations form the base of the operation. Each organization functions to provide continual input into the advocacy program concerning the needs of children and families and how these needs are being met. It provides the citizen board members of the program's neighborhood child development council. It keeps the board and the council staff aimed at the child health and mental health issues of major concern to the neighborhood.

Thus, one can define a neighborhood operational child advocacy organization as a Neighborhood Child Development Council composed of citizens in the neighborhood or rural community, who make up the preprofessionals, and one or more

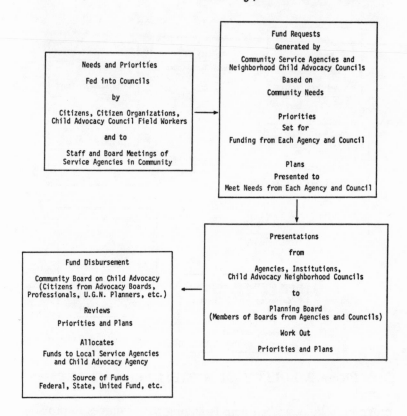

Figure 3. FUNDING FLOW CHART

professionals whose duty it is to work with the board. Examining the needs and devising methods of meeting these needs are followed by assessing how well these methods work. The organization is responsive to its board composed, in the majority, of parents, youth, and professionals from churches, agencies, and schools. Personnel employed by the council are present to account for how the council is working. It is empowered by law to coordinate with all health, education, and welfare agencies in its area to evolve methods of meeting community needs. Thus, it may ask existing agencies to take on one or more tasks, and it may help bring into being one or more new agencies to help with the major tasks not now being dealt with by any agency.

Such creation of a new agency would require planning with community or city-county boards and their help in developing the new agency.

The operational child advocacy organization must keep a broad view of the needs and the efforts to meet them. Thus, its prime function is one of assessment and helping plan with existing agencies how needs of children and families can be better met. Its employees are preprofessionals and a few professionals who develop skills in planning, monitoring, and assessing services and their delivery. For such coordinating functions to be effective, ideally there should be central control of funding for both private and public agencies through a community, county, or city board. Objectives and priorities for each neighborhood and community become defined by the citizen board of the community council in conjunction with the citizen boards of service agencies which serve that community.

The neighborhood or rural community child development agencies combine to form a large community, county, or city agency depending on size. Here the purpose is to coordinate evaluation of needs and overall services required to meet needs and to relate them on a broader basis to what existing or new agency collaborations are required to carry out these functions.

Funding should go to a community agency, composed of several neighborhoods or rural communities, with designated monies to the neighborhood councils which have the final responsibility for assessing both needs and required services.

STATE AGENCY. The state child advocacy agency or child development agency is primarily a planning body to evaluate the variety of needs in the state, to develop a state plan and to plan priorities. It also helps make available those services of state agencies which are based in the community. The state child development agency should have a board composed of a majority of citizens from the neighborhoods and rural communities, citizens-at-large concerned with child health and mental health, some operational executives of the advocacy programs, as well as planning personnel from state agencies. The stipulation is clearly necessary, in view of Head Start experiences, that federal funding cannot be diverted by the state child development agency from the neighborhoods and communities. The tendency

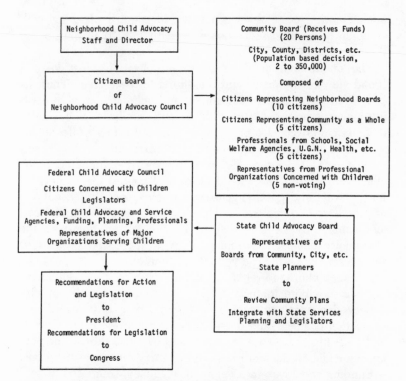

Figure 4. NEIGHBORHOOD CHILD ADVOCACY COUNCIL LINES OF RESPONSIBILITY IN CHILD ADVOCACY HIERARCHY

at every level is to build bureaucracies and thus maintain the status quo in services while maintaining the hierarchy in their agencies. These tendencies must be vigilantly scrutinized by the operational child advocacy agencies to whom federal and state monies must go for development of needed programs. Funds to local child development councils and service agencies are distributed according to plan to carry out the agreed programs.

FEDERAL PROGRAMS. The federal legislation must mandate community and neighborhood autonomy. It must be designed so states cannot sequester funds for their own bureaucracy or channel them into favorite and favored communities where little actual effort will be made to meet child and family needs.

Central issues for community child advocacy programs

PREVENTION. Programs must be prevention-focused to become maximally effective. Such a focus inevitably considers the prenatal, perinatal, birth, and postnatal experiences as critical factors in a fundamental approach to the mental health and health problems of children. A prevention focus also brings operational child advocacy programs to grips with basic community problems of nutrition and health care.

The overwhelming evidence noted elsewhere is that malnutrition of mothers results in malnourished, underweight, often premature infants who are born already brain damaged as a result of protein and vitamin deficiencies. Continued malnutrition during infancy compounds the problem and results in children unable to learn or function adequately in society.

Data also reveal that prenatal and delivery medical care is unavailable to many poor mothers and families. So birth trauma— lack of adequate oxygen due to long, slow, and painful deliveries —further damage the infants' brains.

In middle-class communities, nutrition and medical care are better. However, the incidence of postpartum depression of mothers, which deprives the infants of adequate mothering and stimulation, is increasing. It remains a less serious problem than in poverty populations, where overwhelming problems of existence produce massive postpartum depression.

Thus, the Neighborhood Council also has a role in discovering how it can locally use already effective methods of dealing with early maternal depression. For example, in some communities, there are not only efforts to increase welfare funds for food, but pilot projects for close following of mothers after their infants are born so that neighborhood workers known to the mothers regularly visit to talk with the mothers and to help them engage their infants in mutually satisfying stimulation.

Obviously, the preventive measures of decent nutrition, adequate medical care, and finding a hopeful future through employment, decent housing, etc., are difficult objectives to attain. However, the route to such prevention seems to be through involvement of young parents by community agencies before, during, and after pregnancy on behalf of their infants and young children. Such community involvement in helping parents to work with their own children tends to reduce apathy and directs energies toward more community-wide involvement. Parents who have worked with their children can be involved in helping other prospective and new parents work productively with their children. They also become alert to their very vital role in their children's preschool education and how their presence as regular observers in the classroom, and sometimes as aides, helps children focus on learning. They find that their predictable presence alters teachers' behavior toward children and enhances learning in school.

Family planning. In the context of involvement with their infants and small children, parents learn to evaluate and assess issues which concern them in the community. As they learn how important their efforts are in working with their children to facilitate learning and for how long such efforts need to be continued, many parents become interested in family planning. Family planning activities in the community may be initiated or brought in by the Child Development Council. Staff members assess with parents the relevance to them of birth prevention efforts and find ways of improving the education and services desired by parents. Family planning is also sought out as parents involved in community activities and looking toward the stability of their family relationship recognize their need for time for themselves as well as with each child as the family develops and members have different needs.

Health maintenance. With decent nutrition and medical care prior to, during, and after the baby's birth, general maintenance of health rather than crisis medical care in grossly overcrowded general hospital emergency rooms should be a program objective. The mental health issues in health maintenance are obvious. Parents and children who are healthy physically are a prerequisite to mental health. Good health care indicates a community concern with prevention of all disease and continuity of care for any illness.

Health maintenance also is a difficult objective to achieve. However, there are starting points. In some communities it has been possible to show advantages in reduced human suffering and reduced costs in the maintenance of health of elementary school children in one elementary school or even one age group. Such demonstration efforts lead to a focus on what is possible. As the manpower problems become clear, new ways that manpower and medical services can be redistributed also become more evident. In one community, the local pediatric society undertook such preventive efforts in two elementary schools with startling results. Many children with chronic infections were helped. Thus, children who would almost surely have developed rheumatic fever were treated preventively. Serious neurological and orthopedic problems were prevented by early detection. Class attendance was increased by 200 percent.

Decent housing. Adequate housing for families means space for children, heat, light, and good sanitation at moderate cost. Availability of such housing is also an important mental health issue. Ghetto housing, with its usual environment of bitter cold, overcrowding, rats, lead poisoning, sewage, and garbage, creates a setting where families cannot feel it is worth the effort to create a home. A sense of self-worth is difficult to come by for the vast majority of families in slum housing.

Employment: An essential aspect. Employment of parents is essential to their feeling effective and self-respecting. In our rapidly changing technology, there are fewer jobs in industry and farming every year. For people to have self-respect, they must have decent-paying jobs which permit them to take care of their families. Children raised by parents chronically unemployed, apathetic, and malnourished join the cycle of apathy and revolt through delinquency and drugs to escape the hopeless helplessness.

The employment of adolescents and young adults who make up a large segment of unemployed is critical for their mental health as adults and as prospective parents. Unless they become gainfully employed, their depression, apathy, and anger often result in destructive efforts to escape their stark realities. Unemployment creates a setting in which infants and small children cannot grow or develop with emotional security. Parental hopelessness for the future stunts normal development and reduces the capacity for learning and mastery.

These employment, housing, health, and nutrition issues are interdependent and important in prevention of generational mental and emotional illness. Where neighborhoods and communities have been able to increase employment of young adults effectively, the changes in adult attitudes have altered the entire atmosphere of the community.

Child advocacy programs are one important vehicle in helping find employment positions in mental health and health services in the community. They need to assess their community manpower needs. Then they must help to form interagency training programs for preprofessionals to meet these vast needs. Employment in the health, education, and welfare enterprises in a community is important. It provides help to the young adults and adolescents in finding worthwhile employment. They achieve a sense of personal worth in service in and to their community. As they become skilled they face new challenges to present credentialism. Recognition in status and salary is vital to job satisfaction.

In one community, teacher aides were hired from among young, unemployed males. The aides adopted a blazer and grey slacks as a uniform. In their work in school and in their community activities, they began to serve as models for the young males of this vast housing project. They also became active and outspoken in community affairs. Perhaps their greatest early impact was in enhancing the learning of students in the schools in which they were employed. They gradually began to see their roles in the classrooms not just in carrying out the instructions of teachers. They gave high priority to finding time to spend with kids who were not learning and sticking with them until they began to learn. Their efforts led them to work with parents to help their children. This had major impact since they could give feedback promptly on the results of parent effort. With their encouragement, parents were less fearful of spending time in their children's classrooms.

In small communities, these efforts in health and education quickly begin to indicate how employment can alter the vitality of a slum community.[12] Clearly this has been so in several Indian reservations where small industry, brought in by great effort, has reduced apathy and demoralization on the reservation. Prime examples exist showing the difference where, on neighboring reservations, closely related tribes have treated unemployment differently. One tribe has fought to obtain employment; the other, run by conservative elders, has not fought for it. The difference in viability and vitality of these two tribes is clear to all observers but especially to their young people. The young people now push for intertribal planning and action.

Operational child advocacy means involvement in those aspects of community mental health where beginning impact can be made. The program can enhance mental health through focus on special community concerns which are basic to health, mental health, and even survival of children and families.

The educational system. In Chapter 12, William Morse describes the required changes in education. As a community preventive measure, the effect of school programs on children must be carefully examined. The goals of educators and their means to effect goals need close examination with a view to collaboration in shaping both goals and operations so that they are more congruent with developmental processes and relevance for living in the 1970s.

An operational child advocacy program can have major impact in altering the methods and goals of education in their neighborhoods and communities. School failure, dropouts, and nonlearning are rampant and are destructive to mental health. Education geared to the realities of today's society must be a mental health objective. Nonrelevant education leads to frustration, self-doubt, and defeat. Schools and community, brought together by the child advocacy program, must evaluate the goals and methods.

We have noted that parents engaged in early educational efforts with their infants and young children become interested in evaluating school programs for their children. Parents regularly in the classroom learn to work in helping children learn. Some become paid teacher aides, others recognize their impact as regular observers and unpaid aides on their child's learning and on the quality of teaching important to children's success in school.

Obviously, learning to read, write, and do mathematics is essential to all learning. The question is, how is this best done in today's classrooms?

The central issue for relevant education may be early efforts to help children learn to solve problems. Children can be helped in the third and fourth grades to look at each lesson in history, math, and English as problems to be solved. Later, actual life problems of concern to the community can become problem-solving projects. The details are described in the section on education. An operational child advocacy program must emphasize relevant and therefore mentally stimulating and integrative education. As students learn to state problems, gather and assess data, and propose solutions, they begin a life-long task of conscious effort to work out problems for themselves and to help others learn the process. This is the first step toward informed and participant citizen action. It helps communities educate for involvement in community issues. Hopeful and active citizens are themselves not depressed. They provide stimulation to their children and models which lead to mental health in their families.

EDUCATION FOR LIVING. A major function of the child advocacy program is to facilitate collaboration of agencies in the service of the community. The educational system is not geared to helping students to acquire the knowledge and skills necessary for living in society. A basic problem-solving approach in education will go far to enable students to make choices, to assess issues, and become informed active citizens. However, education has at least two other major contributions to make to students in the schools.

One of these can occur through a collaboration between health and higher education institutions to provide basic information about human biology. Such information provides the basis for factual information about human reproduction. It has been our experience in several communities that high school students of all socioeconomic classes are ignorant about their own physiology and anatomy, especially about their reproductive anatomy and physiology. To provide high interest courses in biology must be a joint enterprise of schools and the health professions.

Learning about human reproduction should lead to courses on human sexual behavior and discussion and study of problems of family living. The psychology of human relations and problems of child-rearing should be related through discussions to practical experiences in child development. Such experiences in well-baby clinics and nursery schools would provide the stimulus for ongoing discussion in the areas of how children learn and how adults, especially parents, affect well children. The planning for courses and various practical experiences with early childhood specialists in colleges would provide mutual stimulation to educators in both institutions.

In one junior high school, a preschool nursery is situated in one wing and serves as a place for observation of small children and actual practical experience in learning to teach and work with preschool children.[11] Practical preparation for understanding human relations and the problems of people living together promotes freer discussion between young children and adolescents and demonstrates how important communication is between people. Child development classes and experiences help students learn how children develop. They come to understand what children's needs are for optimal growth and how they, as eventual parents, contribute to their children's physical and mental health, especially their capacities for learning and developing curiosity and concerned, warm, human relations.

EDUCATION FOR WORK. The second collaboration between educators and community is in the critical area of education for jobs. Currently, school does not prepare adolescents for work of any kind. It is essential for the mental health of young people to learn in actual work experiences so they can be effective workers and will be gainfully employed in a service society. Practical experiences in needed crafts such as electrical repair, carpentry, cabinet work, and plumbing for the many motor-skilled youngsters become essential as preparation for employment. The child advocacy program can help facilitate training in human services through enterprises supported by the Department of Health, Education, and Welfare in the community. Education for work is a vital community concern and focuses on the need to find jobs for the unemployed, and especially for the youth and young adults in the community.

COMBATING RACISM: A PREVENTIVE PROGRAM. Chester Pierce, in Chapter 8, delineates the magnitude of racism as a mental health disorder which affects the white population and has drastic impact on the darker-skinned minority peoples. One function of a child advocate program is to devise ways of combating racism on a local level.

In the white community, it may take the form of educative effort through opportunities to work together with minority individuals on issues of common purpose. It also means vigilance about the images of Blacks and other minorities taught to children in schools. Most important are those efforts to understand how racism spreads—especially, how fears and anxieties, in particular about jobs, are used to spread racist myths. The most prevalent myth is that only by being white and therefore superior can one hope to keep a job or get one. One must, therefore, keep Blacks or other minorities from getting jobs and taking them away from poor whites. It requires vigilant education to help people recognize that poor people who have learned to use this device to feel better about themselves are indeed being taught to perpetuate an illness in themselves. Unless they can learn other ways toward self-esteem, racism ensures that such hatred of others will divide people so that the poor do not get the work they need. The mental illness that persists hurts everyone.

In minority communities, the mental health task is engaging the residents in activities that enhance their sense of competence and worth. There must be a special focus on how they and their children are—historically and in the present—reinforced to feel second class. Schools and community, through subtle and not so subtle teachings, and the attitudes and behavior of white people in all agencies toward them, need to be closely examined and behaviors documented so they can be demonstrated and brought into the open and altered.

Chester Pierce describes several ways minority communities might approach their problem of altering both their set and also the feelings and behavior of whites who come in contact with them.

EARLY INTERVENTION. The prevention goals mentioned above need to be tied to early intervention programs. A child advocate program must help coordinate the forces that can be brought to bear to follow through with all the infants, young children, and their families in various settings to spot troubles early and prevent the occurrence of serious physical and emotional illnesses.

Parental involvement through well-infant and child clinics and infant education programs permits not only close following of families but educates the parents to look for and report early signs of trouble. The health and mental health professionals and preprofessionals need special training to recognize the early signs of physiological and psychological stress. Thus, persistent delays in development as indicated by troubles with sleeping, eating, and normal milestones of physical, cognitive, and emotional growth give early warning of problems.

Developmental diagnosis. As Julius Richmond has emphasized in Chapter 3, all health, mental health, and education professionals and preprofessionals must be trained to understand developmental processes. They then can, with experience, detect variations in development and examine those in terms of severity and duration. As those disturbances which affect the individual child's development are detected, remedial measures can be instituted. Preprofessionals trained in such a setting quickly become developmentally attuned and can not only spot problems in children but also become aware of family problems. They then can try to be helpful to the family and make available to them the community resources. Most developmental problems require a close working partnership with the parents. Parents can learn to be alert to problems and to seek help with them. Health or mental health problems identified in infancy and preschool ages, when worked with, can prevent more serious disturbance and permanent disability.

The most potent force in early intervention is a program which follows all children's and families' health and mental health through regular health maintenance visits. Such a program can use Child Development Council staff to help follow those children and families referred for specific treatment to ensure that in fact the treatment occurs and to help evaluate with the family and the agency the efficacy of the treatment.

Vulnerable children and early intervention. In each neighborhood or community there will be those children who are vulnerable because of trauma at birth, malnutrition, early undetected infections, family troubles and depression, and external stress on the family, such as loss of job, death in the family, etc. As youngsters' vulnerability is recognized, they should be carefully followed so that special help can be given to them as needed. These children need to be observed as they react to separation from mother in preschool or kindergarten or to stresses imposed by a rigid school setting. A common sign of psychological decompensation is anxiety, as indicated by tension, hyperactive behavior, or withdrawal. At such times there should be efforts to reach out to child and family. Often, physiological decompensation, in the form of many or prolonged illnesses, indicates the stress the child is experiencing. Investigation of both the medical and psychological aspects of recurrent, frequent, and severe illnesses is important in determining causes and initiating treatment to help the child to better health.

ADOLESCENT CRISES. Crises in school, especially during the preadolescent and adolescent period, require the presence of trained crisis counselors to whom children can turn when in need. The counselors need to have their time kept free for such work. Through interagency agreements, the counselors must be able to mobilize whatever help the child and family need at such a time.

Adolescents work well in groups. Adolescents in crisis could use groups which meet regularly to help young people through the various identity problems as well as the real-world problems facing them. Groups may be organized in the school or by any health, mental health, or social agency which has access to students as well as trained workers experienced in work with adolescents. Some have noted how often students in the group do the case finding if the group is a viable one and the adults trustworthy.

I have been impressed by the pilot efforts in Indian reservations where elders work with suicidal young people. These elders, who are the culture-bearers in some communities, can help adolescents in crisis find alternatives to suicide by their patient willingness to be with a young person and available to talk as long as needed. This role for the elderly needs to be examined as a potentially important mental health resource in the community. Dane Prugh and Kent Jordan, in Chapter 14, describe how the elderly have been used in hospitals to provide the cuddling and security of a lap and the required attention to infants and children who languish in an impersonal environment.

Those of us who have seen adolescents take care of young children in a hospital or therapeutic nursery school know the mutual benefit to the sick child and the adolescent trained in such work. Adolescent turmoil is helped by group therapy but often equally important is the opportunity to be of real service, to feel needed, important, and competent to help others.

Treatment programs at the community level

All child advocacy programs must concern themselves with treatment for the children and families in need of it in the neighborhood and community. By treatment, we mean the remediation necessary to reduce, eliminate, or stabilize health and mental health problems, keeping the child at home or close to home wherever possible.

Most adults in a community have experienced treatment for medical problems as help that is too hard to get and usually available too late to really do much good. It is usually sought or only available as a last resort when an illness is so severe that immediate treatment is absolutely necessary. Thus, early treatment for health and mental health problems requires both education and a new method of delivering treatment services. Early case finding must occur whenever the child and family are in contact with the human service agencies of a community, especially the schools.

Treatment plans must be made with all the family members concerned present together. Planning should involve those agencies that can help with all or parts of a problem. The process of mutual planning with the family helps to clarify the problems, reduce blaming, and lead to plans that the family can be a participant in from the beginning.

AGENCY COLLABORATION: KEY TO SERVICE DELIVERY. Before describing some of the treatment services that must be available locally, we need to examine the role of a child advocate program in effecting interagency collaboration on behalf of children and families.

Norman Lourie has vividly described in Chapter 7 the problems of hierarchy and turf which lead to possessiveness and defensiveness, obstacles to change and thus to collaboration. There is a need for each agency and profession to believe it can do and actually does do the whole job despite the data to the contrary. Thus, the overriding task of the child advocate program is to devise methods of working with agencies on these inter- and intra-agency issues so that more effective services can be obtained. The issues are more relevant in treatment services because most agencies function in these areas. It is often easier to obtain collaboration in prevention and early intervention services, which are functions of new agencies. These may collaborate more easily since they have had no defined role and are often eager to learn how they can be effective in new mental health or health areas which extend their effectiveness as an agency.

In one community, where an effort was made to bring all known agencies together to plan for improved treatment services, it seemed impossible to overcome the traditional turf problems. It was difficult to focus on the issues concerning what each agency could contribute to better serving a population. Efforts at operational collaboration, through the use of family case conferences to focus on which agencies could be most helpful in particular instances, were similarly difficult. Either an agency said it could not work with severe delinquents or poor minority school dropouts or it said it was equipped to do the whole job by itself. In the last instance, in diagnostic interviews, the client was judged not suitable for treatment and dropped. The county mental health board repeatedly heard of the continued problems in getting agencies to collaborate to provide improved mental health services. Over time, it was able to influence the private agency funding source so that all child-serving agencies not paid by county funds also received their grants through approval of the mental health board. A critical factor for receiving funds was not how "busy" the agency was, but how effective its client services and collaboration with other agencies were. Thus, slowly, community priorities were hammered out. Each agency was committed to carry out agreed-upon priorities which were spelled out as service objectives. Agency heads found they lost little autonomy through collaboration and, for the first time, their relationships to public agencies were changed. Instead of being dumping grounds or resources of last resort, public agencies became part of a system of services to be utilized on the basis of their professional contribution in working on problems of common concern.

The initiation of accountability and case follow-up permitted evaluation of the effectiveness of agency collaboration on behalf of clients. It became clear that more children and families had more appropriate services. Areas of critical shortage could more easily be documented for funding sources to review. Since the referral and dump system no longer worked, each referral had to be reasonably appropriate. To get the schools, Head Start, welfare, juvenile courts, and public health resources as well as private agencies committed to a collaborative service plan is difficult because unit heads may interfere with policy decisions made by their superiors. However, the collaboration is slowly more effective as objectives and tasks for each agency become clarified, not only with directors and staff, but with agency boards.

On a smaller population base, the neighborhood and community may be easier to work in. Collaborating agencies can often recognize more specific goals and can know when they are attained. They experience that it is to their advantage to have multiple agency impact on a problem. The follow-through of the child development council staff begins to focus with agencies on adequacy of referral, intake, and treatment results.

TREATMENT SPECIALIZATION: ACCORDING TO TRAINING. Most workers who perform similar tasks require some help to fully use their specialized expertise. Thus, social workers and elementary school counselors may both work with families and treat children, but it is more efficient and certainly more helpful to have the child's learning and school problems dealt with by the counselor, who is trained in diagnosis of learning problems and who has good relationships with teachers in their mutual efforts to help troubled and nonlearning students. The counselor can then collaborate closely with the social worker's efforts with a family. Also, the elementary school counselor who learns to help children with learning problems in a group, and to help teachers in a group to understand how to work with their students, utilizes his or her capacities most effectively. Similarly, the worker who works with parents in groups capitalizes on both group processes

and the mutual learning and reduction of self-blame and increased openness of inquiry possible in groups of parents whose
children have problems. Professionals also maximize the use of
skills, often by combining some brief individual case work
through trained preprofessionals to provide extra help where
needed. Such efforts complement each other and provide training opportunities for preprofessionals.

The ways in which such collaboration opens new avenues of
service delivery are fascinating. In one instance, a mothers'
group to help families with children about to enter first grade
uncovered the fact that several children had severe allergic
problems that had not been dealt with at the public health clinic
or, in one instance, by a private physician. Parents hoped that
school would uncover the problems and then deal with them.
The referral to the public health clinic for diagnostic evaluations
suggested by the nurse carried the name of the parent group as
referring source. Prompt and comprehensive diagnosis and treatment ensued. The parent group then expressed its appreciation
by letter and paved the way for further referral and help to children in the kindergarten through a formalized parent group.
With the leadership of health and mental health professionals
they used the organized parent group to obtain diagnostic and
treatment services from community resources.

Other experiences indicate that from collaboration in delivery
of services, other collaborative possibilities open up in prevention and early intervention. It is also evident that identifying the
needed and lacking treatment resources in a community and
working in collaboration to obtain them are important efforts of
the collaboration, leading to greater mutual support and a sense
of greater effectiveness of all agency personnel and board members.

In one neighborhood, the neighborhood health committee
recognized the need for a therapeutic nursery school after some
20 children of nursery school age were referred to a local health
department children and youth program. A city-wide nursery
school organization offered to staff a regular nursery school for
a small fee per child. However, they had no facilities or personnel to help deal with child and family problems. The neighborhood committee then asked for help from the county health

department who brought in, for consultation, staff and faculty from the mental health center and the medical school. Their collaboration established some guidelines for the therapeutic nursery school and offers of consultation to the teachers and mental health workers hired for the therapeutic nursery school. In time, with O.E.O. funds, such a school was opened and a part-time psychiatric social worker was obtained from the local family-service agency. Consultants from the Department of Psychiatry in the medical school helped form a team to work with problem children and their parents and to develop a therapeutic nursery school program. After a time, the program developed very effective teachers and became more flexible and sophisticated and was able to deal with a larger community of children. They then affiliated with several agencies which had other programs to provide specific remedial services to both preschool and elementary school children and their parents of a larger community. The new program provided social work placement from the school of social work, observation and training for a junior college parent education center, and was included in the outreach services of the community mental health center.

TREATMENT NEEDS IN A NEIGHBORHOOD OR COMMUNITY. These needs range from inpatient care to home mental health (or community-home liaison) workers responding to calls for help or carrying out education and interventions for minor problems. Special classes and schools for all ages, usually attached to regular schools along with outpatient services, are intermediate steps. Foster care for children who need to be away from home for a time is an important community service. Inpatient care for children who require specialized intensive care in a therapeutic milieu is the most specialized and expensive service.

Obviously only the first service, a community-home liaison or home health or mental health worker, can be totally contained in a neighborhood. That service also is part of the early intervention, education, and prevention service to be offered in the community. In practice it is the least developed service and the preprofessionals the poorest trained. In several communities where ongoing training and consultation occur, these workers become expert in both diagnostic and remedial work and avail themselves of consultation to render better service and to enhance their own learning. Experienced, trained public health nurses who are psychiatrically trained have proved to be extremely effective consultants and service coordinators in a number of communities. Their experience in working with families in the home is very important.

Most special services require a large population base; thus, a community of several neighborhoods can put together special school services from therapeutic nursery and day school classes to part-time outpatient mental health services available in a local health center or hospital on a regular basis from a larger mental health center.

Foster care services require a social agency or mental health service to find good foster homes and to develop a training program for foster parents. Continuing education and consultation with mental health personnel are vital to foster parents' development so their foster children receive not only well-intentioned care, but care specially designed for a child through a collaboration of foster parents and mental health workers. Foster parents who understand their role and function with a child can anticipate troubles rather than calling for help after the crisis when it is often too late.

Inpatient care may be required for a few children, usually for a limited time. The aim is to return the child to the home and community as promptly as possible. An intensive treatment program combines every known modality of work with a disturbed child. A therapeutic milieu, developmentally designed to provide specific remediation through individual and social experiences in therapeutic educational and recreational programs, is critical. Development of a treatment plan with skilled staff, which utilizes the child's ego strengths to work toward solving the emotional difficulties, is important. Work with the family either in the community or at the inpatient setting is essential to help most severely disturbed children to return to their home.

ROLE OF CHILD ADVOCATE AGENCY IN TREATMENT. As an example, let us take outpatient treatment for a child and parents. The advocate agency in its role of following and evaluating treatment would usually have a staff person present at the family conference where the recommendation is made. This representative would note when referral is made and when intake at the outpatient facility is expected. Thus, one week after such intake is planned, a phone call or visit would be made to determine if intake occurred and what the plans are for continued work.

With some families, where confusion is evident at the conference, the child development council staff might call to go over the findings and reasons for referral and remind the family of the intake as well as to find out if there are any special problems such as need for babysitter or help with an ill family member so that family members could be free to go.

After intake, any confusion or indecision in the family noted by the staff member would be reviewed with the agency to help them recognize the family's unclarity or the family's inability to hear what the recommendations were. The agency can plan to reinforce the recommendations and clarify any treatment program. They can involve the child advocate agency at any point of miscommunication.

Regular, periodic inquiries of family and agency indicate both the advocate's continued concern and whether help is ongoing. When child or family is discharged, community agencies and some staff of the advocate agency need to meet briefly to decide what more needs to be done in the neighborhood, school, etc., to consolidate the work of the agency and specify how and by whom such plans will be carried out and monitored.

INTERRELATED HEALTH AND MENTAL HEALTH PROBLEMS. Many health and mental health problems are closely allied. This means that the child advocate agency staff must be available to local health clinics and must concern itself with facilitating the development of both health and mental health facilities. The same kind of tracking is required to make sure health care is provided and received. Aftercare programs are often important and community-home workers may be the key to maintenance of medication, limitation of activities, or other medical aftercare instructions.

In the instance of inpatient care, there must also be local follow-through. Local council staff interest insures continued interest of hospital personnel. It also indicates that the child advocacy agency will evaluate progress and outcome with the patient, family, and hospital. It stands ready to assist with plans for return to home or other community placements. Inpatient care in all but rare instances needs to be short-term and goal-oriented.

MULTIPLE USE OF COMMUNITY HEALTH, EDUCATION, AND MENTAL HEALTH FACILITIES. An operational child advocacy program has a unique opportunity to examine the facilities in the neighborhood and immediate community. Such a review with existing agencies can lead to appraisal of the present function of each facility, be it a school, health clinic, residential setting, church, etc., and how it might be used to meet current problems and concerns in the neighborhood or community.

In at least three communities in one city, the institutions for care of unwed mothers were no longer able to operate viable programs. These institutions had religious affiliations and served an entire county, but now were being assessed in terms of how they might serve the surrounding community since, in each instance, the population of unwed mothers had sharply dropped with freer dissemination of contraceptive knowledge and the pill, except in the ghetto, which none of these agencies served.

In each community there were needs for buildings for day care, 24-hour emergency child care, and therapeutic day care and group living situations for adolescents. These were some of the options discussed.

In one community, the board of the agency felt that its infant nursery and excellent medical facilities, as well as dormitories and kitchen, might be best used as a child development center where a few disturbed and especially inexperienced young mothers might stay with their infants while they learned to care for the infants. While there they could be helped to find housing, work out financial support, and could be worked into the day care program. In this context, a large day care program which helped mothers to learn to care for their infants and was related to a well-baby public health clinic would make fullest use of the facility. Thus, they negotiated for the 24-hour care for some mothers and infants who required it as well as emergency care for young children whose parents had to be away for a short time.

The planning for the use of these buildings served as a model for the other two homes for unwed mothers as community facilities. The elementary and junior high school in the community were also influenced by the presence of a 24-hour facility in the community. They learned it was possible to have their buildings used by the community for evening classes, community meetings, etc., with little increased cost to the schools and much greater involvement of the school in the community's life. The shop and sewing facilities in the junior high school were used almost 18 hours a day, 6½ days a week, and became the first joint parent-child activity center in the country.

In another community, a private residential treatment center found they couldn't make ends meet with the increasing cost of care. The community, with the help of a mental health center, proposed a multi-use facility. Therapeutic day care for children from the whole community was proposed. The elementary school a block away relocated some of its special classes for the very young children at the center so that the students could be more involved with other young children on the playground, etc. It also offered fuller utilization of the staff of the residential center consultants. Financing was partially provided for when the planning group approached the juvenile court and the welfare department. They made some resources available to provide care of dependent children previously badly housed and cared for in the juvenile hall.

Neighborhood and community planning can effectively utilize in new forms currently nonfunctional agencies, their buildings, and staff.

Funding and interagency collaboration

Funding for operational advocacy must be primarily a federal effort. Federal legislation for community child advocacy programs must be of sufficient magnitude and variation so that all communities—whether within a ghetto or in a middle-class neighborhood—are able to take advantage of it to begin programs which meet the particular unmet needs of each community. Such legislation might require the state to be involved with matching funds on the 25 percent basis as is presently true of certain mental health programs. For some states there needs to be total federal support. Those states which are extremely poor or in which there are large ghettoized cities are going to require total federal support in order to provide effective programs.

The legislated federal funding must require the coordination of voluntary and federal funds on behalf of the child and the family programs and these must be available on a community-wide basis. The majority on the boards of neighborhood and community child advocacy programs must be parents and other citizens in the community. A few professionals from schools, courts, welfare, and those who represent current services and the state and local planning personnel, working with a community-wide board of citizens, should make up the primary agency which determines priorities and methods of dealing with the needs through interagency collaboration. They can help set up those new agencies that are required for the community, and especially the neighborhood, to develop effective services.

It is the job of community child advocacy boards, through the parents and other citizens and through citizen organizations from each of the neighborhoods, to help them exercise the leadership required so that each neighborhood has its own child development council or operational advocacy program. It is clear that this kind of collaboration among citizens, agency professionals, and community officials is vital. Collaboration of the heads and boards of the city-county agencies such as schools, health departments, welfare, and courts can begin to produce a new pattern of service and early intervention and prevention.

INTERAGENCY PLANNING. An interagency citizen board planning for the needs in the community also evaluates staff duplication and the need for reeducation of staff. New functions emerge for a variety of professionals and preprofessionals in each of the communities, especially in the schools and the various other city and private agencies. Such an interagency organization would have a new look at probation, welfare, health, and mental health services and how they can better serve the community. The focus needs to be on how agencies might coordinate their activities to begin to act in prevention, rather than only in a holding operation or inadequate rehabilitation.

The needless duplication of function and bureaucratic structure is difficult to deal with. It can only be examined critically and constructively by an operational program which knows the needs and examines all possible resources available for filling these needs. Thus, such operational community child advocate agencies begin to expect the operational arms of service agencies that carry out the prevention and treatment programs to be accountable for their programs and operations. The job of many of the employed child advocates is that of monitoring with the families and children in the neighborhood how services are being carried out and whether critical needs are being met.

One could make comparisons of the few effective Head Start programs in the country with those that have not been effective, and extrapolate to how operational advocacy programs in the neighborhood might be best developed. The effective programs had large numbers of citizens from each neighborhood vitally involved. There was heavy parent involvement, both working in the classroom programs themselves as unpaid helpers and as aides. There was good attendance at the various classes which helped the parents understand the Head Start program and its specific efforts so parents could work more effectively in the classroom. The most successful programs were those in which parents were a large part of the policy making boards and where the professionals, preprofessionals, teachers, and teachers' aides were accountable to their citizen boards.

Some aspects of program review

Part of the effort in any program must be the teaching of research methodology and accountability to some citizen workers. Thus, a number of parents and young people in the program learn how one assesses the effectiveness and success of programs. It is clear, from the work of Riessman, Cohen and Pearl [18] and Kellam and Schiff,[10] that many individuals in the community can be trained for research jobs. These community persons are trained for new roles, not only for employment, but also in community responsibility. Program review can only be effective when done by a combination of parents, citizens, and professionals from agencies, along with the government officials at the local and state level. Citizen involvement permits a clear assessment of program effectiveness. The program objectives, the deployment of resources, their utilization, and examination of unmet needs must be constantly scrutinized in each community.

This chapter focuses on one particular model of operational child advocacy—a model based on a prevention/early intervention approach. The treatment aspects which are so important are more readily available, more varied, and have greater resources in such a model than one which focuses primarily on meeting treatment needs and enhancing treatment capabilities. Like all models, it needs operational testing to assess its feasibility and validity for a community. Any model requires time to work out problems and to effect consolidation of effort. This model embodies many of the elements discussed in Joint Commission meetings, although not all.

The purpose of the chapter is to evoke response from communities and professionals, to achieve some feeling about what is likely to work and what is not. Essentially, only efforts to work operationally in neighborhoods and communities will highlight effective models and pinpoint problem areas for refinement and change.

The federal legislation discussed briefly is a critical factor in making operational advocacy possible. The elements of such legislation described all come from Joint Commission recommendations.

REFERENCES

1. BLATT, B. A hypothesis of theories and methods in special education, mental retardation, and cultural deprivation. In J. Hellmuth (Ed.), *Disadvantaged Child*. Vol. 1. New York: Brunner/Mazel, 1967. Pp. 65–76.
2. CHRISTMASS, J. J. Group methods in training and practice: Nonprofessional mental health personnel in a deprived community. *American Journal of Orthopsychiatry*, 1966, *36*, 414–419.
3. EISENBERG, L. Reading retardation: Psychiatric and sociologic aspects. In J. Hellmuth (Ed.), *Disadvantaged Child*. Vol. 1. New York: Brunner/Mazel, 1967. Pp. 409–431.
4. GOLDBERG, G. Untrained neighborhood workers in a school work program. In A. Pearl and F. Riessman (Eds.), *New Careers for the Poor*. New York: Free Press, 1965.
5. HUTCHESON, B. R., BLOOM, L., & CHORAS, P. New delivery systems for children's services. *American Journal of Orthopsychiatry*, 1970, *40*, 282–283.
6. JOHN, V. P., & GOLDSTEIN, L. S. The social context of language acquisition. In J. Hellmuth (Ed.), *Disadvantaged Child*. Vol. 1. New York: Brunner/Mazel, 1967. Pp. 455–469.
7. KATZ, A. H. Self-help in rehabilitation: Some theoretical aspects. *Rehabilitation Literature*, 1967, *28*, 10–11, 30.
8. KELIHER, A. V. Parent and child centers: What they are, where they are going. *Children*, 1969, *16*:2, 63–66.

9. KELLAM, S. G., & SCHIFF, S. K. Adaptation and mental illness in the first-grade classrooms of an urban community. *Psychiatric Research Reports,* American Psychiatric Association, 1967, No. 21, 79–91.

10. KELLAM, S. G., & SCHIFF, S. K. The Woodlawn Mental Health Center: A community mental health center model. *Social Service Review,* 1966, *40,* 255–263.

11. KOHLER, M. The rights of children, an unexplored constituency. *Social Policy,* 1971, *1,* 36–44.

12. LEIGHTON, D. A contribution of population studies: Ameliorative measures for the disadvantaged. *Acta Psychiatrica Scandinavica,* 1970, *46* (Suppl. 219), 103–108.

13. MCHARDY, L. W. The court, the police, and the school. *Federal Probation,* 1968, 32:1, 47–50.

14. MULFORD, R. Protective services for children. In R. Morris (Ed.), *Encyclopedia of Social Work.* Vol. 2. New York: National Association of Social Workers, 1971. Pp. 1007–1013.

15. NICHTERN, S. The care of dependent children. *Journal of the American Academy of Child Psychiatry,* 1973, *12,* 393–399.

16. O'DONNELL, E. J., & REID, O. M. The multi-service neighborhood center: Preliminary findings from a national survey. *Welfare in Review,* 1971, 9:3, 1–8.

17. PERLMAN, R., & JONES, D. *Neighborhood Service Centers.* Washington, D.C.: Office of Juvenile Delinquency and Youth Development, 1967.

18. RIESSMAN, F., COHEN, J., & PEARL, A. *Mental Health of the Poor: New Treatment Approaches for Low-Income People.* New York: Free Press, 1964.

19. SCHIFF, S. K., & KELLAM, S. G. A community-wide mental health program of prevention and early treatment in first grade. *Psychiatric Research Reports,* American Psychiatric Association, 1967, No. 21, 92–102.

20. WARD, S. A. Components of a child advocacy program. *Children Today,* 1972, *1*:2, 38–40.

One day, perhaps, unimaginable generations
hence, we will evolve into the knowledge that
human beings are more important than real estate
and will permit this knowledge to become the
ruling principle of our lives. For I do not
for an instant doubt, and I will go to my grave
believing, that we can build Jerusalem, if
we will.

R. AVEDON and J. BALDWIN in *Nothing Personal*

_____ **17**

Now and
the Way It Should Be

IRVING N. BERLIN, M.D.

Family problems: Who helps?

Family problems, such as the physical illness of a parent, a
runaway, delinquent behavior of a child, a child with school
and neighborhood problems due to retardation, or mental illness, usually result in appeals to a variety of agencies for help.

When the Andersons faced each of these problems in their
family, here is what happened.

Mrs. Anderson at age 40 began to experience pain and swelling in her joints, especially of her hands and feet. After trying
several home remedies for two months with no relief, she went
to the county hospital clinic. She waited five hours to see the
resident who did the physical examination, took some blood for
chemical tests, and asked her to return in two weeks. In the
meanwhile he placed her on aspirin medication regularly. The
aspirin helped a bit with the swelling of her joints but not the
pain which made every movement extremely difficult. The medical resident also suggested some rest in bed for a couple of
weeks. Mrs. Anderson thought, "He didn't even ask if I had any

kids at home." With four children, of whom two were preschoolers and one was a disturbed child, it was impossible to stay in
bed.

After another very long wait on her return to the clinic, the
medical resident informed Mrs. Anderson that she had severe
rheumatoid arthritis. Remembering, she thought, "Now I'll be
crippled for life like my aunt and have to be nursed and fed.
God, how I hated feeding her!" She heard the resident say that
an expensive medicine was necessary and there needed to be
very close following to make sure that she did not get sick from
the medication. Mr. Anderson worked for the city as a laborer.
The medical insurance option they had chosen, the least expensive one, covered only hospitalization and, because of father's
job, they were not eligible for Medicaid medical care. Mrs. Anderson went to the county hospital clinic for family medical
problems because the only doctors in the area were two terribly
overworked elderly men who could spend only a few minutes
with a patient and usually were so busy with injuries and infections that they had little time for their patients who required
thorough examinations and follow-up. Besides, Mrs. Anderson
and her friend believed these two old doctors had had no time
to keep up with medical advances; they did little or no laboratory tests and they looked so exhausted that many patients did
not want to trouble them.

How to get the expensive medication on their budget was a
major problem for the Andersons. They did manage it, however, and Mrs. Anderson got considerable relief of her symptoms, but her face became puffy and she began to feel dizzy.
When she returned to the hospital clinic there was a new medical resident who quickly read her chart, took her off that medication and prescribed something else for the pain in addition to
the aspirin. Through five changes of residents in a year, Mrs.
Anderson was placed on five different pain relievers and sleeping pills. Each time Mrs. Anderson hoped the new medication
and pain reliever would help her feel good again. It never happened. She was soon hooked on both pain relievers and sleeping pills, her joints becoming more painful and stiff so that she
could hardly walk or use her hands. During a brief hospitalization in the summer in a small private hospital, she was put on

small doses of the first medication and her pain killers and sleeping pills taken away. This reduced the swelling, joint stiffness, and most of the pain and made her feel alive and well as long as she was in the hospital, away from the burdens of home. But once home again she went back to her pain killers and sleeping pills. She could always get these from each new resident. By now Mrs. Anderson was not able to do much housework or cooking. Her oldest girl, 15-year-old Anne, did those jobs when she came home from school.

THE HISTORY OF A RUNAWAY AND ITS RESULTS. When Anne at 16 decided she'd had it at home with her addicted and out-of-it mother and her crazy brother who could not be managed, she ran away with several other girls to a nearby town to find work. Within a week police found them and returned them home. After four more runaways Anne was declared incorrigible and at 16½ was placed in a girls' school for delinquents. No one from the juvenile probation department had the time to find out why Anne ran away, to recognize Mrs. Anderson's troubles and the burdens on the family with a psychotic boy. The overwhelmed court workers did not take the time to get Mr. Anderson's opinions and to talk with the other children to find out what was going on in the home. Now with Mrs. Anderson spaced out on drugs, Mr. Anderson was constantly feeling both angry and helpless about where to turn.

Anne had a pleasant time at the special school for delinquents and learned how to take care of herself in the streets. The last the Andersons heard of Anne she was working in a house of prostitution and had been arrested in a raid. She left town later and never thereafter contacted her family.

MENTAL ILLNESS AND FAMILY STRESS. Henry, now 11½, is in constant trouble in school. In a special class for the emotionally disturbed his temper outbursts and destructive and assaultive behavior disrupted all class work. As he grew older he became more willful and demanding, was very difficult at home, and could only be handled by Mr. Anderson. Mr. Anderson was firm and clear about his expectations and Henry enjoyed working with his dad in the garden. In the garden Henry carried out instructions; he was pleased at his father's approving comments. He knew his dad liked to garden with him. He often told his doctor this. Henry looked forward to weekends when father could garden with him.

As Mrs. Anderson became more addicted, her husband became more depressed, and spent less time with Henry. Henry, already difficult in school and at home, felt neglected and became overtly hostile toward his siblings, actually hurting them. He became more destructive to toys and his own clothing. In school, in the class for the emotionally disturbed children, he had always been a sullen, angry, explosive child who was difficult to teach, and who was either teased by older children to evoke his temper flareups or who teased the younger children unmercifully himself and was in trouble with teachers for his difficult behavior. His accelerated troubles in school and at home finally led to his being hospitalized in the children's ward of a nearby state mental hospital.

Henry's history. Henry was a very large—almost nine pounds—baby. Since their medical insurance did not cover obstetrical care during pregnancy or delivery, like thousands of low-income employed, Mrs. Anderson went without obstetrical care and was delivered at the county hospital. The obstetrical residents at the county hospital were not prepared for such a large baby, and although it was Mrs. Anderson's second baby, she was in labor for 36 hours and on the delivery table for six hours. They finally had to get help from the staff doctor on call who performed a high forceps. Mrs. Anderson was in such pain on the delivery table that they gave her gas anesthesia intermittently for the six hours.

Henry was born blue, lifeless, and with a badly marked head from the high forceps. With the use of oxygen and a respirator they finally brought him back to life. From earliest days Henry's sleeping and feeding were irregular; he was colicky. His sleeplessness and Mrs. Anderson's need also to care for her aged, sickly parents kept her chronically tired and angry at Henry and her husband, who could not stay awake with Henry and work the next day. There seemed no way out of this terrible nightmare until her parents had been sick so long that they were feeble and, despite her guilt feelings, they went to the county old age home. Mrs. Anderson spent little time with Henry. He was very clumsy in walking and coordination but there had been slow improvement. He learned to talk slowly, but was mostly moody and kept to himself. Their neighborhood doctor said Henry would grow out of it and be okay. At age four Henry did not talk except for a few words, was not really communicative except by grunting and pointing to make his needs known, could not coordinate to run, did not dress himself, was not toilet trained, had frequent temper tantrums, and preferred to be alone with his furry animals and an old toy phonograph playing the same record over and over, watching the record spin.

Finally Mrs. Anderson braved the long wait in the county hospital's children's clinic. There, after examinations and psychological testing, they told her that Henry was disturbed, perhaps psychotic, and certainly had brain damage. They gave her the feeling that she was to blame for all of Henry's problems. The only advice they gave her was that Henry would have to go to a special school. Since the hospital had no services for disturbed or brain-damaged children, and no liaison with local agencies, especially the schools, they simply made the diagnosis and left the Andersons, like thousands of other families with disturbed, hard-to-diagnose children, to fend for themselves.

Like so many other seriously disturbed children who are not given special help in early childhood and whose parents are not taught to work realistically with their child, Henry became a tyrant, difficult to manage or to teach. In essence, his behavior problems were like those of some mentally ill children, those who communicate their feelings in action rather than words. They relate poorly to peers and adults. The sudden violence and disruptive behavior are ostensibly not predictable. Not having been in a milieu program with special treatment, Henry looked more strange and more antisocial as time passed. He was constantly demanding and provoking at home. By the time Henry got to special class at age six, his learning could not be assessed and by intelligence tests he appeared retarded with islands of normal functioning in memory test and vocabulary. Henry loved to look up words in the dictionary. His angry willfullness was encouraged by mother's giving in to his every desire; she fed him and ran to do his bidding. She also insisted that his sisters and brothers give in to him. Thus Henry developed few self-care skills. Others did for him what he could and would have learned to do for himself in a treatment center. His brothers and sister resented him but knew no way out.

Henry and his problems dominated the family; the other children got less than their share of care and the older sister bitterly resented Henry. Much of the psychological complications of Mrs. Anderson's arthritis and her need for pain killers and sleeping pills may have been the result of trying to avoid the strain and problems of dealing with this strange, angry, uncommunicative, destructive, and demanding boy at home.

In most families an emotionally disturbed, organically disordered, or developmentally disturbed child who is not helped to learn to accept discipline and to behave in order to gain love and approval disrupts the family and creates a living hell which adversely affects every family member. These disturbed children themselves suffer because they never succeed in learning to react realistically to their social situation and they find their family and others hiding their true feelings of how the child's behavior impinges on them and how much anger and hate they feel. The guilt of parents with an emotionally disturbed child is based on self-blame and real circumstances, as with Mrs. Anderson, where her parents' illness deprived Henry of the care and love she'd given her other babies. Often the self-blame is a feeling of having brought a strange child into the world and that it must be something in the parents' families which is at fault. That blame is increased by most contacts with professionals, especially in the mother's case where she is often told it is her fault. Being blamed makes any firm behavior and clear expectations of the child, rather than propitiation and giving in to demands, extremely difficult if not impossible.

The Andersons, as do many families of low and middle income levels, depend upon the health and social agencies in a community at the very least to provide help in times of stress. In the case of severe disorder they require more continuous help and support.

A neighborhood child advocate program at work

The neighborhood worker of the program would know all of the households in each area. When a woman became noticeably pregnant, the worker would inquire about prenatal care and, if it had not been arranged for, would help make an appointment at the obstetrical clinic. The worker would follow up to find out if the appointment was kept and help arrange for each newly pregnant woman to join a class on health care during pregnancy. The group would also discuss the baby's growth in the mother and the process of delivery, as well as basics of child development and the common medical and emotional problems of pregnancy.

Under such a program, Mrs. Anderson would have gone to the clinic for regular checkups. Both parents would have attended the classes because Mr. Anderson enjoyed learning new things and meeting new people. He would have helped his wife to attend and become interested in learning about how babies grow. He would have been more attentive to his wife as he understood the process of pregnancy and they could have talked together about the information in the classes for prospective parents.

In her sixth-month x-ray at the clinic the doctors, having discovered the large size of the baby and the small size of Mrs. Anderson's pelvis, would probably have talked with the Andersons about taking the baby by a Caesarean operation so there would be no injury, oxygen deficiency, or brain damage. The clinic would also have offered birth control advice to the Andersons if they wanted to space their children.

The birth of a baby who is normal may produce stress on the mother in a family where other children are very young and require a great deal of attention. In this case, even if Henry had had no sleep, colic, or hyperactive behavior problems in infancy, the coincident illness of his mother's aged parents would have caused stress and resulted in fragmenting Mrs. Anderson's time and attention and certainly would have disturbed her peace of mind with a new baby so that she would have experienced less pleasure than she had found in nurturing the older child.

In an advocacy program the regular follow-up visits of the public health nurse would have uncovered the multiple problems both in the child and with the grandparents. In the case conference several kinds of help would have been discussed and offered to the family to help with these problems.

To relieve mother of the stress of ill parents, a housekeeper as well as an outreach medical service to determine the nature of the parents' illnesses might have been offered. In this case the mild stroke of the maternal grandmother and the cardiac decompensation of the maternal grandfather would have required both specific medical help and continued medication for both grandparents provided by a nurse practitioner after initial diagnosis. Care for both grandparents by a trained homemaker would have been both less expensive than hospitalization and more psychologically helpful to the grandparents. It also might have permitted, with treatment and help, mild to moderate compensation in the physical illnesses so they could again care for each other with minimal outside assistance, thus, hopefully, as has been demonstrated in geriatric screening programs, keeping these elderly people out of a home for the aged as long as they could and wanted to function independently.

Mrs. Anderson, relieved of this burden, could have spent more time with Henry. Since his basic rhythms of sleep and feeding were disturbed, she also might have needed relief at night so she could better function with him during the day. In addition, the neighborhood Developmental Deviations Clinic would have provided for this mother and others regular classes in child development, teaching them to stimulate and to interact playfully with their babies, activities which are usually very difficult for most mothers with such children.

Such classes make individual assessments of each baby in terms of normal maturation and in Henry's case would have provided visual-tactile methods for learning and stimulation as well as the usual vocal stimulation through mother's singing, rhymes, music, etc., which many such children are not very responsive to initially.

Most important, mothers with similar problems, as their anxieties are reduced, can talk together, even plan together on mutual babysitting. Reduction of anxiety occurs primarily as they see that a variety of developmentally appropriate playful stimuli which they have been helped to use in teaching their child reduces the hyperactivity, tends to help development, and encourages stabilization of the sleep cycle.

Oddly enough, or perhaps not oddly at all, a wide variety of developmental problems, from nonresponsive babies with noninteracting, frightened new mothers to babies with obvious mon-

golism, congenital blindness, deafness, and other clear neurologic diseases like cerebral palsy, all benefitted from the
Developmental Deviations Stimulation Clinic. The weekly
meetings, and the individual sessions at home with the child
developmental aides who worked with each mother on their
specific stimulation and interaction programs, gave each mother
mutual support and individual help. The charted changes in the
infants made clear how well each child was doing according to
his or her particular problems. Mothers who failed to come to
meetings were not only helped at home but any interferences,
like babysitting problems, transportation, etc., were worked out
in the child advocacy program. Mothers of children with similar
problems were eager to help new mothers recognize the benefits
of the programs and would make home visits with the child development aide.

In such a program, cerebral palsied children, who have major
muscle paralysis but no mental deficits, were helped early because mothers could see how rapidly their babies progressed
intellectually and were helped to expect them to do well there,
so that, despite paralysis, they would not be penalized in the
intellectual areas because of mothers' great anxieties about their
handicapped babies, anxieties which increase rather than
ameliorate the handicap. Also, in the process of passive exercise
to the paralyzed limbs the babies obviously enjoy the stimulation and the muscles become stronger.

Children with Henry's problem did very well when playfully
stimulated through the modalities of motor and visual sensory
intake. Such children, who moved into the neighborhood when
they were three to five years of age, would have special preschool experiences to help them control their impulses, to use
their muscles fully, and to learn to socialize, using behavior modification approaches which rewarded every positive behavior.
Those children whose sensori-motor patterns indicated possible
brain damage, developmental lags, or immaturity due to premature birth could be tried on stimulant drugs under pediatric
care. The parents of these children were helped by involving
them in developing home reward systems to encourage behavior
patterns and expectations that aided these children to become

part of the family rather than permitting their impulsive behavior to tyrannize the family.

Clearly autistic and psychotic young children were part of this therapeutic day care experience. Their mothers were expected also to participate in the day care program to learn how to best work with them at home. Careful evaluation of organic components and sensori-motor skills helped develop learning programs for each child. The troubled interactions of very depressed and disorganized mothers with their disturbed children were decreased as they were taught, through carefully monitored instruction in the center and at home, how they might more effectively help in the child's development. Depression and disorganization appear to be reduced as mothers who feel helpless and to blame for their child's disorder find they can indeed learn to work effectively with them. Modeling techniques and behavior modification techniques are used to help mother and father to observe how someone else works with their child. They are then helped to imitate such work, beginning with simple tasks in which they learn how to reinforce their child's approximations of successful efforts. They thus learn how to influence their child's behavior in a positive way at home.

For school-age children who are still seriously disturbed, day treatment centers attached to the school permit a combination of milieu activities, group activities, use of recreation and occupational therapy, special education methods and, where indicated, individual treatment. Such a program avoids a state hospital where the least skilled mental health workers do treatment and where loss of home support means rejection to the child and results in regression and more severe behavior disturbance.

In the day treatment center, as in the preschool, parents must be involved in order to learn how to use at home the techniques that work in the center. Home visits of center staff to help parents learn to work with their child around the specific issues of living at home—self-care, social interactions, taking responsibilities, etc.—make the program one of total push to help the child improve enough to benefit from normal schooling and contact with normal children.

Where children's behavior requires hospitalization, use of antipsychotic medication, and use of a 24-hour milieu program, such programs must be close enough to the community to permit weekend visits home. Parents must also be participant in such programs so they can learn what attitudes and specific remedial work seem to be helpful to their child in the hospital, the goal being to return the child to the day treatment center after being helped to better integration in the hospital.

Thus, for Henry the community could have provided a variety of options emphasizing early intervention, education, socialization, and parental involvement to help Henry begin to make it in school and at home.

When Mrs. Anderson became ill and could not care for Henry at home, temporary foster homes or group homes could have been used if a home care aide could not have dealt with Henry. At the same time, the health clinic's doctor would have explained to her about the treatment, what reactions she could expect, how long it would take for the medicine to work and relieve most of the pain, and how the dosage would have to be carefully adjusted. The visits of the public health nurse and the outreach worker to check on the effects of medication would also have cheered Mrs. Anderson. The fact that someone was interested in her would have helped her to bear the discomfort and realize that she was being cared about and for and that her pain was recognized. She would have been confident that the medication would reduce the discomfort and stiffness in time. Such confidence, which comes from continued concern, permits living and working with moderate pain with the reassurance that the pain is not being ignored. It is a prime feature of comprehensive care. Although medical residents rotate through the clinic, the regular clinic doctor, the public health nurses, and the outreach workers all provide ongoing care to make sure that people in the community are taken care of and that their chronic problems are not neglected. These are all essential components of comprehensive, continuous care—a rare phenomenon today.

In the event that a child or adolescent runs away from home or otherwise gets into trouble with the juvenile court, the outreach worker tries to piece together from the youth and family members the family problems which affect the youth. In the

Andersons' case, the worker could have offered help from the mental health clinic's social workers to both Anne and the Andersons. The social worker would have used her relationship with the family to ensure that they kept the appointment. Without infringing on the social worker's relationships with the Andersons, the outreach worker would have at least kept in touch with the social worker and the court to see if the family required neighborhood support, such as care for Henry and the youngest child when they went for appointments.

With the family problems at least honestly aired, some effort would be made to relieve Anne and Mr. and Mrs. Anderson of some of their stress by continued counseling to increase family communication. Temporary placement of Henry outside the home to give Mrs. Anderson a chance to work out both her medical and psychological problems could have been arranged with help from the therapeutic day treatment center. The concentration of a family's attention on a disturbed child often shortchanges other children in the family. They do not receive the amount of concern, attention, and responsiveness required for their development. A system is required which considers the family's needs as a whole and tries to help the family recognize the needs of their other children and how Henry may be helped to accept his place in the family through the work in the treatment center. The pediatricians, health care workers, and school personnel need to collaborate on behalf of all the children and family members to pick up signs of incipient troubles and begin to provide the family with the help they need to look at and manage problems. Camp experiences for Henry and weekends free from Henry may be very important to this family. There need to be community resources to help families with such added burdens.

In the community mental health agency Anne would not only have had a worker of her own with whom to talk but also would have been offered a chance to work in an adolescent group with young people of her age who had similar problems. As young people share their feelings and their troubles, they can be helped to examine together what alternative courses of action might be best for them. In the group they learn how to talk about their feelings, to discuss family problems and their own problems, and consider solutions. They also have the opportunity to discuss and learn together what adolescents want and need to know about human physiology, anatomy, and sexuality. In the course of these discussions they begin to understand a variety of impulses—sexual, angry, jealous, self-destructive, wanting and needing to be babied, etc. As they understand their feelings better they can examine their behavior and their needs and consider how these can be met in relationships and what they want for themselves in the future. As they discuss human relationships which occur in their own families and understand how these come about, they can discuss the kinds of relationships they would like to have, their life ambitions. They discuss family size and family planning as one aspect of planning their lives.

In times of great stress Mr. Anderson would have known he could turn for help to the neighborhood worker and the health or mental health clinic which would aid him in dealing with his wife or Henry or Anne and help reduce his tensions and keep his relationship with Anne and the other children open.

Finally, a community health and mental health advocacy program would be concerned with scope and continuity of care. Any illness of any member of the Anderson family would have been treated at the health clinic promptly. The doctor and the medical aides, having known the Andersons and how they might react to a serious illness in a child, would be able to counsel them and reduce their anxieties. They would also have known the children in the family and how best to work with a child so that treatment would be carried out most effectively and anxiety reduced. They would have understood how to interpret Mrs. Anderson's illness to her and her family and how to help them give aid to the mother without reducing her status in the family. They would know about Henry and his impact on the family. Health care personnel would also be alert to the impact of any chronic disease on a person and family. In the Anderson family both Henry and Mrs. Anderson have such chronic diseases and need special attention around other illnesses.

Only if severe emotional or organic illness in a child is considered developmentally, dealt with early and with an eye to continuous care in a family setting, are the child and family likely to make a healthy adaptation to the disorder. Such an adaptation gives hope for ever better functioning of the disturbed child in the family and society. It also means the family will become more integrated and learn through their experiences with a disturbed child about themselves as human beings and about how a family, with appropriate help, can live and solve problems together.

REFERENCES

1. ADAMS, J. K. School ombudsmen explore student rights. *Opportunity* (Published by the Office of Economic Opportunity), 1972, 2:3, 24–29.
2. ALPER, B. S. The training school: Stepchild of public education. *Federal Probation*, 1969, 33:4, 24–28.
3. BAYLEY, N. Value and limitations of infant testing. *Children*, 1958, 5, 129.
4. BOWLBY, J., AINSWORTH, M., BOSTON, M., & ROSENBLUTH, D. Effects of mother-child separation: Follow-up study. *British Journal of Medical Psychology*, 1956, 29, 211–247.
5. BRAMWELL, D. M. Changing concepts of residential care. In I. Philips (Ed.), *Prevention and Treatment of Mental Retardation*. New York: Basic Books, 1966. Pp. 334–345.
6. DAVIS, L. T. (Ed.) *Who Speaks for Children?* Raleigh, North Carolina: Study Commission on North Carolina's Emotionally Disturbed Children, 1970.
7. FANSHEL, D., & SHINN, E. B. *Dollars and Sense in the Foster Care of Children: A Look at Cost Factors*. New York: Child Welfare League of America, 1972.
8. GOLDFARB, W. Effects of psychological deprivation in infancy and subsequent stimulation. *American Journal of Psychiatry*, 1945, 102, 18–33.
9. GROSSER, C. *Helping Youth: A Study of Six Community Organization Programs*. Washington, D.C.: Office of Juvenile Delinquency and Youth Development, 1968.
10. KAHN, A. J. The delivery of social services at the local level. In A. J. Kahn, *Studies in Social Policy and Planning*. New York: Russell Sage Foundation, 1969. Pp. 245–294.
11. KATZ, S. N. *When Parents Fail: The Law's Response to Family Breakdown*. Boston: Beacon Press, 1971.
12. KNOBLOCH, H., & PASAMANICK, B. Environmental factors affecting human development before and after birth. *Pediatrics*, 1960, 26, 210–218.
13. KRAMER, R. M. *Participation of the Poor*. Englewood Cliffs, New Jersey: Prentice-Hall, 1969.

14. MEYER, D. A. A community assesses its needs. *Children Today,* 1972, *1*:2, 37.
15. MOELLER, H. G. Corrections and the community: New dimensions. *Federal Probation,* 1968, 32:2, 25–29.
16. PASAMANICK, B., & KNOBLOCH, H. Epidemiologic studies on the complications of pregnancy and the birth process. In G. Caplan (Ed.), *Prevention of Mental Disorders in Children.* New York: Basic Books, 1961. Pp. 74–94.
17. RIEGER, N. I. Problems in treating children in a state mental hospital. *Hospital and Community Psychiatry,* 1970, *21,* 251–255.
18. SCHEPSES, E. Delinquent children and wayward children. *Federal Probation,* 1968, 32:2, 42–46.
19. SCHORR, A. L. *Poor Kids: A Report on Children in Poverty.* New York: Basic Books, 1966.
20. SILBERMAN, C. E. *Crisis in the Classroom.* New York: Vintage Books, 1971.
21. SUNLEY, R. Family advocacy: From case to cause. *Social Casework,* 1970, *51,* 347–357.
22. WERRY, J. S., et al. Studies on the hyperactive child. IV. Neurological status compared with neurotic and normal children. *American Journal of Orthopsychiatry,* 1962, *42,* 441–450.
23. WHEELER, G. R., & INSKEEP, H., III. Youth in the gauntlet. *Federal Probation,* 1968, 32:4, 21–25.

There is no substitute for the enlightened
action of an aroused citizenry.

THOMAS JEFFERSON

_____**18**

Child Advocacy: Political and Legislative Implications

NORMAN V. LOURIE, A.C.S.W.
IRVING N. BERLIN, M.D.

We can. Will we?

We can markedly reduce mental retardation, developmental
disabilities, infantile or early childhood mental illness. Will we?
We can either prevent or intervene early into a wide variety of
learning and behavior disorders of childhood. We can alter educational patterns to enhance learning and promote problem solving skills in school. Will we? We can work effectively with
parents to help them help their own children to learn. We can
show parents how to assume responsibility for reducing children's psychotic symptoms and disability from a wide variety of
neurophysiologic disorders noted shortly after birth. Will we?
We can change patterns of health and mental health care and
provide neighborhood advocacy for children and families. Will
we? We can reduce crime, delinquency, drug and alcohol abuse.
We can eliminate poverty and reduce racism. Will we?

Yes, recent research and model programs show we can achieve
all these important goals for our children, our citizens. Research
shows we stand on the doorstep of opportunity for change in all
these areas. As was once true in the purification of water and
sterilization of milk, technical capability exists. We have the

311

know-how and the capacity to realize human rights in health and mental health. Will we, as professionals, as concerned lay citizens, as legislators, be excited by the promise of accomplishment and give these goals high priority?

Elements of progress in social welfare legislation

The history of social welfare services in this country includes the impact of the Townsend movement of elderly citizens, centering in California. The vigorous educational campaigns and pressures on legislators, which took on a national flavor, helped bring about the first social security legislation in the 1930s.

There are about one thousand human services programs in the United States. They arise as federal laws; they complement and supplement thousands of state and local laws and programs in the human services field. The American social welfare scene is younger than that of most other industrialized countries. In general, it probably provides, as our standard of living does, higher income maintenance levels and more investment in a wide variety of categorical programs. However, relative to the wealth of our nation and its place in the scale of things as compared to other nations, there are a great many anachronisms in the American scene.

While we have reduced poverty through our economy, our Social Security Act, our public assistance programs, and now our recently enacted Supplemental Security Income program (new federal guaranteed minimum income program for the aged, blind, and disabled), we are far from eliminating poverty. Medicaid and Medicare have certainly not solved our health problems. Even the surge of massive federal education laws and monies in the 1960s failed to complete the promises and resolutions of the White House Conference on Children. There are still a great many educationally disadvantaged children in the United States.

While categorical programs are important and the consumer groups, including parents, have made great inroads in pushing legislators, bureaucrats, and courts, our programs are characterized by fragmentation, duplication, overlapping, and incompleteness. We talk integration and coordination. We have strong rhetoric about these, but we have not achieved them. They are largely myths. The concepts of human services and human services systems are more faddist discussion terms than they are realities.

In comparison with underdeveloped and perhaps even some of the developed countries, what we have appears to be better than most in some fields, but we have nothing that parallels some nations' health programs and total social insurance coverage.

Aside from the issue of how we want to use our resources, there is still the fundamental issue of whether we are using our citizens' capacities and rights to produce legislative and programmatic results that can meet the objectives of our theories about human services coverage. How do we take advantage of our political and legislative structure to see to it that all of the human risks are known, that human needs are known, and that systems are then designed which guarantee that the needs are met?

It isn't that we do not have legislation and programs. We have too many. They are not well articulated and not one of them, even when directly administered by the federal government and its leaders, has ever been given the resources needed to do the job for children.

Human rights and politics

Human rights in health, welfare, and education are attained not only in response to manifest need, but almost always through education of the public, of legislators, and of public officials. Such educational campaigns result in important public pressures.

The political potential of all concerned professionals committed to the attainment of fundamental health, mental health, education, and basic income rights could be a potent force for public education and social action.

Some observers have suggested that moves to destroy programs in mental health—including training of mental health professionals, community mental health programs, day care, preschool and primary school programs, and especially antipoverty programs—have occurred because some people fear an educated, informed, healthy, and vigorous citizenry that may pose a threat to certain vested interests and political forces.

History clearly shows that the health, education, and welfare professionals and their organizations can take important political stands to help influence social legislation and create new rights, a step toward a better life.

POWER OF SPECIAL INTEREST GROUPS. It is characteristic of the political process that special interests wield power. Through the efforts of concerned parents and citizens in state chapters of national organizations, new legislation has been written to benefit many disabled children in some states. Concerned parents, mental health professionals, and citizens have helped to enact new legislation in a few states to provide excellent services for autistic or severely emotionally disturbed children. Professional and citizen groups have provided impetus in many states for legislation on child abuse. Recently parents of developmentally disabled and retarded youngsters in 20 states have filed "Right to Education" suits. A major one was won in Pennsylvania courts. These are aimed at equal protection under the law to provide all children education equivalent to that provided for normal children. Many states have such laws that seem to cover *all* children, but many disabled are excluded.

It is clear that concerned citizens, especially parents, concerned professionals, especially those who work with the most seriously emotionally or developmentally handicapped children, and concerned legislators can have profound impact on the health and mental health of children.

CONTINUED VIGILANCE A REQUISITE FOR STATE FUNDING AND CARE. On the state level where many human services legislative triumphs have occurred, they must be followed through. For instance, in the State of Washington an "Education for All" bill has passed, but without the appropriations to make the law fiscally operable. In California, vigilant parents of severely retarded children now in state hospitals have prevented the closing of these hospitals, because, as is typical, *no* community facilities have been funded and established specifically to provide comparable, much less better, programs for these children. In all too many states, state mental hospitals have been closed without provision for community living facilities, medication funds, support for day care and rehabilitation services for the chronically ill patients. Here, too, with adequate planning and funds, we can provide community services and facilities. Will the pressures and priorities be great enough? Who will undertake the social action tasks?

A recapitulation of our research information

We can, if we will, eliminate malnutrition and prematurity, which research shows lead to so much of our retarded population. We can do much about prenatal and delivery care to vastly reduce the number of developmentally handicapped infants and small children. We can even detect much of the maternal depression during and after pregnancy which has been indicted as a major cause of infantile psychosis.

Sufficient experimental programs have been conducted in early infancy and the preschool years to show that we can either prevent or intervene early in a wide variety of early childhood disorders so they will be markedly reduced in severity; some disorders can be totally eliminated by early intervention. Especially effective has been continued work with children and their parents in groups and in pairs. Teaching parents to stimulate and work in developmental ways with their children has been successful at home as well as in the child development centers.[24,25]

We already know a great deal about the preschool years and the influence of parents on their child's capacity and eagerness to learn. And we know from several massive studies that parental attitudes are the single most important determinants of their child's ability to learn in school.[64,82]

We have data from some programs that previously nonlearning children in noneducating schools do learn when educators work with parents to help them teach their children. Thus parents become their child's advocates in preschool, primary school, etc.

We also know a considerable amount about developmental issues and about teaching and learning processes which can make learning exciting, viable, and rewarding. In preadolescence and adolescence we have examples of how all of learning can be used to develop problem-solving skills and produce more involved and concerned citizens.

We have data about what it takes to reduce and treat delinquency. We know that a number of legal decisions have insisted on the right to treatment of children adjudicated as delinquent or adults diagnosed as mentally ill. We also know that legal decisions, like some legislative acts, do not create the monies to provide that treatment. Nor do legal decisions alter the environments of poverty and racism.

Public health objectives require political action

While new educational patterns, adequate medical care of children, changes in hospital care patterns, and viable neighborhood advocacy programs depend on legislation at the federal and state levels, the cry, the demand, and the pressure for legislation depend on an awakened and informed citizenry. Informing the citizenry, involving parents on their children's behalf, and helping inform and educate legislators are professional tasks and responsibilities.

Every public health measure, from vaccination for smallpox, measles, and polio to elimination of lead in paint or purification of contaminated drinking water to eliminate typhoid, has depended on professional action to educate both the public and legislators. It has depended on professional leadership and political pressure, and each such effort costs money plus the time and concern of professionals. No public health legislation has ever come to fruition without political pressure.

BUDGETS: POLITICS AND PEOPLE. In this light we are beginning to learn that *every public budget is a political document.* Health and mental health professionals need to learn more about political behavior and political participation, personal and organizational. We need to learn how to be part of the political system —to be actors in framing the actions, rather than merely reactors in times of crisis.

Every institution in a democratic society that professes concern for people is a political institution. Its budget reflects decisions about people, decisions to which professionals have rarely contributed responsible political action, political action which now should have as high a priority for us as has professional responsibility. The two are inseparable. Political action for professionals and professional organizations is a professional responsibility, since the well-being of our fellow citizens and decisions on their hunger, pain, illness, and survival are realistically equally professional and political concerns. Dr. Abraham C. Bergman, a pioneering pediatrician in political efforts who helped to promote legislation against flammable fabrics through the Flammable Fabrics Act and helped influence the Poison Prevention Packaging law, has said, "Politicians can potentially save (and sacrifice) more lives than doctors." [6]

Professions exist and are given sanctions by members of a society. It is natural for professions to develop self-interest. But a profession has both professional self-interest and public interest responsibilities. Professional self-interest to protect the profession and its institutions must be primarily related to assuring high standards of practice. Public interest must assure that the public is being protected, that appropriate human values are established and maintained.

Political and professional interests in many areas are inseparable. If no sound public social policy exists, professional interests cannot develop rationally and with any predictability. The professional organizations in a democracy are therefore in part political institutions. The government, the public's main vehicle of expression and value translation, influences professional institutions. Current issues around health care, safety, and consumer health and mental health rights have made this clear to all health, welfare, and education professionals.

Violence of professional-political concern

Some professional concerns for the political issues of today are found in the recommendations of the Joint Commission on Mental Health of Children. One such concern focuses on the factors which lead to violence, and their mental health implications.

The Joint Commission was created because of a concern with violence resulting from the assassination of President Kennedy. Oswald had been seen in a child guidance clinic and diagnosed as psychologically disturbed but no follow-up had occurred. Thus investigation of the etiologic factors which lead children and adults to violent behavior was a charge of the Commission. In that context we examined the research on many of the environmental factors that influence violence. One can translate the human and nonhuman elements like loss of a job into psychological factors which are noted in the violence of parents who abuse their children as well as the experiences which result in acts of violence in childhood and adolescence.

It is clear that in one sense real violence is the misuse of power. Poverty and racism are prime factors in mental health problems. Poverty and racism are real violence against people —physical, mental, spiritual, psychological, intellectual, emotional, and social. Powerlessness felt by the poor and minorities is violence against humanity. All of these—poverty, racism, and a sense of powerlessness—also create violence in the people affected.

> A Black ghetto in most American cities operates very much like any system of slavery. Relatively little overt violence is needed to keep the institution going, and yet the institution violates the human beings involved because they are systematically denied the options which are open to the vast majority in the society. A systematic denial of options is one way to deprive men of autonomy. . . . We are social beings; our whole sense of what we are is dependent on the fact that we live in society, and have open to us socially determined options. What access we have to the socially defined options is much more important than what language or what system of property rights we inherit at birth. The institutional form of quiet violence operates when people are deprived of choices in a systematic way by the very manner in which transactions normally take place. It is as real, and as wicked, as the thief with a knife.[32]

> But God help the Negro—or the young militant—who rejects the game itself; or who does not see people as expendable counters in a game, even if all have an equal chance to compete. It is these who constitute America's favorite victims of violence, for they undercut the very basis of society's legitimacy and threaten to halt the game. White America's fear of looters, intense as it is, is far less, I believe, than would be its fear of Negroes who did not want whiskey or TV, or who joined white leaders in a promising effort to improve not only the distribution of rewards in our society but the common view of what is rewarding.[31]

Violence may have many causes, but it cannot be separated from poverty and racism. No matter what the causes, violence poses both professional and political issues.

A new professional responsibility

It is a professional responsibility—a professional-political responsibility—to alert the American people and provide informed leadership in realizing a new American dream, a dream that rejects poverty, racism, injustice, misuse of power for private gain, and inappropriate distribution of wealth.

We need a new American dream—a dream based on full employment, elimination of private *poverty* by assuring every person an adequate standard of living, the elimination of public poverty by expanding our economy, taxing ourselves enough and allocating our resources to remedy the glaring deficiencies represented by our decaying cities, obsolescent transportation systems, neglected natural resources, polluted air and waters, rural blight. We need a dream which emphasizes actual educational opportunity for all in accord with ambitions, abilities, and the needs of an advancing technology and provides full health and social care to those who need it. All are health, mental health, social welfare, and education related issues.

PROFESSIONAL RESPONSIBILITIES EXTENDED. Professional responsibilities can in part be related to how our expertise, our research, and our clinical knowledge can be used on behalf of the people we serve. We can wage a campaign for a new child development act based on our knowledge that certain opportunities and experiences, for instance, food and vitamins to pregnant women and infants, and stimulation to infants, will help our citizens become more effective. These efforts have been characterized by some as token efforts and partial solutions and signs of "charitable" concern of professionals. However, history reveals that such efforts lead not only to increased education of legislators and public awareness of need, but to some beginning solutions, the first steps in a long process of attaining human rights.

Our professionals and our professions should be a primary political force to carry such a message and to create the necessary social policy. No other force is more logical for the task.

THE RIGHT TO HUMAN SERVICES. Human services as a right

rather than as a charitable impulse is a sound political platform. We have enough evidence to prove that "charitable" approaches created in crises are rarely broad enough or effective enough and do not endure.

We are at an important point in history. With hundreds of human services programs (not one of them complete or fully funded), we seemed to be on our way to realizing parts of the promised American dream. However, after a century of gradual forward movement, we are in danger of being turned around— reversing the trend.

We have come far enough to know that realization is within our capacity. The human resources share of the federal budget is close to 41 percent. The defense budget has declined to 34 percent. While for the first time the health, education, and welfare budget is larger than the defense budget, in total billions spent there is no decrease in spending for defense.

Some feel comfortable about what gains have been made, comfortable because they advocate piecemeal, bite-sized solutions to overwhelming problems. The real issue is one of values and commitment. In such fields as defense and space programs we have never taken piecemeal approaches to national problem solving. In human services a high value is placed on a bits-and-pieces approach, as if a comprehensive approach causes apprehension.

For our professions the political obligations are clear. We have no right to ask for more unless we take vigorous political positions on the hard issues. We cannot ask for more unless we agree that those who can should pay more. Redistribution of fiscal resources and creation of additional fiscal resources cannot be avoided. This means taxes. What are we willing to pay?

It is clear that many Americans want more and better social welfare services and are willing to pay for them. Defeat of the California proposition to limit taxes is one recent evidence. Another was the more than 200,000 letters sent to the Secretary of Health, Education, and Welfare in opposition to proposed restrictive Social Security Act social services. Still another indication is the current interest in social and health services by the Senate Finance and the House Ways and Means Committees, the tax committees in Congress.

THE PROFESSIONS' EDUCATIONAL ROLE. The social and health professions have a tremendous educational task to perform in provision of basic human rights. The task is basically a political one. This battle can be won only in the political arena. There is no substitute for national social policy, for national leadership.

The major battleground is the federal budget, federal law, and federal regulations. Our professional responsibilities must include political activity to deal with the hard, complex issues.

We are involved in the dilemmas of categorical programming, with its overlaps, gaps, and fragmentations. We professionals have contributed to the rhetoric leading to lack of coordination and to inefficient and inadequate delivery systems. We must not try to escape our own responsibility for many difficulties and problems. We should not defend what is unsound. We must also examine how our own diverse special interests compound the problems of service delivery. Our own behavior and our own integrity are very much involved.

The helping professions have a major leadership role to play in the human services. Setting standards for our practice is only one part of the obligation. Setting goals and criteria for improved service delivery is another. Without minimizing our achievements we should not be reluctant to admit our service delivery failures, as well as the obvious hazards of our own intense struggles for turf.

We need ecumenical movements within our own ranks. We need to support criteria and arrangements for human services delivery systems which indeed guarantee that all of the risks are known, that the needs are known, and that the delivery methods can ensure, can guarantee, that the needs are met. We need to set up performance measures by which programs can be evaluated and the effectiveness of successful ones validated.

ADVOCACY. We have created a fad for advocacy. Advocacy is simply any action in behalf of a cause. Advocacy in the final sense is operative only when organizations work to guarantee that needs are met. In this sense advocacy depends on consumer control of programs to meet urgent needs at the neighborhood level. This is inherent in operational advocacy.

LEGISLATIVE ROLES. Legislative bodies create programmatic and bureaucratic arrangements based on professional information. It is a cop-out to moan about what legislatures have done to citizens and to the social and health professions. Doing something better includes electing good people to public office and then working with them toward sound solutions which do not result in incomplete and competitive programs. In addition, we have to support legislators in efforts to get fiscal resources and priorities shifted by engaging in the political process of educating the public about programs and resource needs—including taxes.

LEARNING FROM PAST EXPERIENCES. While no health, mental health, social welfare, or educational programs have been fully funded, throwing additional money and services into a community is no guarantee that problems will be solved. Political action cannot be successful if it is fragmented by competitive professionals and interest groups each seeking to maintain their own power. Just as a political party or a political machine has to "get itself together" for a campaign, we have some pre-political-action issues to resolve.

Confusions confounded

CONFUSION OF SCOPE. Who owns which turf? Do we own it together? Can we agree on which of our institutional forms should have which responsibilities? Or are we unalterably committed to operational competition, our literally competing for prerogative, for functional authority? In reality, do we own *any* turf? To whom are we professionally obligated? Does the consumer have any real say about the quantity and the quality of services?

CONFUSION OF METHODOLOGY. Absent are clear definitions of problems and clear classification systems. Our reluctance to be accountable may relate to the need for clarification of what we are responsible for, what our specific goals are, how they are to be attained, and how we can evaluate our efforts and alter them to be more effective for the citizens we serve.

CONFUSION OF CONCEPTUAL FOCUS. We are organized for service delivery along categorical lines rather than along problem-solving lines. Each program seeks to be the comprehensive one. In using resources to support certain fiefdoms rather than to solve certain problems, professions and interest groups have helped create fragmented, self-serving, and overlapping legislation. The failure of many competitive programs to demonstrate effectiveness has resulted in funding difficulties and problems in finding the best solutions to service problems.

Mutual functional analysis of need and capacity to deliver particular services by particular institutions may reduce the confusion and competition. There really is enough work to go around. Our goals must be to assure that needs are known and met on a priority basis. Specialties are needed but they are seldom put together effectively at operational levels. Perhaps the general hospital, in this context, is a model worth attention. How disastrous if the general hospital service components were spread around town each under separate management. The resulting pulling, hauling, referring, and transferring would leave many more sick people dangling in the cracks than already occurs.

Fragmentation of service which now occurs in community mental health centers is a current example. Health, mental health, education, and welfare are viewed as separate dimensions of human needs to be dispensed separately without regard for the total human being who is served. The most needy children are not served enough in health and mental health centers, and are served questionably in the schools.

Action beyond profession or guild

We Americans are responsible for Watergate and have no right to bemoan what it represents unless we have been active in the political process. Even then we should examine our mistakes. The present Washington payoffs should teach us some lessons.

One is that the executive and legislative branches of government, at all levels, are of our own creation. Professionals, as citizens, must take responsibility for who holds office and who makes social policy. When human services social policy is the victim of an administration and we have neglected to develop our professional organizations for political action, then we must accept some blame. We have no right to complain that the American political system is not working if we are not an active part of it. If we believe there are serious problems, we must be an integral part of the efforts toward solution.

Human services professionals belong in the political arena. We are already a service society. More than half of all American workers are engaged in providing services. It is only from within the political system that effective interpretation of human services needs can be adequately exposed and given publicity which can lead to action.

Professional responsibility is incomplete when it concentrates on professional self-interest or on categorical lobbying alone.

Professional public interest is incomplete if it is not carried into the heart of the political process.

Professionals have the same responsibility as, if not more than, non-professionals for involving themselves in partisan politics, for joining political clubs, and taking an active role in choosing candidates and in elections. Professionals' awareness and concern with social policy in aspects of health, mental health, education, and welfare make it essential.

POLITICS AND PROFESSIONAL RELUCTANCE TO PARTICIPATE. Still lingering is a sense that political participation is not appropriate for professionals. Some publicly employed professionals use federal or state "Hatch" acts as barriers to avoid political activity. Politics is for someone else. Both arguments are cop-outs.

Public employees may not be able to run for office or manage campaigns in some jurisdictions. But they can belong to political clubs. They can be politically active by speaking out on the relevant issues about which they have expert knowledge or research data. They can have important impact on policy and candidates.

Professions which claim inappropriateness as the reason for being nonpolitical remind one of how such political paralysis is dropped when issues of fluoridation or universal medical care arise.

Today we must not be paralyzed at all. We have built some coalitions with each other on the national scene. Professionals have a major professional contribution to make in the political party. Political party platform committees, especially at local and state levels and to some extent nationally, have reached out to selected professionals for advice. Our presence, however, is not consistently sought, available, or felt. Planning and writing party policy and priorities are important steps in the process that precedes legislative and budget actions, and can have a major effect on results. Party platforms are not always carried out, nor are the positions stated by the candidates; however, positive party platform statements and candidates' positions at least provide an historical record and are in themselves public education. A political commitment provides a point of reference and a unity that groups can reuse when a subsequent issue has to be faced.

DECISIONS WHICH OVERRIDE PROFESSION. The professional planning and policy contributions go deeper than prose. They are more complex. Often they represent hard decisions not easy to achieve and not easy to face. The options are sometimes difficult. Sometimes they involve deep professional differences. That is part of the challenge.

It is not hard for professionals to make a decision to combat a proposed budget which eliminates basic services, training, and research. The task is tougher when more basic strategic choices have to be made.

For instance, mental health and physical health depend heavily on many circumstances clearly outside the direct province of health and mental health. Known relationships exist between unemployment and health, between poverty and health, between poor housing and health. Health and mental health are basically interrelated.

Where should the emphasis be at a particular time? At a point where fiscal choices have to be made? No one can avoid the fact that fiscal choices are real and have to be made. While we can advocate a constantly larger pie, at any moment of decision the pie is only so large and has to be divided. How much energy and resources should go to services as opposed to support for a minimal standard of living, including income, jobs, and housing?

For instance, at the recent American Public Health Association meetings one resolution in a section meeting called only for redesign of housing and cars. Professional organizations' official deliberations these days need to respond to basic issues. Resolutions and action statements on the need for a guaranteed minimum income or a decent standard of living are appropriate and necessary to make. The dissemination of such resolutions through local organizations to the grass roots level of the organization is critically important. The grass roots members of any professional organization are in contact daily with people whom they can educate. The health, mental health, and human welfare aspects of these key issues are within the professional educational domain. No one else will do it.

A KEY PROFESSIONAL-POLITICAL ROLE. There is also, quite obviously, a professional-political role that is clinical-political. The political atmosphere is a highly personalized one in which relationships and their management are vital. Human services professionals, theoretically, should fare well in the political atmosphere because they understand the intricacies and dynamics of relationships that the average politician knows by instinct or as a result of the behavior modification experiences he has had in the political arena.

Perhaps the most important clinical-political role is the interpretive, the educational one. Review the list of lobbyists published by most legislative bodies. They cover every conceivable field. The competition for legislative interest is fierce and competitive. Legislative structure and operational mode produce specialized committees and specialized individual interests, particularly committee chairmen and staffs.

No legislator has the staff to gather material with sufficient detail and clarity to be useful in clarifying a complex piece of legislation being written, reducing the ambivalence or lack of clarity that administration personnel in Health, Education, and Welfare departments on state and federal levels may create by basing their recommendations on self-serving data or *at least* faulty reasoning, and distortion of facts and history which require correction by a clear presentation of past and current data.

Some few of us do undertake a job of legislative education. Some of us do reasonably well with these committees, especially when not biased professionally and when we emphasize clearly the consumers' needs. The political system and its complexities and pressures of special interests do not produce enough well-informed legislators. While it is important to keep our key, knowledgeable, more influential legislative leaders informed, there are still major educational tasks to be performed among the large mass of legislators and particularly among non-elected political leaders. It is necessary to help these political leaders view human services not as cash benefits, benevolences, or charities, but as vital human rights, human services rights. In this area professionals and their organizations have a huge task of education. They must be prepared not only to document the savings in human resources, but the current cost, inefficiency, and future impact of legislation on the community and nation. Most politicians have difficulty in being future-oriented, being pressed with the realities of today. When we can combine present and future issues into rational legislation, we can educate not only politicians, but our fellow citizens as well.

CONSUMER AND PROFESSIONAL. For professionals, particularly in a service society, the consumer ultimately makes the decisions at the ballot box. Therefore the citizen consumer in a democratic society is our best ally. Indeed the consumer is our most unused resource. Not only do some consumers have a potential as paraprofessional colleagues, but they have actual experience with and understanding of service delivery patterns and how they work. They can and do assess effectiveness or lack of it which makes them essentially better allies for support of programs of human service delivery.

If we think of consumers of human services as only the poor or powerless, we may wonder if they can be really helpful in influencing politicians. We have seen that these consumers can be aroused to speak up and to use their voting power, and to influence the thinking and voting of members of their groups or neighborhoods—then to reach out as advocates in the political arena.

On the other hand, users of human services in our society are not only those in poverty. Mental retardation, drug and alcohol abuse, delinquency, and other social problems exist at all socioeconomic levels. The impression of human services as welfare for the poor needs to be replaced in the minds of both politicians and citizens with the view of human services as a human right and a human need existing among all citizens.

Many struggles for human rights legislation have been led by community social and financial leaders who have experienced the needs firsthand as parents or observed them as volunteers. Such persons can be strong allies for professionals.

In today's political atmosphere what better ally for professionals than those who need and use our range of services? Consumers, citizens, are the heart and mass of the American electorate.

Professions seeking human service objectives need political partnership with this electorate. After all, they are the ones whose sanctions we need in order to profess.

A possible future for human services

The future will call for more rather than less concentration on human services such as neighborhood advocacy systems, each ultimately designed to work best for its particular constituents.

If we do our work right, including our political work, human care and development in the next century will be marked by at least two thrusts: first, advances in social policy and its technology at least the equal of the technology of industry; and second, coalescence of health, education, and welfare programs into an integrated human services system. There will be major new public responsibility for human welfare at all levels of government, particularly at the federal level.

How to achieve this condition, this translation into a full national commitment for human well-being, is clearly a political question. Sound social policy will not emerge without political action on the part of all professionals in the allied fields of health, mental health, education, and social welfare.

At present, such action, when it does occur, is too often designed to protect self-interest more than it does citizen interest. Concern for children and families, for those in pain, the helpless or hopeless in our present society, requires our best thinking professionally and politically. Professional interest and citizen interest can no longer be separated.

We can best emphasize our position by paraphrasing a Chinese proverb [15] quoted earlier:

> The superior "professional effort" prevents human disease and disorder and suffering.
> The mediocre "professional effort" tries for early cure.
> The inferior "professional effort" concentrates only on curing fully developed conditions.

Let us all strive toward becoming superior professionals through full use of the political process. In that effort we can not only bring about prevention, but enhance our capacities to cure early and to treat the full-blown troubles of people.

REFERENCES

1. An Act to Amend Chapter 110 of the General Statutes to Establish the Governor's Advocacy Commission on Children and Youth. Chapter 935, House Bill 203. Raleigh: General Assembly of North Carolina, July 20, 1971.
2. ADAMS, P., et al. *Children's Rights.* London: Panther Books, 1972.
3. Ad Hoc Committee on Child Mental Health. *Report to the Director.* Washington, D.C.: National Institute of Mental Health, February, 1971.
4. ALINSKY, S. D. *Reveille for Radicals.* New York: Vintage Books, 1969.
5. *The American Health Empire: Power, Profits, and Politics.* Report of the Health Policy Advisory Center (Health-PAC). New York: Vintage Books, 1971.
6. BERGMAN, A. C. In "Rx for progress: Political medicine." *Health Science Review,* 1974, 3:3, 2.
7. BERLIN, I. N. Professionals' participation in community activities: Is it part of the job? *American Journal of Orthopsychiatry,* 1971, *41,* 494–500.
8. BERLIN, I. N., et al. The psychiatrist, the APA, and social issues: A symposium. *American Journal of Psychiatry,* 1971, *128,* 677–687.
9. BLATT, B. *Exodus from Pandemonium: Human Abuse and a Reformation of Public Policy.* Boston: Allyn & Bacon, 1970.
10. BREMNER, R. H. *American Philanthropy.* Chicago: University of Chicago Press, 1960.
11. BREMNER, R. H. (Ed.) *Children and Youth in America.* Vol. 1. Cambridge, Mass.: Harvard University Press, 1971. Parts 1–6.
12. CAHN, E. S., & CAHN, J. C. Power to the people or the profession? —The public interest in public interest law. *Yale Law Journal,* 1970, *79,* 1005–1048.
13. CARTER, J. H. Psychiatry's insensitivity to racism and aging. *Psychiatric Opinion,* 1973, *10:6,* 21–25.
14. CHAMBERS, C. (Ed.) *National Conference on Social Welfare: A Century of Concern.* Columbus, Ohio: National Conference on Social Welfare, 1973.
15. Chinese Proverb. Quoted by Irvin Emanuel in "New leader stresses problem solving at CDMRC." *Health Science Review,* 1974, 3:3, 3.
16. COHEN, J. Advocacy and the children's crisis. *American Journal of Orthopsychiatry,* 1971, *41,* 807–808.
17. COHEN, N. *Social Work in the American Tradition.* New York: Dryden Press, 1958.
18. COLEMAN, J. S., et al. *Equality of Educational Opportunity.* Washington, D.C.: U. S. Government Printing Office, 1966.

19. COLES, R. Death of the heart in ghetto children. *Federal Probation*, 1968, 32:3, 3–7.
20. Columbia Human Rights Law Review (Eds.) *Legal Rights of Children: Status, Progress and Proposals.* Fair Lawn, New Jersey: R. E. Burdick, 1972.
21. *Crisis in Child Mental Health: Challenge for the 1970s.* Report of the Joint Commission on Mental Health of Children. New York: Harper & Row, 1970.
22. DE SCHWEINITZ, K. *England's Road to Social Security.* Philadelphia: University of Pennsylvania Press, 1947.
23. DIMOND, P. Towards a children's defense fund. *Harvard Educational Review*, 1971, *41*, 386–400.
24. DMITRIEV, V. *Infant Learning.* Seattle, Washington: University of Washington Experimental Education Unit publication, 1973.
25. DMITRIEV, V. *Multidisciplinary Programs for Down's Syndrome in Children.* University of Washington Experimental Education Unit publication, 1973.
26. DORSEN, N. (Ed.) *The Rights of Americans: What They Are— What They Should Be.* New York: Vintage Books, 1970.
27. *Encyclopedia of Social Work.* Washington, D.C.: National Association of Social Workers, 1971.
28. FILLER, L. *A Dictionary of American Social Reforms.* New York: Philosophical Library, 1963.
29. *Five Decades of Action for Children: A History of the Children's Bureau.* Washington, D.C.: U.S. Government Printing Office, 1962.
30. FREED, H. M. The community psychiatrist and political action. *Archives of General Psychiatry*, 1967, *17*, 129–134.
31. FRIEDENBERG, E. Z. "Legitimate violence." *The Nation*, June 24, 1968, 822.
32. GARVER, N. What violence is. *The Nation*, June 24, 1968, 819–822.
33. GELLES, R. J. Child abuse as psychopathology: A sociological critique and reformulation. *American Journal of Orthopsychiatry*, 1973, *43*, 611–621.
34. GOLD, E. M., & STONE, M. L. Total maternal and infant care: A realistic appraisal. *American Journal of Public Health*, 1968, *58*, 1219–1229.
35. GOODMAN, L. (Ed.) *Economic Progress and Social Welfare.* New York: Columbia University Press, 1966.
36. GOODMAN, P. What rights should children have? *New York Review of Books*, September 23, 1971, 20–22.
37. GOULD, R. J. Children's rights: More liberal games. *Social Policy*, 1971, *1*, 50–52.
38. HANCOCK, P. L. The ordeal of change. *Federal Probation*, 1969, 33:1, 16–22.
39. *Having the Power, We Have the Duty.* Report to the Secretary of

Health, Education, and Welfare. Washington, D.C.: Advisory Council on Public Welfare, June 29, 1966.

40. HEINZE, W. O. Equal rights for all children. *Parents Magazine,* 1969, *40,* 12–13.

41. *Hunger, U.S.A.* Report of the Citizen's Board of Inquiry into Hunger and Malnutrition in the United States. Washington, D.C.: New Community Press, 1968.

42. JORGENSEN, J. D. Crime in a free society: Choice or challenge? *Federal Probation,* 1970, *34:*1, 14–18.

43. KAHN, A. J., KAMERMAN, S., & MCGOWAN, B. G. *Child Advocacy: Report of a National Baseline Study.* New York: Columbia University School of Social Work, 1972.

44. KAMERMAN, S. B., KAHN, A. J., & MCGOWAN, B. G. Research and advocacy. *Children Today,* 1972, *1:*2, 35–36.

45. KLEIN, P. *From Philanthropy to Social Welfare.* San Francisco: Jossey-Bass, 1968.

46. KNITZER, J. Advocacy and the children's crisis. *American Journal of Orthopsychiatry,* 1971, *41,* 799–806.

47. KOHLER, M. The rights of children, an unexplored constituency. *Social Policy,* 1971, *1,* 36–44.

48. LEIGHTON, D. C. A contribution of population studies: Ameliorative measures for the disadvantaged. *Acta Psychiatrica Scandinavica,* 1970, *46*(Suppl. 219), 103–108.

49. LEIGHTON, D. C. Measuring stress levels in school children as a program-monitoring device. *American Journal of Public Health,* 1972, *62,* 799–806.

50. LEONE, R. C. Public interest advocacy and the regulatory process. *Annals of the American Academy of Political and Social Science,* 1972, *400,* 46–58.

51. LEVINE, M., & LEVINE, A. *A Social History of Helping Services: Clinic, Court, School, and Community.* New York: Appleton-Century-Crofts, 1970.

52. LEVITAN, S. A. *The Great Society's Poor Law: A New Approach to Poverty.* Baltimore, Md.: Johns Hopkins Press, 1969. Pp. 177–190.

53. LEWIS, W. L. Child advocacy and ecological planning. *Mental Hygiene,* 1970, *54,* 475–483.

54. LUBOVE, R. *Poverty and Social Welfare in the United States.* New York: Holt, Rinehart & Winston, 1970.

55. MARKER, G., & FRIEDMAN, P. R. Rethinking children's rights. *Children Today,* 1973, *2:*6, 8–11.

56. MCCORMICK, M. J. Social advocacy: A new dimension in social work. *Social Casework,* 1970, *51,* 3–12.

57. MECHANIC, D. *Mental Health and Social Policy.* Englewood Cliffs, New Jersey: Prentice-Hall, 1969.

58. MENNINGER, W. W. Some perspectives on violence in America today. *Federal Probation,* 1969, *33:*4, 5–11.

59. MEYER, C. *Social Work Practice: A Response to the Urban Crisis.* New York: Free Press, 1970.
60. *A National Program for Comprehensive Child Welfare Services.* New York: Child Welfare League of America, 1971.
61. PEATTIE, L. R. Reflections on advocacy planning. *Journal of the American Institute of Planners,* 1968, *34:*2, 80–88.
62. PERKINS, R. F. Community health patterns. *American Journal of Public Health,* 1968, *58,* 1154–1161.
63. PIVEN, F. Whom does the advocate planner serve? *Social Policy,* 1970, *1:*1, 32–38.
64. PLOWDEN, B. *Children and Their Primary Schools: A Report of the Control Advisory Council for Education.* Vol. 2. London: Her Majesty's Stationery Office, 1967.
65. POUSSAINT, A. F. *Why Blacks Kill Blacks.* New York: Emerson Hall, 1972.
66. PUMPHREY, R., & PUMPHREY, M. *The Heritage of American Social Work.* New York: University of Columbia Press, 1961.
67. REID, J. H., & PHILLIPS, M. Child welfare since 1912. *Children Today,* 1972, *1:*2, 13–18.
68. REIN, M. Social planning: The search for legitimacy. In M. Rein, *Social Policy: Issues of Choice and Change.* New York: Random House, 1970. Pp. 193–220.
69. RILEY, P. V. Family advocacy: Case to cause and back to case. *Child Welfare,* 1971, *50,* 374–383.
70. ROMANYSHYN, J. M. *Social Welfare: From Charity to Justice.* New York: Random House, 1971.
71. ROTHSTEIN, J. Corrections is based on the dignity of man. *Federal Probation,* 1970, *34:*1, 38–40.
72. SELDES, G. *The Stammering Century.* New York: Harper & Row, 1965.
73. SHORE, M. F. Whither child advocacy? *American Journal of Orthopsychiatry,* 1971, *41,* 798.
74. SMITH, E. A. *Social Welfare, Principles and Concepts.* New York: Association Press, 1965.
75. SMITH, R. "For every child . . .": A commentary on developments in child welfare 1962–1967. *Child Welfare,* 1968, *47:*3, 125–132.
76. *Statistical Abstracts of the United States.* Washington, D.C.: U.S. Government Printing Office, 1972.
77. TOBY, J. Violence and the masculine ideal: Some qualitative data. *Annals of the American Academy of Political and Social Science,* 1966, *364,* 19–27.
78. TOCH, H. *Violent Men.* Chicago: Aldine Publishing, 1969.
79. VESEY, W. *Government and Social Welfare.* New York: Henry Holt, 1958.
80. WALTERS, P. Mississippi: Children and politics. In J. Larner and

I. Howe (Eds.), *Poverty: Views from the Left.* New York: William Morrow, 1968. Pp. 221–244.

81. WEISSMAN, H. (Ed.) *Justice and the Law in the Mobilization for Youth Experience.* New York: Association Press, 1969.

82. WERNER, E. E., BIERMAN, J. M., & FRENCH, F. E. *The Children of Kauai.* Honolulu: University of Hawaii Press, 1971.

83. White House Conference on Youth. *Recommendations and Resolutions.* Washington, D.C.: U.S. Government Printing Office, 1971.

84. WINEMAN, D., & JAMES, A. The advocacy challenge to schools of social work. *Social Work,* 1969, *14*:2, 23–32.

85. YETTE, S. F. *The Choice: The Issue of Black Survival in America.* New York: G. P. Putnam, 1971.

Index